T0211589

Lecture Notes in Computer Science   10200

Commenced Publication in 1973
Founding and Former Series Editors:
Gerhard Goos, Juris Hartmanis, and Jan van Leeuwen

More information about this series at http://www.springer.com/series/7407

Giovanni Squillero
Kevin Sim et al. (Eds.)

Applications of Evolutionary Computation

20th European Conference, EvoApplications 2017
Amsterdam, The Netherlands, April 19–21, 2017
Proceedings, Part II

 Springer

Editors

see next page

ISSN 0302-9743   ISSN 1611-3349   (electronic)
Lecture Notes in Computer Science
ISBN 978-3-319-55791-5   ISBN 978-3-319-55792-2   (eBook)
DOI 10.1007/978-3-319-55792-2

Library of Congress Control Number: 2017934329

LNCS Sublibrary: SL1 – Theoretical Computer Science and General Issues

Printed on acid-free paper

This Springer imprint is published by Springer Nature
The registered company is Springer International Publishing AG
The registered company address is: Gewerbestrasse 11, 6330 Cham, Switzerland

Volume Editors

Giovanni Squillero
Politecnico di Torino, Italy
giovanni.squillero@polito.it

Kevin Sim
Edinburgh Napier University, UK
k.sim@napier.ac.uk

Gerd Ascheid
RWTH Aachen University, Germany
gerd.ascheid@ice.rwth-aachen.de

Jaume Bacardit
Newcastle University, UK
jaume.bacardit@newcastle.ac.uk

Anthony Brabazon
University College Dublin, Ireland
anthony.brabazon@ucd.ie

Paolo Burrelli
Aalborg University Copenhagen,
   Denmark
pabu@create.aau.dk

Stefano Cagnoni
University of Parma, Italy
cagnoni@ce.unipr.it

Matt Coler
INCAS[3], The Netherlands
mattcoler@incas3.eu

Carlos Cotta
Universidad de Málaga, Spain
ccottap@lcc.uma.es

Fabio D'Andreagiovanni
Zuse Insitute Berlin, Germany
f.dandreagiovanni@gmail.com

Federico Divina
Universidad Pablo de Olavide Sevilla,
   Spain
fdivina@upo.es

Anna I. Esparcia-Alcázar
Universitat Politècnica de València, Spain
aesparcia@pros.upv.es

Francisco Fernández de Vega
University of Extremadura, Spain
fcofdez@unex.es

Kyrre Glette
University of Oslo, Norway
kyrrehg@ifi.uio.no

Evert Haasdijk
Vrije Universiteit Amsterdam,
   The Netherlands
e.haasdijk@vu.nl

Jacqueline Heinerman
Vrije Universiteit Amsterdam,
   The Netherlands
j.v.heinerman@vu.nl

J. Ignacio Hidalgo
Universidad Complutense de Madrid,
   Spain
hidalgo@ucm.es

Ting Hu
Memorial University St. John's NL,
   Canada
ting.hu@mun.ca

Giovanni Iacca
INCAS[3], The Netherlands
giovanniiacca@incas3.eu

Michael Kampouridis
University of Kent, UK
m.kampouridis@kent.ac.uk

Paul Kaufmann
University of Paderborn, Germany
paul.kaufmann@gmail.com

Michalis Mavrovouniotis
Nottingham Trent University, UK
michalis.mavrovouniotis@ntu.ac.uk

Antonio M. Mora García
Universidad de Granada, Spain
amorag@geneura.ugr.es

Trung Thanh Nguyen
Liverpool John Moores University, UK
t.t.nguyen@ljmu.ac.uk

Robert Schaefer
AGH University of Science
   and Technology, Poland
schaefer@agh.edu.pl

Sara Silva
Faculdade de Ciências,
   Universidade de Lisboa, Portugal
sara@fc.ul.pt

Ernesto Tarantino
ICAR/CNR, Italy
ernesto.tarantino@icar.cnr.it

Alberto Tonda
INRA, France
alberto.tonda@grignon.inra.fr

Neil Urquhart
Edinburgh Napier University, UK
n.urquhart@napier.ac.uk

Mengjie Zhang
Victoria University of Wellington,
   New Zealand
mengjie.zhang@ecs.vuw.ac.nz

Preface

This two-volume set contains proceedings of EvoApplications 2017, the European Conference on the Applications of Evolutionary Computation. The event was held in Amsterdam, The Netherlands, during April 19–21.

EvoAPPS, as it is called, is part of EVO*, the leading European event on bio-inspired computation. EvoAPPS aimed to show the latest applications of research, ranging from proof of concepts to industrial case studies. At the same time, under the EVO* umbrella, EuroGP focused on the technique of genetic programming, EvoCOP targeted evolutionary computation in combinatorial optimization, and EvoMUSART was dedicated to evolved and bio-inspired music, sound, art, and design. The proceedings for all of these co-located events are available in the LNCS series.

If EVO* coalesces four different conferences, EvoAPPS exhibits an even higher granularity: It started as a collection of few workshops and slowly grew into a 14-track conference, steadily able to attract more than 100 papers per year. This year marked our 20th anniversary, but, despite the success, we do not want to stop to celebrate. In an ever-evolving scientific landscape, EvoAPPS needs to mutate to adapt and survive: its scope is constantly broadening or shrinking according to new developments, new tracks are proposed while others are merged or suspended.

This edition covered 14 different domains: business analytics and finance (Evo-BAFIN track); computational biology (EvoBIO track); communication networks and other parallel and distributed systems (EvoCOMNET track); complex systems (Evo-COMPLEX track); energy-related optimization (EvoENERGY track); games and multi-agent systems (EvoGAMES track); image analysis, signal processing, and pattern recognition (EvoIASP track); real-world industrial and commercial environments (EvoINDUSTRY track); knowledge incorporation in evolutionary computation (Evo-KNOW track); continuous parameter optimization (EvoNUM track); parallel architectures and distributed infrastructures (EvoPAR track); evolutionary robotics (EvoROBOT track); nature-inspired algorithms in software engineering and testing (EvoSET track); and stochastic and dynamic environments (EvoSTOC track).

This year, we received 108 high-quality submissions, most of them well suited to fit in more than one track. We selected 46 papers for full oral presentation, while 26 works were given limited space and were shown as posters. All such contributions, regardless of the presentation format, appear as full papers in these two volumes (LNCS 10199 and LNCS 10200).

Many people contributed to this edition: We express our gratitude to the authors for submitting their works, and to the members of the Program Committees for devoting such a big effort to review papers within our tight schedule.

The papers were submitted, reviewed, and selected through the MyReview conference management system, and we are grateful to Marc Schoenauer (Inria, Saclay-Île-de-France, France) for providing, hosting, and managing the platform.

We thank the local organizers, Evert Haasdijk and Jacqueline Heinerman, from the Vrije Universiteit Amsterdam.

We thank Pablo García Sánchez (University of Cádiz, Spain) for maintaining the EVO* website and handling publicity.

We thank the invited speakers, Kenneth De Jong and Arthur Kordon, for their inspiring presentations.

We thank SPECIES, the Society for the Promotion of Evolutionary Computation in Europe and Its Surroundings, and its individual members (Marc Schoenauer, President; Anna I. Esparcia-Alcázar, Secretary and Vice-President; Wolfgang Banzhaf, Treasurer) for the coordination and financial administration.

And we all express our special gratitude to Jennifer Willies for her dedicated and continued involvement in EVO*. Since 1998, she has been essential for building our unique atmosphere.

February 2017

Giovanni Squillero	Jacqueline Heinerman
Kevin Sim	J. Ignacio Hidalgo
Gerd Ascheid	Ting Hu
Jaume Bacardit	Giovanni Iacca
Anthony Brabazon	Michael Kampouridis
Paolo Burelli	Paul Kaufmann
Stefano Cagnoni	Michalis Mavrovouniotis
Matt Coler	Antonio M. Mora Garcia
Carlos Cotta	Robert Schaefer
Fabio D'Andreagiovanni	Sara Silva
Federico Divina	Ernesto Tarantino
Anna I. Esparcia-Alcázar	Trung Thanh Nguyen
Francisco Fernández de Vega	Alberto Tonda
Kyrre Glette	Neil Urquhart
Evert Haasdijk	Mengjie Zhang

Organization

EvoApplications Coordinator

Giovanni Squillero   Politecnico di Torino, Italy

EvoApplications Publication Chair

Kevin Sim   Edinburgh Napier University, UK

Local Chairs

Evert Haasdijk   Vrije Universiteit Amsterdam, The Netherlands
Jacqueline Heinerman   Vrije Universiteit Amsterdam, The Netherlands

Publicity Chair

Pablo García Sánchez   University of Cádiz, Spain

EvoBAFIN Chairs

Anthony Brabazon   University College Dublin, Ireland
Michael Kampouridis   University of Kent, UK

EvoBIO Chairs

Jaume Bacardit   Newcastle University, UK
Federico Divina   Universidad Pablo de Olavide, Spain
Ting Hu   Memorial University, St. John's, Canada

EvoCOMNET Chairs

Ernesto Tarantino   ICAR/CNR, Italy
Fabio D'Andreagiovanni   Zuse Insitute Berlin, Germany
Giovanni Iacca   INCAS^3, The Netherlands

EvoCOMPLEX Chairs

Carlos Cotta   Universidad de Málaga, Spain
Robert Schaefer   AGH University of Science and Technology, Poland

EvoENERGY Chairs

Paul Kaufmann   University of Paderborn, Germany
Kyrre Glette   University of Oslo, Norway

EvoGAMES Chairs

Paolo Burrelli   Aalborg University Copenhagen, Denmark
Antonio M. Mora García   Universidad de Granada, Spain
Alberto Tonda   INRA, France

EvoIASP Chairs

Stefano Cagnoni   University of Parma, Italy
Mengjie Zhang   Victoria University of Wellington, New Zealand

EvoINDUSTRY Chairs

Kevin Sim   Edinburgh Napier University, UK
Neil Urquhart   Edinburgh Napier University, UK

EvoKNOW Chairs

Giovanni Iacca   INCAS^3, The Netherlands
Matt Coler   INCAS^3, The Netherlands
Gerd Ascheid   RWTH Aachen University, Germany

EvoNUM Chair

Anna I. Esparcia-Alcázar Universitat Politècnica de València, Spain

EvoPAR Chairs

Francisco Fernández   University of Extremadura, Spain
  de Vega
J. Ignacio Hidalgo   Universidad Complutense de Madrid, Spain

EvoROBOT Chairs

Evert Haasdijk   Vrije Universiteit Amsterdam, The Netherlands
Jacqueline Heinerman   Vrije Universiteit Amsterdam, The Netherlands

EvoSET Chairs

Anna I. Esparcia-Alcázar Universitat Politècnica de València, Spain
Sara Silva   Faculdade de Ciências, Universidade de Lisboa, Portugal

EvoSTOC Chairs

| Trung Thanh Nguyen | Liverpool John Moores University, UK |
| Michalis Mavrovouniotis | Nottingham Trent University, UK |

Program Committees

Eva Alfaro	Instituto Technològico de Informàtica, Spain [EvoBAFIN]
Jhon Edgar Amaya	Universidad Nacional Experimental del Táchira, Venezuela [EvoCOMPLEX]
Michele Amoretti	University of Parma, Italy [EvoIASP]
Anca Andreica	Universitatea Babeş-Bolyai, Romania [EvoCOMPLEX]
Jarosław Arabas	Warsaw University of Technology, Poland [EvoKNOW]
Ignacio Arnaldo	PatternEx, USA [EvoPAR]
Maria Arsuaga Rios	CERN, Switzerland [EvoINDUSTRY]
Jason Atkin	University of Nottingham, UK [EvoINDUSTRY]
Joshua Auerbach	Champlain College, USA [EvoROBOT]
Jaume Bacardit	Newcastle University, UK [EvoBIO]
Lucia Ballerini	University of Edinburgh, UK [EvoIASP]
Tiago Baptista	Universidade de Coimbra, Portugal [EvoCOMPLEX]
Bahriye Basturk Akay	Erciyes University, Turkey [EvoINDUSTRY]
Vitoantonio Bevilacqua	Politecnico di Bari, Italy [EvoIASP]
Hans-Georg Beyer	Vorarlberg University of Applied Sciences, Austria [EvoNUM]
Leonardo Bocchi	University of Florence, Italy [EvoIASP]
János Botzheim	Tokyo Metropolitan University, Japan [EvoKNOW]
Nicola Bova	University of Edinburgh, UK [EvoIASP]
Anthony Brabazon	University College Dublin, Ireland [EvoBAFIN]
Juergen Branke	University of Warwick, UK [EvoSTOC]
Nicolas Bredeche	Institut des Systèmes Intelligents et de Robotique, France [EvoROBOT]
Cédric Buche	ENIB, France [EvoGAMES]
Doina Bucur	University of Twente, The Netherlands [EvoCOMNET, EvoKNOW]
Aleksander Byrski	AGH University of Science and Technology, Poland [EvoCOMPLEX]
Antonio Córdoba	Universidad de Sevilla, Spain [EvoCOMPLEX]
David Camacho	Universidad Autónoma de Madrid, Spain [EvoGAMES]
Fabio Caraffini	De Montfort University, UK [EvoKNOW]
Hui Cheng Cheng	Liverpool John Moores University, UK [EvoSTOC]
Francisco Chicano	Universidad de Málaga, Spain [EvoSET]
Anders Christensen	University Institute of Lisbon, ISCTE-IUL, Portugal [EvoROBOT]
Myra Cohen	University of Nebraska, USA [EvoSET]
José Manuel Colmenar	Universidad Rey Juan Carlos, Spain [EvoPAR]

Stefano Coniglio	University of Southampton, UK [EvoCOMNET]
Ernesto Costa	University of Coimbra, Portugal [EvoSTOC]
Sam Cramer	University of Kent, UK [EvoBAFIN]
Fabio Daolio	Shinshu University, Japan [EvoIASP]
Christian Darabos	Dartmouth College, USA [EvoBIO]
Ivanoe De Falco	ICAR-CNR, Italy [EvoIASP]
Antonio Della	Cioppa University of Salerno, Italy [EvoIASP]
Igor Deplano	Liverpool John Moores University, UK [GENERAL]
Laura Dipietro	Cambridge, USA [EvoIASP]
Federico Divina	Universidad Pablo de Olavide, Spain [EvoBIO]
Stephane Doncieux	Institut des Systèmes Intelligents et de Robotique, France [EvoROBOT]
Bernabé Dorronsoro	Universidad de Cádiz, Spain [EvoCOMPLEX]
Marc Ebner	Ernst Moritz Arndt University, Greifswald, Germany [EvoIASP]
Aniko Ekart	Aston University, UK [EvoINDUSTRY]
Andries P. Engelbrecht	University of Pretoria, South Africa [EvoSTOC]
Şima Etaner-Uyar	Istanbul Technical University, Turkey [EvoNUM]
Edoardo Fadda	Politecnico di Torino, Italy [GENERAL]
Carlos Fernandes	Universidade de Lisboa, Portugal [EvoCOMPLEX]
Florentino Fernandez	Universidad de Vigo, Spain [EvoBIO]
Antonio Fernández Ares	Universidad de Granada, Spain [EvoGAMES]
Antonio Fernández Leiva	Universidad de Málaga, Spain [EvoGAMES]
Gianluigui Folino	ICAR-CNR, Italy [EvoPAR]
Francesco Fontanella	University of Cassino, Italy [EvoIASP]
Gordon Fraser	University of Sheffield, UK [EvoSET]
Alex Freitas	University of Kent, UK [EvoBIO]
José Enrique Gallardo	Universidad de Málaga, Spain [EvoCOMPLEX]
Pablo García Sánchez	University of Cádiz, Spain [EvoCOMPLEX, EvoGAMES]
Gregory Gay	University of South Carolina [EvoSET]
Carlos Gershenson	Universidad Nacional Autónoma de México, México [EvoCOMPLEX]
Mario Giacobini	Universita di Torino, Italy [EvoBIO]
Raffaele Giancarlo	Universitá degli Studi di Palermo, Italy [EvoBIO]
Kyrre Glette	University of Oslo, Norway [EvoROBOT]
Francisco Gomez Vela	Universidad Pablo de Olavide, Spain [EvoBIO]
Antonio González Pardo	Universidad Autónoma de Madrid, Spain [EvoGAMES]
Casey Greene	University of Pennsylvania, USA [EvoBIO]
Michael Guckert	University of Applied Sciences, Germany [EvoINDUSTRY]
Francisco Luis Gutiérrez Vela	Universidad de Granada, Spain [EvoGAMES]
Evert Haasdijk	Vrije Universiteit Amsterdam, The Netherlands [EvoROBOT]
Johan Hagelback	Blekinge Tekniska Hogskola, Sweden [EvoGAMES]

John Hallam	University of Southern Denmark, Denmark [EvoGAMES]
Ahmed Hallawa	RWTH Aachen University, Germany [EvoKNOW]
Heiko Hamann	University of Paderborn, Germany [EvoROBOT]
Jin-Kao Hao	University of Angers, France [EvoBIO]
Jacqueline Heinerman	Vrije Universiteit Amsterdam, The Netherlands [EvoROBOT]
Daniel Hernández	Instituto Tecnológico Nacional, Mexico [EvoPAR]
Malcom Heywood	Dalhousie University, Canada [EvoBAFIN]
Ronald Hochreiter	WU Vienna University of Economics and Business, Austria [EvoBAFIN]
Rolf Hoffmann	Technical University Darmstadt, Germany [EvoCOMNET]
Ting Hu	Memorial University, Canada [EvoBIO]
Joost Huizinga	University of Wyoming, USA [EvoROBOT]
Óscar Ibáñez	Universidad de Granada, Spain [EvoIASP]
Juan Luis Jiménez Laredo	University of Le Havre, France [EvoCOMPLEX, EvoPAR]
Michael Kampouridis	University of Kent, UK [EvoBAFIN]
Andreas Kassler	Karlstad University, Sweden [EvoCOMNET]
Ahmed Kattan	EvoSys.biz, Saudi Arabia [EvoBAFIN]
Shayan Kavakeb	AECOM, UK [EvoSTOC]
Graham Kendall	University of Nottingham, UK [EvoCOMNET]
Marouane Kessentini	University of Michigan, USA [EvoSET]
Mario Koeppen	Kyushu Institute of Technology, Japan [EvoIASP]
Oliver Kramer	University of Oldenburg, Germany [EvoENERGY]
Wacław Kuś	Politechnika Śląska, Poland [EvoCOMPLEX]
William B. Langdon	University College London, UK [EvoNUM, EvoPAR]
Raúl Lara Cabrera	Universidad Autónoma de Madrid, Spain [EvoGAMES]
Claire Le Goues	Carnegie Mellon University, USA [EvoSET]
Kenji Leibnitz	National Institute of Information and Communications Technology, Japan [EvoCOMNET]
Changhe Li	China University of Geosciences, China [EvoSTOC]
Antonios Liapis	University of Malta, Malta [EvoGAMES]
Federico Liberatore	Universidad Carlos III, Spain [EvoGAMES]
Piotr Lipinski	University of Wroclaw, Poland [EvoBAFIN]
Francisco Luna	Universidad de Málaga, Spain [EvoPAR]
Evelyne Lutton	Inria, France [EvoIASP]
Chenjie Ma	Fraunhofer Institute for Wind Energy and Energy System Technology, Germany [EvoENERGY]
Penousal Machado	University of Coimbra, Portugal [EvoIASP]
Tobias Mahlmann	Lund University, Sweden [EvoGAMES]
Domenico Maisto	ICAR-CNR, Italy [EvoCOMNET]
Carlo Mannino	SINTEF Oslo, Norway [EvoCOMNET]
Andrea Marcelli	Politecnico di Torino, Italy [GENERAL]

Elena Marchiori	Radboud Universiteit van Nijmegen, The Netherlands [EvoBIO]
Ingo Mauser	Karlsruhe Institute of Technology, Germany [EvoENERGY]
Michalis Mavrovouniotis	Nottingham Trent University, UK [EvoSTOC]
Michael Mayo	University of Waikato, New Zealand [EvoBAFIN]
Jorn Mehnen	Cranfield University, UK [EvoSTOC]
Tim Menzies	University of Nebraska, USA [EvoSET]
Juan Julián Merelo	Universidad de Granada, Spain [EvoNUM, EvoCOMPLEX]
Pablo Mesejo	Santiago Inria, France [EvoIASP]
Krzysztof Michalak	Wroclaw University of Economics, Poland [EvoBAFIN]
Martin Middendorf	University of Leipzig, Germany [EvoENERGY]
Wiem Mkaouer	University of Michigan, USA [EvoSET]
Maizura Mokhtar	Edinburgh Napier University, UK [EvoENERGY]
Jean-Marc Montanier	Softbank Robotics Europe, France [EvoROBOT]
Roberto Montemanni	IDSIA, Switzerland [EvoCOMNET]
Jean-Baptiste Mouret	Inria Larsen Team, France [EvoROBOT, GENERAL]
Nysret Musliu	Vienna University of Technology, Austria [EvoINDUSTRY]
Boris Naujoks	TH - Köln University of Applied Sciences, Germany [EvoNUM]
Antonio Jesús Nebro	Universidad de Málaga, Spain [EvoCOMPLEX]
Ferrante Neri	De Montfort University, UK [EvoIASP, EvoKNOW, EvoNUM, EvoSTOC]
Trung Thanh Nguyen	Liverpool John Moores University, UK [EvoSTOC]
Geoff Nitschke	University of Cape Town, South Africa [EvoROBOT]
Rafael Nogueras	Universidad de Málaga, Spain [EvoCOMPLEX]
Stefano Nolfi	Institute of Cognitive Sciences and Technologies, Italy [EvoROBOT]
Gustavo Olague	CICESE, México [EvoPAR]
Kai Olav Ellefsen	University of Wyoming, USA [EvoROBOT]
Carlotta Orsenigo	Politecnico di Milano, Italy [EvoBIO]
Ender Ozcan	University of Nottingham, UK [EvoINDUSTRY]
Michael O'Neill	University College Dublin, Ireland [EvoBAFIN]
Patricia Paderewski Rodriguez	Universidad de Granada, Spain [EvoGAMES]
Peter Palensky	Technical University of Delft, The Netherlands [EvoENERGY]
Anna Paszyńska	Jagiellonian University, Poland [EvoCOMPLEX]
David Pelta	Universidad de Granada, Spain [EvoSTOC]
Justyna Petke	University College London, UK [EvoSET]
Sanja Petrovic	University of Nottingham, UK [EvoINDUSTRY]
Nelishia Pillay	University of KwaZulu-Natal, South Africa [EvoINDUSTRY]
Clara Pizzuti	ICAR-CNR, Italy [EvoBIO]

Riccardo Poli	University of Essex, UK [EvoIASP]
Arkadiusz Poteralski	Politechnika Śląska, Poland [EvoCOMPLEX]
Simon Powers	Edinburgh Napier University, UK [EvoINDUSTRY]
Petr Pošík	Czech Technical University in Prague, Czech Republic [EvoNUM]
Mike Preuss	University of Münster, Germany [EvoNUM, EvoGAMES]
Abraham Prieto	University of La Coruña, Spain [EvoROBOT]
Jianlong Qi	Ancestry, USA [EvoBIO]
Mauricio Resende	Amazon, USA [EvoCOMNET]
Jose Carlos Ribeiro	Politécnico de Leiria, Portugal [EvoPAR]
Hendrik Richter	Leipzig University of Applied Sciences, Germany [EvoSTOC]
Simona Rombo	Università degli Studi di Palermo, Italy [EvoBIO]
Claudio Rossi	Universidad Politecnica de Madrid, Spain [EvoROBOT]
Günter Rudolph	University of Dortmund, Germany [EvoNUM]
Jose Santos Reyes	Universidad de A Coruña, Spain [EvoBIO]
Federica Sarro	University College London, UK [EvoSET]
Ivo Fabian Sbalzarini	Max Planck Institute of Molecular Cell Biology and Genetics, Germany [EvoNUM]
Robert Schaefer	University of Science and Technology, Poland [EvoCOMNET]
Thomas Schmickl	University of Graz, Austria [EvoROBOT]
Sevil Sen	Hacettepe University, Turkey [EvoCOMNET]
Chien-Chung Shen	University of Delaware, USA [EvoCOMNET]
Sara Silva	Universidade de Lisboa, Portugal [EvoIASP]
Anabela Simões	Institute Polytechnic of Coimbra, Portugal [EvoSTOC]
Moshe Sipper	Ben-Gurion University, Israel [EvoGAMES]
Stephen Smith	University of York, UK [EvoIASP]
Maciej Smołka	AGH University of Science and Technology, Poland [EvoCOMPLEX]
Ana Soares	EnergyVille, VITO, Belgium [EvoENERGY]
Andy Song	RMIT, Australia [EvoIASP]
Giovanni Squillero	Politecnico di Torino, Italy [EvoIASP, GENERAL]
Marcin Szubert	Poznań University of Technology, Poland [EvoCOMPLEX]
Ke Tang	University of Science and Technology of China USTC, China [EvoNUM]
Andrea Tettamanzi	University of Nice Sophia Antipolis/I3S, France [EvoBAFIN]
Ruppa Thulasiram	University of Manitoba, Canada [EvoBAFIN]
Renato Tinós	Universidade de São Paulo, Brazil [EvoSTOC]
Julian Togelius	New York University, USA [EvoGAMES]
Pawel Topa	AGH University of Science and Technology, Poland [EvoCOMNET]

Krzysztof Trojanowski	Cardinal Stefan Wyszyński University in Warsaw, Poland [EvoSTOC]
Ha Chi Trung	Liverpool John Moores University, UK [EvoSTOC]
Wojciech Turek	AGH University of Science and Technology, Poland [EvoCOMPLEX]
Tommaso Urli	Csiro Data61, Australia [EvoGAMES]
Andrea Valsecchi	European Center of Soft Computing, Spain [EvoIASP]
Leonardo Vanneschi	Universidade Nova de Lisboa, Portugal [EvoBIO, EvoIASP]
Sebastien Varrete	Université du Luxembourg, Luxembourg [EvoPAR]
José Manuel Velasco	Universidad Complutense de Madrid, Spain [EvoPAR]
Vinícius Veloso de Melo	UNIFESP-SJC, Brazil [EvoKNOW]
Marco Villani	University of Modena and Reggio Emilia, Italy [EvoCOMNET]
Rafael Villanueva	Universitat Politècnica de València, Spain [EvoPAR]
Tanja Vos	Open University, The Netherlands [EvoSET]
Markus Wagner	University of Adelaide, Australia [EvoENERGY]
Ran Wang	Liverpool John Moores University, UK [EvoSTOC]
Jarosław Was	AGH University of Science and Technology, Poland [EvoCOMNET]
David White	University College London, UK [EvoSET]
Tony White	Carleton University, Canada [EvoCOMNET]
Bing Xue	Victoria University of Wellington, New Zealand [EvoBIO, EvoIASP]
Anil Yaman	Technical University of Eindhoven, The Netherlands [EvoKNOW]
Shengxiang Yang	De Montfort University, UK [EvoSTOC]
Georgios N. Yannakakis	University of Malta, Malta [EvoGAMES]
Danial Yazdani	Liverpool John Moores University, UK [EvoSTOC]
Aleš Zamuda	University of Maribor, Slovenia [EvoKNOW]
Mengjie Zhang	Victoria University of Wellington, New Zealand [EvoBIO]
Nur Zincir-Heywood	Dalhousie University, Canada [EvoCOMNET]

Contents – Part II

General

Contents – Part I

EvoCOMNET

EvoCOMPLEX

EvoROBOT

EvoSET

Hybrid Algorithms Based on Integer Programming for the Search of Prioritized Test Data in Software Product Lines

Javier Ferrer$^{(\boxtimes)}$, Francisco Chicano, and Enrique Alba

Universidad de Málaga, Málaga, Spain
{ferrer,chicano,eat}@lcc.uma.es

Abstract. In Software Product Lines (SPLs) it is not possible, in general, to test all products of the family. The number of products denoted by a SPL is very high due to the combinatorial explosion of features. For this reason, some coverage criteria have been proposed which try to test at least all feature interactions without the necessity to test all products, e.g., all pairs of features (pairwise coverage). In addition, it is desirable to first test products composed by a set of priority features. This problem is known as the Prioritized Pairwise Test Data Generation Problem. In this work we propose two hybrid algorithms using Integer Programming (IP) to generate a prioritized test suite. The first one is based on an integer linear formulation and the second one is based on a integer quadratic (nonlinear) formulation. We compare these techniques with two state-of-the-art algorithms, the Parallel Prioritized Genetic Solver (PPGS) and a greedy algorithm called prioritized-ICPL. Our study reveals that our hybrid nonlinear approach is clearly the best in both, solution quality and computation time. Moreover, the nonlinear variant (the fastest one) is 27 and 42 times faster than PPGS in the two groups of instances analyzed in this work.

Keywords: Combinatorial Interaction Testing · Software Product Lines · Pairwise testing · Feature models · Integer Linear Programming · Integer Nonlinear Programming · Prioritization

1 Introduction

A *Software Product Line (SPL)* is a set of related software systems, which share a common set of features providing different products [1]. The effective management of *variability* can lead to substantial benefits such as increased software reuse, faster product customization, and reduced time to market. Systems are being built, more and more frequently, as SPLs rather than individual products because of several technological and marketing trends. This fact has created an

---

This research is partially funded by the Spanish Ministry of Economy and Competitiveness and FEDER under contract TIN2014-57341-R, the University of Málaga, Andalucía Tech and the Spanish Network TIN2015-71841-REDT (SEBASENet).

© Springer International Publishing AG 2017
G. Squillero and K. Sim (Eds.): EvoApplications 2017, Part II, LNCS 10200, pp. 3–19, 2017.
DOI: 10.1007/978-3-319-55792-2_1

increasing need for testing approaches that are capable of coping with large numbers of feature combinations that characterize SPLs. Many testing alternatives have been put forward [2–5]. Salient among them are those that support *pairwise testing* [6–12]. The pairwise coverage criterion requires that all pairs of feature combinations should be present in at least one test product. Some feature combinations can be more important than others (e.g., they can be more frequent in the products). In this case, a weight is assigned to each feature combination (usually based on product weights). In this context, the optimization problem that arises consists in finding a set of products with minimum cardinality reaching a given accumulated weight. This problem has been solved in the literature using only approximated algorithms.

The use of exact methods, like Mathematical Programming solvers, has the drawback of a poor scalability. Solving integer linear programs (ILP) is NP-hard in general. Actual solvers, like CPLEX[1] and Gurobi[2], include modern search strategies which allow them to solve relatively large instances in a few seconds. However, the size of the real instances of the problem we solve in this paper is too large to be exactly solved using ILP solvers. For this reason, we propose a combination of a high level heuristic (greedy) strategy and a low level exact strategy. The combination of heuristics and mathematical programming tools, also called *matheuristics*, is gaining popularity in the last years due to its great success [13].

In this paper we present two novel proposals: a Hybrid algorithm based on Integer Linear Programming (HILP) and another Hybrid algorithm based on Integer Nonlinear Programming (HINLP). We compare our proposals with two state-of-the-art algorithms: a greedy algorithm that generates competitive solutions in a short time, called prioritized-ICPL (pICPL) [14] and a hybrid algorithm based on a genetic algorithm, called *Prioritized Pairwise Genetic Solver* (PPGS) [15], which obtains higher quality solutions than pICPL but generally using more time. Our comparison covers a total of 235 feature models with a wide range of features and products, using three different priority assignments and five product prioritization selection strategies. Our main contributions in this paper are as follows:

- Two novel hybrid algorithms based on Integer Programming. One models the problem using linear functions (HILP) and the other one using nonlinear functions (HINLP).
- A comprehensive evaluation of the performance of HILP and HINLP. In the experimental evaluation 235 feature models and different prioritization schemes were used. We also compared the new approaches with those of state-of-the-art methods: PPGS and pICPL.

The remainder of the article is organized as follows. The next section presents some background on SPLs and feature models. In Sect. 3 the Prioritized Pairwise Test Data Generation Problem in SPL is formalized. Next, Sect. 4 details

[1] http://www-03.ibm.com/software/products/en/ibmilogcpleoptistud.
[2] https://www.gurobi.com.

our algorithmic proposals. In Sect. 5 we briefly present the other algorithms of the comparison, the priority assignments and experimental corpus used in the experiments. Section 6 is devoted to the statistical analysis of the results and Sect. 7 describes possible threats to the validity of this study. Finally, Sect. 8 outlines some concluding remarks and future work.

2   Background: Feature Models

Feature models have become the *de facto* standard for modelling the common and variable features of an SPL and their relationships, collectively forming a tree-like structure. The nodes of the tree are the features which are depicted as labelled boxes, and the edges represent the relationships among them. Feature models denote the set of feature combinations that the products of an SPL can have [16].

Figure 1 shows the feature model of our running example for SPLs, the *Graph Product Line (GPL)* [17], a standard SPL of basic graph algorithms that has been widely used as a case study in the product line community. In GPL, a product is a collection of algorithms applied to directed or undirected graphs. In a feature model, each feature (except the root) has one parent feature and can have a set of child features. A child feature can only be included in a feature combination of a valid product if its parent is included as well. The root feature is always included. There are four kinds of feature relationships:

- *Mandatory features* are selected whenever their respective parent feature is selected. They are depicted with a filled circle. For example, features *Driver* and *Algorithms*.
- *Optional features* may or may not be selected if their respective parent feature is selected. An example is the feature *Search*.
- *Exclusive-or relations* indicate that exactly one of the features in the exclusive-or group must be selected whenever the parent feature is selected. They are depicted as empty arcs crossing over a set of lines connecting a parent feature with its child features. For instance, if feature *Search* is selected, then either feature *DFS* or feature *BFS* must be selected.
- *Inclusive-or relations* indicate that at least one of the features in the inclusive-or group must be selected if the parent is selected. They are depicted as filled arcs crossing over a set of lines connecting a parent feature with its child features. As an example, when feature *Algorithms* is selected then at least one of the features *Num*, *CC*, *SCC*, *Cycle*, *Shortest*, *Prim*, and *Kruskal* must be selected.

In addition to the parent-child relations, features can also relate across different branches of the feature model with the *Cross-Tree Constraints (CTC)*. Figure 1 shows the CTCs of our feature model in textual form. For instance, *Num requires Search* means that whenever feature *Num* is selected, feature *Search* must also be selected. These constraints as well as those implied by the hierarchical relations between features are usually expressed and checked using propositional logic.

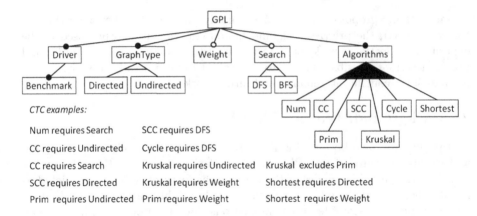

Fig. 1. *Graph Product Line* feature model.

3 Problem Formalization: *Prioritized Pairwise Test Data Generation*

Combinatorial Interaction Testing (CIT) is a testing approach that constructs samples to drive the systematic testing of software system configurations [18,19]. When applied to SPL testing, the idea is to select a representative subset of products where interaction errors are more likely to occur rather than testing the complete product family [18]. In the following we provide the basic terminology of CIT for SPLs[3].

Definition 1 (Feature list). *A feature list FL is the list of features in a feature model.*

Definition 2 (Feature set). *A feature set fs is a pair* $(sel, \overline{sel})$ *where the first and second components are respectively the set of selected and not-selected features of a SPL product. Let FL be a feature list, thus* $sel, \overline{sel} \subseteq FL$, $sel \cap \overline{sel} = \emptyset$, *and* $sel \cup \overline{sel} = FL$. *Wherever unambiguous we use the term* product *as a synonym of feature set.*

Definition 3 (Valid feature set). *A feature set fs is valid with respect to a feature model fm iff fs.sel and fs.$\overline{sel}$ do not violate any constraints described by fm. The set of all valid feature sets represented by fm is denoted as* FS^{fm}.

The focus of our study is pairwise testing, thus our concern is on the combinations between two features. The coming definitions are consequently presented with that perspective; however, the generalization to combinations of any number of features is straightforward.

---

[3] Definitions based on [20,21].

Definition 4 (Pair[4]). *A pair ps is a 2-tuple (sel, $\overline{sel}$) involving two features from a feature list FL, that is, $ps.sel \cup ps.\overline{sel} \subseteq FL \wedge ps.sel \cap ps.\overline{sel} = \emptyset \wedge |ps.sel \cup ps.\overline{sel}| = 2$. We say pair ps is* covered *by feature set fs iff $ps.sel \subseteq fs.sel \wedge ps.\overline{sel} \subseteq fs.\overline{sel}$.*

Definition 5 (Valid pair). *A pair ps is* valid *in a feature model fm if there exists a valid feature set fs that covers ps. The set of all valid pairs of a feature model fm is denoted with VPS^{fm}.*

Let us illustrate pairwise testing with the GPL running example. Some samples of pairs are: *GPL* and *Search* selected, *Weight* and *Undirected* not selected, *CC* not selected and *Driver* selected. An example of invalid pair, i.e., not denoted by the feature model, is features *Directed* and *Undirected* both selected. Notice that this pair is not valid because they are part of an exclusive-or relation.

Definition 6 (Pairwise test suite). *A pairwise test suite pts for a feature model fm is a set of valid feature sets of fm. A pairwise test suite is* complete *if it covers all the valid pairs in VPS^{fm}, that is: $\{fs|\forall ps \in VPS^{fm} \Rightarrow \exists fs \in FS^{fm}$ such that fs covers ps$\}$.*

In GPL there is a total of 418 valid pairs, so a complete pairwise test suite for GPL must have all these pairs covered by at least one feature set. Henceforth, because of our focus and for the sake of brevity we will refer to pairwise test suites simply as *test suites*.

In the following we provide a formal definition of the priority scheme based on the sketched description provided in [14].

Definition 7 (Prioritized product). *A prioritized product pp is a 2-tuple (fs, w), where fs represents a valid feature set in feature model fm and $w \in \mathbb{R}$ represents its weight. Let pp_i and pp_j be two prioritized products. We say that pp_i has higher priority than pp_j for test-suite generation iff pp_i's weight is greater than pp_j's weight, that is $pp_i.w > pp_j.w$.*

As an example, let us say that we would like to prioritize product *p0* with a weight of 17. This would be denoted as $pp0 = (p1,17)$.

Definition 8 (Pairwise configuration). *A pairwise configuration pc is a 2-tuple (sel, $\overline{sel}$) representing a partially configured product, defining the selection of 2 features of feature list FL, i.e., $pc.sel \cup pc.\overline{sel} \subseteq FL \wedge pc.sel \cap pc.\overline{sel} = \emptyset \wedge |pc.sel \cup pc.\overline{sel}| = 2$. We say a pairwise configuration pc is covered by feature set fs iff $pc.sel \subseteq fs.sel \wedge pc.\overline{sel} \subseteq fs.\overline{sel}$.*

Definition 9 (Weighted pairwise configuration). *A weighted pairwise configuration wpc is a 2-tuple (pc,w) where pc is a pairwise configuration and $w \in \mathbb{R}$ represents its weight computed as follows. Let PP be a set of prioritized products*

---

[4] This definition of pair differs from the mathematical definition of the same term and is specific for SPLs. In particular, it adds more constraints to the traditional definition of pair.

and PP_{pc} be a subset, $PP_{pc} \subseteq PP$, such that PP_{pc} contains all prioritized products in PP that cover pc of wpc, i.e., $PP_{pc} = \{pp \in PP | pp.fs \text{ covers } wpc.pc\}$. Then $w = \sum_{p \in PP_{pc}} p.w$

Definition 10 (Prioritized pairwise covering array). *A prioritized pairwise covering array $ppCA$ for a feature model fm and a set of weighted pairwise configurations WPC is a set of valid feature sets FS that covers all weighted pairwise configurations in WPC whose weight is greater than zero: $\forall wpc \in WPC$ $(wpc.w > 0 \Rightarrow \exists fs \in ppCA \text{ such that } fs \text{ covers } wpc.pc)$.*

Given a prioritized pairwise covering array $ppCA$ and a set of weighted pairwise configurations WPC, we define coverage of $ppCA$, denoted by $cov(ppCA)$, as the sum of all weighted pairwise configurations in WPC covered by any configuration in $ppCA$ divided by the sum of all weighted configurations in WPC, that is:

$$cov(ppCA) = \frac{\sum_{\substack{wpc \in WPC \\ \exists cc \in ppCA, cc \text{ covers } wpc.pc}} wpc.w}{\sum_{wpc \in WPC} wpc.w}. \tag{1}$$

The optimization problem we are interested in consists of finding a *prioritized pairwise covering array, $ppCA$,* with the minimum number of feature sets $|ppCA|$ maximizing the coverage, $cov(ppCA)$.

4   Hybrid Algorithms Based on Integer Programming

In this work we propose two different hybrid algorithms combining a heuristic and Integer Programming. The first one is based on an integer linear formulation (HILP) and the second is based on a quadratic (nonlinear) integer formulation (HINLP). Throughout this section we highlight the commonalities and differences between the proposals.

The two algorithms proposed in this work use the same high level greedy strategy. In each iteration they try to find a product that maximizes the weighted coverage. This could be expressed by the following objective function h:

$$h(x) = \sum_{wpc \in I(x) \cap U} wpc.w \tag{2}$$

where x is a product, U the set of not covered pairwise configurations and $I(x)$ the set of pairwise configurations covered by x.

Once the algorithm found the best possible product, it is added to the set of products, the pairs covered are removed from the set of all weighted pairs, and then it seeks for the next product. The algorithms stop when it is not possible to add more products to increase the weighted coverage. This happens when all pairs of features with weight greater than zero are covered.

Let us first describe the common part related to the integer program which is the base of the computation of the best product in each iteration. The transformation of the given feature model is common in the two algorithms. However, the expressions used for dealing with pairwise coverage are different in the linear and nonlinear approaches.

Let f be the number of features in a model fm, we use decision variables $x_j \in \{0,1\}$ and $j \in \{1,2,\ldots,f\}$ to indicate if we should include feature j in the next product $(x_j = 1)$ or not $(x_j = 0)$. Not all the combinations of features form valid products. According to Benavides et al. [20] we can use propositional logic to express the validity of a product with respect to a FM. These Boolean formulas can be expressed in Conjunctive Normal Form (CNF) as a conjunction of clauses, which in turn can be expressed as constraints in an integer program. The way to do it is by adding one constraint for each clause in the CNF. Let us focus on one clause and let us define the Boolean vectors v and u as follows [22]:

$$v_j = \begin{cases} 1 \text{ if feature } j \text{ appears in the clause,} \\ 0 \text{ otherwise,} \end{cases}$$

$$u_j = \begin{cases} 1 \text{ if feature } j \text{ appears negated in the clause,} \\ 0 \text{ otherwise.} \end{cases}$$

With the help of u and v we can write the constraint that corresponds to one CNF clause for the i-th product as:

$$\sum_{j=1}^{f} v_j(u_j(1-x_j) + (1-u_j)x_j) \geq 1. \tag{3}$$

Finally, Algorithm 1 represents the general scheme used by our algorithmic proposals based on integer programming. In Line 1 the list of products $ppCA$ is initialized to the empty list. Then, the execution enters the loop (Line 2) that tries to find the best product maximizing the coverage with respect to the configurations not covered yet, U (Line 3). The new product is added to the list of products $ppCA$ (Line 4) and the covered pairs are removed from the set U (Line 5).

Algorithm 1. Scheme of hybrid algorithms based on integer programming

Require: U //Set of configurations with weights greater than zero
Ensure: $ppCA$ // List of products
1: $ppCA \leftarrow []$
2: **while** $U \neq \emptyset$ **do**
3:    $z \leftarrow$ solve (max $h(x)$ subject to valid x)
4:    $ppCA \leftarrow ppCA + z$
5:    $U \leftarrow U/covered(z)$ // Remove pairs covered by product z
6: **end while**

4.1   Linear Approach

In the linear approach we need decision variables to model the pairwise configurations that are covered by a product. These variables are denoted by $c_{j,k}$, $c_{j,\overline{k}}$, $c_{\overline{j},k}$ o $c_{\overline{j},\overline{k}}$, depending on the presence/absence of the features j, k in a configuration. They will take value 1 if the product covers a configuration and 0 otherwise. The values of variables c depends on the values of the x variables. To reflect this dependency in our linear program, we need to add the following constraints for all pairs of features $1 \leq j < k \leq f$:

$$2c_{\overline{j},\overline{k}} \leq (1 - x_j) + (1 - x_k), \tag{4}$$
$$2c_{\overline{j},k} \leq (1 - x_j) + x_k, \tag{5}$$
$$2c_{j,\overline{k}} \leq x_j + (1 - x_k), \tag{6}$$
$$2c_{j,k} \leq x_j + x_k. \tag{7}$$

It is not necessary to add all possible variables c, but only those corresponding to a pair not yet covered. Finally, the goal of our program is to maximize the weighted pairwise coverage, which is given by the sum of variables $c_{j,k}$ weighted with $w_{j,k}$. Let us denote with U the set of configurations not covered yet. The expression to maximize is, thus:

$$\sum_{(j,k)\in U} w_{j,k}c_{j,k}, \tag{8}$$

where (abusing notation) j and k are used to represent the presence/absence of features.

4.2   Nonlinear Approach

In the nonlinear approach we avoid using the decision variables that represent the presence/absence of particular pairs in a product, reducing the number of variables and constraints compared to the linear approach. As a counter part we need to use nonlinear functions to represent the objective function. In this case the objective function to maximize is as follows:

$$\sum_{(j,k)\in U} w_{j,k}x_jx_k + \sum_{(\overline{j},k)\in U} w_{\overline{j},k}(1 - x_j)x_k + \tag{9}$$

$$\sum_{(j,\overline{k})\in U} w_{j,\overline{k}}x_j(1 - x_k) + \sum_{(\overline{j},\overline{k})\in U} w_{\overline{j},\overline{k}}(1 - x_j)(1 - x_k). \tag{10}$$

This problem formulation results in a more concise problem representation because the objective function is smaller and the inequalities (4)–(7) are not required.

5   Experimental Setup

This section describes how the evaluation was performed. First, we describe the PPGS and pICPL algorithms, object of the comparison. Next, we present the methods used to assign priorities, the feature models used as experimental corpus, and the experiments configuration.

5.1   Prioritized Pairwise Genetic Solver

Prioritized Pairwise Genetic Solver (PPGS) is a constructive genetic algorithm that follows a master-slave model to parallelize the individuals' evaluation. In each iteration, the algorithm adds the best product to the test suite until all weighted pairs are covered. The best product to be added is the product that adds more weighted coverage (only pairs not covered yet) to the set of products.

The parameter settings used by PPGS are the same of the reference paper for the algorithm [15]. It uses binary tournament selection and a one-point crossover with a probability 0.8. The population size of 10 individuals implies a more exploitation than exploration behaviour of the search with a termination condition of 1,000 fitness evaluations. The mutation operator iterates over all selected features of an individual and randomly replaces a feature by another one with a probability 0.1. The algorithm stops when all the weighted pairs have been covered. For further details on PPGS see [15].

5.2   Prioritized-ICPL (pICPL) Algorithm

Prioritized-ICPL is a greedy algorithm to generate n-wise covering arrays proposed by Johansen et al. [14]. pICPL does not compute covering arrays with full coverage but rather covers only those n-wise combinations among features that are present in at least one of the prioritized products, as was described in the formalization of the problem in Sect. 3. We must highlight here that the pICPL algorithm uses *data parallel execution*, supporting any number of processors. Their parallelism comes from simultaneous operations across large sets of data. For further details on prioritized-ICPL please refer to [14].

5.3   Priority Assignment Methods

We considered three methods to assign weight values to prioritized products: *rank-based values*, *random values*, and *measured values*.

Rank-based Values. In the rank-based weight assignment, the products are sorted according to how dissimilar they are. More dissimilar products appear first in the ranking and have a lower rank. Then, they are assigned priority weights based on their rank values, low ranked products are assigned higher priorities. Giving the same weight value to two of the most SPL-wide dissimilar products, the weight values will be more likely spread among a larger number of pairwise configurations making the covering array harder to compute. In addition, this enables us to select different percentages of the number of products for prioritization. The selected percentages used are: 5%, 10%, 20%, 30% and 50%.

Random Values. In the random weight assignment, the weights are randomly generated from a uniform distribution between the minimum and maximum values obtained with the rank-based assignment. A percentage of the products denoted by each individual feature model was used for product prioritization. The selected percentages are: 5%, 10%, 20%, 30%, and 50%.

Measured Values. For this third method, the weights are derived from non-functional properties values obtained from 16 real SPL systems, that were measured with the SPL Conqueror approach [23]. This approach aims at providing reliable estimates of measurable non-functional properties such as performance, main memory consumption, and footprint. These estimations are then used to emulate more realistic scenarios whereby software testers need to schedule their testing effort giving priority, for instance, to products or feature combinations that exhibit higher footprint or performance. In this work, we use the actual values taken on the measured products considering pairwise feature interactions.

Table 1. Measured values benchmark

SPL name	Prop	NF	NP	NC	PP%
Prevayler	F	6	32	24	75.0
LinkedList	F	26	1440	204	14.1
ZipMe	F	8	64	64	100.0
PKJab	F	12	72	72	100.0
SensorNetwork	F	27	16704	3240	19.4
BerkeleyDBF	F	9	256	256	100.0
Violet	F	101	≈1E20	101	≈0.0
Linux subset	F	25	≈3E7	100	≈0.0
LLVM	M	12	1024	53	5.1
Curl	M	14	1024	68	6.6
x264	M	17	2048	77	3.7
Wget	M	17	8192	94	1.15
BerkeleyDBM	M	19	3840	1280	33.3
SQLite	M	40	≈5E7	418	≈0.0
BerkeleyDBP	P	27	1440	180	12.50
Apache	P	10	256	192	75.0

Footprint, **M**ain memory consumption, **P**erformance, **N**umber of **F**eatures, **N**umber of **P**roducts, **N**umber of **C**onfigurations, **P**ercentage of **P**rioritized products.

Table 1 summarizes the SPL systems evaluated, their measured property (Prop), number of features (NF), number of products (NP), number of configurations measured (NC), and the percentage of prioritized products (PP%) used in our comparison.

5.4 Benchmark of Feature Models

In this work we use two different groups of feature models. The first one (G1) is composed of 219 feature models which represent between 16 and 80,000 products using rank-based and random weight priority assignments. The second group (G2) is composed of 16 real feature models which represent between 16 and ≈3E20 products for which the measured values strategy for weight assignment was used. In total, we used 235 distinct feature models: 16 feature models from SPL Conqueror, 5 from Johansen et al. [14], and 201 from the SPLOT website [24]. Note that for G1, two priority assignment methods are used with five different prioritization selection percentages. For feature models which denote less than 1,000 products we use 20%, 30% and 50% of the prioritized products. For feature models which denote between 1,000 and 80,000 products we use 5%, 10% and 20%. This yields a grand total of 1,330 instances analyzed with the four algorithms in our comparison (Table 2).

Table 2. Benchmark summary

	G1	G2	Summary
NFM	219	16	235
NP	16–80 K	32–≈3E24	16–≈3E24
NF	10–67	6–101	6–101
WPA	RK,RD	M	RK, RD, M
PP%	5, 10, 20, 30, 50	≈0.0–100	≈0.0–100
PI	1314	16	1330

NFM: Number Feature Models, NP: Number Products, NF: Number of Features, WPA: Weight Priority Assignment, RK: Rank based, RN: Random, M: Measured, PP%: Prioritized Products Percentage, PI: Problem Instances

5.5 Hardware

PPGS and pICPL are non-deterministic algorithms, so we performed 30 independent runs for a fair comparison between them. As performance measures we analyzed both the number of products required to test the SPL and the time required to run the algorithm. In both cases, the lower the value the better the performance, since we want a small number of products to test the SPL and we want the algorithm to be as fast as possible. All the executions were run in a cluster of 16 machines with Intel Core2 Quad processors Q9400 (4 cores per processor) at 2.66 GHz and 4 GB memory running Ubuntu 12.04.1 LTS and managed by the HT Condor 7.8.4 cluster manager. Since we have four cores available per processor, we have executed only one task per single processor, so we have used four parallel threads in each independent execution of the analyzed algorithms. HILP and HINLP were executed once per instance and weight assignment, because they are deterministic algorithms. Four cores were used as in the other algorithms.

6 Results Analysis

In this section, we study the behaviour of the proposed approaches using statistical techniques with the aim of analyzing the computed best solutions and highlighting the algorithm that performs the best.

6.1 Quality Analysis

In Table 3 we summarize the results obtained for group G1, feature models with up to 80,000 products. Each column corresponds to one algorithm and in the rows we show the number of products required to reach 50% up to 100% of total weighted coverage. The data shown in each cell is the mean and the standard deviation of the independent runs of 219 feature models. We highlight the best value for each percentage of weighted coverage.

At first glance we observe that the algorithms based on integer programming are the best in solution quality for all percentages of weighted coverage. Between HILP and HINLP the differences are almost insignificant except for 100% coverage, so it is difficult to claim that one algorithm is better than the other. It is also noteworthy that PPGS is the worst algorithm for 100% coverage while pICPL is the worst for the rest of percentages of coverage.

Table 3. Mean and standard deviation for G1 instances (219 FMs).

Coverage	HILP	HINLP	PPGS	pICPL
50%	$1.18_{0.39}$	$1.18_{0.38}$	$1.19_{0.39}$	$1.24_{0.55}$
75%	$1.96_{0.49}$	$1.96_{0.49}$	$1.96_{0.50}$	$2.11_{1.01}$
80%	$2.19_{0.58}$	$2.19_{0.58}$	$2.22_{0.59}$	$2.42_{1.13}$
85%	$2.52_{0.70}$	$2.52_{0.70}$	$2.54_{0.70}$	$2.76_{1.31}$
90%	$2.98_{0.86}$	$2.99_{0.87}$	$3.00_{0.87}$	$3.36_{1.56}$
95%	$3.93_{1.14}$	$3.93_{1.14}$	$3.95_{1.17}$	$4.43_{2.07}$
100%	$9.21_{6.31}$	$8.99_{5.06}$	$9.45_{6.81}$	$9.23_{6.41}$

In order to check if the differences between the algorithms are statistically significant or just a matter of chance, we applied the non-parametric Kruskal-Wallis test with a confidence level of 95% (p-value under 0.05). In summary the number of times that one algorithm is statistically better than the other algorithms is as follows: HILP in 11 out of 21 comparisons (7% and 3 other algorithms), HINLP in 10 out of 21, PPGS in 7 out of 21, and pICPL 1 out of 21. These results confirm that for G1 the algorithms based on integer programming are statistically better than the other proposals, so they are able to compute better sets of prioritized test data than PPGS and pICPL.

Let us now focus on group G2, feature models with measured weight values. In Table 4 we show the results for this group of real instances. Here, pICPL and PPGS are the best algorithms in one percentage of coverage, 50% and 80% respectively. Nevertheless HILP and HINLP are able to compute better test suites for most percentages of coverage, so the conclusions extracted are similar than those extracted from the experiments with G1 instances. For 50% and 100% coverage there are no significant differences among the four algorithms, but in the rest of scenarios there are significant differences with respect to pICPL. Therefore, it is clear that pICPL is the worst algorithm for G2 instances. We want to highlight that there is no difference again between HILP and HINLP.

Table 4. Mean and standard deviation for G2 instances (16 FMs).

Coverage	HILP	HINLP	PPGS	pICPL
50%	$1,56_{0,50}$	$1,56_{0,50}$	$1,58_{0,49}$	$1,56_{0,50}$
75%	$2,63_{0,78}$	$2,63_{0,78}$	$2,66_{0,77}$	$2,75_{0,75}$
80%	$2,81_{0,81}$	$2,81_{0,81}$	$2,81_{0,73}$	$3,25_{0,97}$
85%	$3,44_{0,86}$	$3,44_{0,86}$	$3,46_{0,87}$	$3,81_{0,95}$
90%	$4,06_{1,03}$	$4,00_{0,94}$	$4,12_{1,04}$	$4,56_{1,27}$
95%	$5,37_{1,05}$	$5,38_{1,05}$	$5,45_{1,14}$	$6,06_{1,44}$
100%	$11,69_{5,51}$	$11.63_{5.33}$	$12,08_{6,50}$	$12,19_{5,68}$

6.2 Performance Analysis

In Fig. 2 we show the boxplots of the execution time (logarithmic scale) required by each algorithm in the two group of instances to reach 100% of weighted coverage. The median is also shown in text. Regarding the computation time, pICPL is clearly the fastest algorithm with statistically significant differences with the rest of algorithms in G1. Actually, in G1 all algorithms are significantly different from each other. In a closer look at the data, we observe that pICPL has a first and second quartiles lower than HINLP's, nevertheless the third pICPL's quartile is far from HINLP's. This means that the performance of pICPL decreases as the instance increases in size. In contrast, HINLP has a smaller inter-quartile range, then HINLP seems to scale better than pICPL.

Besides, in the comparison between HILP and HINLP, all quartiles are lower for HINLP, so from these results, it is clear that HINLP produce a boost in computation time due to the reduction of clauses in comparison with the linear variant of the algorithm (HILP).

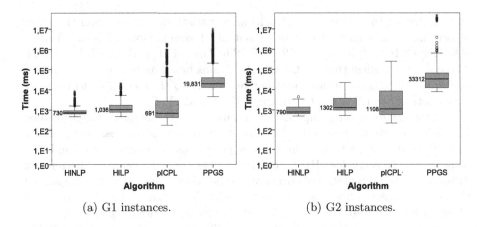

(a) G1 instances.   (b) G2 instances.

Fig. 2. Comparison of algorithms' execution time in logarithmic scale.

With regard to the G2 group of instances, HINLP is the fastest with significant differences with the rest of algorithms. In this group of instances, there are not significant differences between HILP and pICPL. Again, pICPL's third quartile is far from the values of HILP and HINLP, then it scales worse than the integer programming approaches. Although PPGS is not the worst algorithm in solution quality, in computation time is the worst of the comparison in the two groups of instances.

As a general conclusion we can say that the two proposed hybrid algorithms obtain good quality solutions while they are also very competitive in runtime. Between them, the variant using nonlinear functions is the best in the comparison with statistical significant differences. For the benchmark of feature models analyzed here our proposals do not have scalability problems. Note that some of the feature models denote $\approx 1E20$ products. Part of our future work is to verify if this trend holds for feature models with a larger number of products.

7   Threats to Validity

There are two main threats to validity in our work. The first one is related to the parameters values of the genetic algorithm (PPGS). A change in the values of these parameters could have an impact in the results of the algorithm. Thus, we can only claim that the conclusions are valid for the combination of parameter values that we used, which are quite standard in the field. Second, the selection of feature models for the experimental corpus can indeed bias the results obtained. In order to mitigate this threat, we used three different priority assignment methods, five percentages of prioritized products, and different sources for our feature models. From them we selected a number of feature models as large as possible, with the widest ranges in both, number of features and number of products.

8   Conclusions and Final Remarks

In this paper we have studied the Prioritized Pairwise Test Data Generation Problem in the context of SPL with the aim of proposing two novel hybrid algorithms. The first one is based on an integer linear formulation (HILP) and the second is based on a integer quadratic (nonlinear) formulation (HINLP). We have performed a comparison using 235 feature models of different sizes, different priority assignment methods and four different algorithms, the two proposed algorithms and two algorithms of the state-of-the-art (pICLP and PPGS). Overall, the proposed hybrid algorithms are better in solution quality. In computation time HINLP is the best with significant difference, except for pICPL in G1.

Regarding the comparison between HILP and HINLP, there is no significant difference in solution quality. The slight existing differences are due to the different solvers used for dealing with linear and nonlinear functions. In contrast, concerning the execution time, there are significant differences between them. The nonlinear variant outperformed the linear variant. The reason behind this improvement in performance could be the number of clauses (constraints) not needed by the nonlinear variant to represent the covered pairs. Then, we can avoid considering a maximum of $f*(f-1)*2$ constraints[5] (total number of valid pairs). Moreover, the nonlinear technique has no scalability issues computing the feature models analyzed here. Therefore, with no doubt the best algorithm in our comparison is HINLP.

There are two promising future lines possible after the work contained in this paper. Broadly speaking, these lines are search for the limits of the nonlinear approach applying this technique to larger feature models and the test suites computation using the whole test suite approach [25]. In this last regard, the hybrid approaches do not assure the optimum because they are constructive algorithms that only deal with one product at a time. Obtaining the Pareto front would require the computation of several products at a time and multiple executions of the algorithm with different upper bounds in number of products. Preliminary results suggest that the number of variables and constraints grow very fast with the number of products computed, what could be an issue for the integer programming solver. Further research will be needed in that direction.

References

1. Pohl, K., Bockle, G., van der Linden, F.J.: Software Product Line Engineering: Foundations, Principles and Techniques. Springer, Heidelberg (2005)
2. Engström, E., Runeson, P.: Software product line testing - a systematic mapping study. Inf. Softw. Technol. **53**(1), 2–13 (2011)
3. da Mota Silveira Neto, P.A., do Carmo Machado, I., McGregor, J.D., de Almeida, E.S., de Lemos Meira, S.R.: A systematic mapping study of software product lines testing. Inf. Softw. Technol. **53**(5), 407–423 (2011)
4. Lee, J., Kang, S., Lee, D.: A survey on software product line testing. In: de Almeida, E.S., Schwanninger, C., Benavides, D. (eds.) SPLC, vol. 1, pp. 31–40. ACM (2012)

---

[5] f is the number of features in a feature model.

5. do Carmo Machado, I., McGregor, J.D., de Almeida, E.S.: Strategies for testing products in software product lines. Softw. Eng. Notes **37**(6), 1–8 (2012)
6. Perrouin, G., Sen, S., Klein, J., Baudry, B., Traon, Y.L.: Automated and scalable t-wise test case generation strategies for software product lines. In: ICST, pp. 459–468. IEEE Computer Society (2010)
7. Oster, S., Markert, F., Ritter, P.: Automated incremental pairwise testing of software product lines. In: Bosch, J., Lee, J. (eds.) SPLC 2010. LNCS, vol. 6287, pp. 196–210. Springer, Heidelberg (2010). doi:10.1007/978-3-642-15579-6_14
8. Garvin, B.J., Cohen, M.B., Dwyer, M.B.: Evaluating improvements to a meta-heuristic search for constrained interaction testing. Empirical Softw. Eng. **16**(1), 61–102 (2011)
9. Hervieu, A., Baudry, B., Gotlieb, A.: PACOGEN: automatic generation of pairwise test configurations from feature models. In: ISSRE, pp. 120–129 (2011)
10. Lochau, M., Oster, S., Goltz, U., Schürr, A.: Model-based pairwise testing for feature interaction coverage in software product line engineering. Softw. Qual. J. **20**(3–4), 567–604 (2012)
11. Cichos, H., Oster, S., Lochau, M., Schürr, A.: Model-based coverage-driven test suite generation for software product lines. In: Whittle, J., Clark, T., Kühne, T. (eds.) MODELS 2011. LNCS, vol. 6981, pp. 425–439. Springer, Heidelberg (2011). doi:10.1007/978-3-642-24485-8_31
12. Ensan, F., Bagheri, E., Gašević, D.: Evolutionary search-based test generation for software product line feature models. In: Ralyté, J., Franch, X., Brinkkemper, S., Wrycza, S. (eds.) CAiSE 2012. LNCS, vol. 7328, pp. 613–628. Springer, Heidelberg (2012). doi:10.1007/978-3-642-31095-9_40
13. Blum, C., Blesa, M.J.: Construct, Merge, Solve and Adapt: Application to the Repetition-Free Longest Common Subsequence Problem. Springer International Publishing, Cham (2016). 46–57
14. Johansen, M.F., Haugen, Ø., Fleurey, F., Eldegard, A.G., Syversen, T.: Generating better partial covering arrays by modeling weights on sub-product lines. In: France, R.B., Kazmeier, J., Breu, R., Atkinson, C. (eds.) MODELS 2012. LNCS, vol. 7590, pp. 269–284. Springer, Heidelberg (2012). doi:10.1007/978-3-642-33666-9_18
15. Lopez-Herrejon, R.E., Ferrer, J., Chicano, F., Haslinger, E.N., Egyed, A., Alba, E.: A parallel evolutionary algorithm for prioritized pairwise testing of software product lines. In: GECCO 2014, pp. 1255–1262. ACM, New York (2014)
16. Kang, K., Cohen, S., Hess, J., Novak, W., Peterson, A.: Feature-oriented domain analysis (FODA) feasibility study. Technical report CMU/SEI-90-TR-21, Software Engineering Institute, Carnegie Mellon University (1990)
17. Lopez-Herrejon, R.E., Batory, D.: A standard problem for evaluating product-line methodologies. In: Bosch, J. (ed.) GCSE 2001. LNCS, vol. 2186, pp. 10–24. Springer, Heidelberg (2001). doi:10.1007/3-540-44800-4_2
18. Cohen, M.B., Dwyer, M.B., Shi, J.: Constructing interaction test suites for highly-configurable systems in the presence of constraints: a greedy approach. IEEE Trans. Softw. Eng. **34**(5), 633–650 (2008)
19. Nie, C., Leung, H.: A survey of combinatorial testing. ACM Comput. Surv. **43**(2), 11:1–11:29 (2011)
20. Benavides, D., Segura, S., Cortés, A.R.: Automated analysis of feature models 20 years later: a literature review. Inf. Syst. **35**(6), 615–636 (2010)
21. Johansen, M.F., Haugen, Ø., Fleurey, F.: An algorithm for generating t-wise covering arrays from large feature models. In: Proceedings of the International Software Product Lines Conference, pp. 46–55 (2012)

22. Sutton, A.M., Whitley, D., Howe, A.E.: A polynomial time computation of the exact correlation structure of k-satisfiability landscapes. In: Proceedings of the Annual Conference on Genetic and Evolutionary Computation, pp. 365–372 (2009)

23. Siegmund, N., Rosenmüller, M., Kästner, C., Giarrusso, P., Apel, S., Kolesnikov, S.: Scalable prediction of non-functional properties in software product lines: footprint and memory consumption. Inf. Softw. Technol. **55**(3), 491–507 (2013)

24. Mendonca, M.: Software Product Line Online Tools (SPLOT) (2013). http://www.splot-research.org/

25. Arcuri, A., Fraser, G.: On the Effectiveness of Whole Test Suite Generation. Springer International Publishing, Cham (2014). 1–15

On the Use of Smelly Examples to Detect Code Smells in JavaScript

Ian Shoenberger[1], Mohamed Wiem Mkaouer[1(✉)], and Marouane Kessentini[2]

[1] Department of Software Engineering, Rochester Institute of Technology, Rochester, USA
{ian.shoenberger,mwmvse}@rit.edu
[2] Department of Computer and Information Science, University of Michigan, Ann Arbor, USA
marouane@umich.edu

Abstract. JavaScript has become one of the widely-used languages. However, as the size of JavaScript-based applications grows, the number of defects grows as well. Recent studies have produced a set of manually defined rules to identify these defects. We propose, in this work, the automation of deriving these rules to ensure scalability and potentially the detection of a wider set of defects without requiring any extensive knowledge on rules tuning. To this end, we rely on a base of existing code smells that is used to train the detection rules using Genetic Programming and find the best threshold of metrics composing the rules. The evaluation of our work on 9 JavaScript web projects has shown promising results in terms of detection precision of 92% and recall of 85%, with no threshold tuning required.

1 Introduction

JavaScript (JS) has been revolutionizing the web by combining services, libraries, and services from various third party providers. It was initially born to exclusively serve as a scripting standard at the browser level but it has drastically expanded to take over the lead in managing web N-tier architectures and as a result, 98% of the most visited websites incorporate JS [1]. The popularity of JS is issued from its dynamically-typed nature [2] and the wide variety of features it can quickly and dynamically include on the fly [3]. On the other hand, dynamically-typed languages, in general, have proven to be difficult to analyze, and thus, their catalog of development supporting tools suffers, and JavaScript is no exception [4]. With the rapid growth of JS applications in terms of size, rich interpolated functionalities at the expense of complexity and the lack of tools support, it is becoming a maintenance nightmare of developers [5]. Just like any other language, JS suffers from bad programming decisions, known as code smells [6], that can be introduced during the initial software development or during adding new features or applying debugging patches. The existence of code smells indicates the poor software quality and it increases the risk of introducing bugs. With the fact that JS is an interpreted language, the absence of a compiler that may raise warnings about potential runtime errors, adding to that the ability to include more code on the runtime through prototyping

© Springer International Publishing AG 2017
G. Squillero and K. Sim (Eds.): EvoApplications 2017, Part II, LNCS 10200, pp. 20–34, 2017.
DOI: 10.1007/978-3-319-55792-2_2

makes it hard to maintain a defect-free JS code base [7]. So code smells detection can be seen as a preventive task to minimize the number of bugs.

Unlike Object-Oriented (OO) languages, in which code smell detection and correction have been widely studied in the literature, there isn't much work tackling these smells in JS for various reasons, for instance, JS naturally does not necessarily comply with object oriented design rules, although it supports their implementation, furthermore, the lack of modeling support for JS prevents the automated identification of any high-level design anti-patterns. Still, several studies have approached the detection of bad development behavior in JS, in which, the most developed family of tools is for static analysis of programs, mostly for detecting very low-level errors in the code. Although tools such as JSLint [8], and JSHint [9] are great for syntactical issues like missing semi-colons and enforcing organizational policy, they do not support the high-level detection of structural defects within the source code that may not be as obvious.

The main challenge of detecting code smells in JS is the inability of statically calculate structural measurements e.g., coupling and cohesion, which can be combined to create code smells detection rules. To capture these interaction properties between JS objects, static analysis has to be augmented with dynamic analysis. On the flipside, dynamic analysis is more costly in terms of time and performance, also, in many statements and dependencies cannot be analyzed at runtime until triggered by a given input or scenario. Still, various studies have been conducted in the context of dynamic analysis to detect type inconsistencies [10], event related [11] cross-browser testing [12] and code smell detection [13]. The latter work labeled JSNOSE [13] extracts a set of static metrics from the static analysis of JS objects and monitor their behavior during the application runtime. Using this combination, it uses the rule-based approach to identify high-level disharmonies, which are similar to a subset of the code smells that exist in literature, as well as smells that exist specific to JavaScript. In addition, JSNOSE allows developers to extend the list of possible smells to detect. In this approach, rules are manually defined to identify the key symptoms that characterize a code-smell using a set of limited quantitative metrics. However, in a more concrete setting, the number of possible code-smells to manually characterize with rules can be large. Moreover, for each code-smell, rules that are expressed in terms of metrics require continuous calibration efforts to find the right threshold especially in a highly dynamic environment like JS.

To cope the above-mentioned limitations, we propose in this paper the automated tuning of code-smells detection rules using a dataset of existing code-smells. The process aims at finding, for each JS object, a subset of similar objects in the base of examples, then, using this subset of objects with their known smells, we use the Genetic Programming to tune the threshold of quantitative metrics in order to maximize the coverage of the detected smells in the subset. These calibrated metrics will be later on used to detect smells in JS. The evaluation of our work on 9 JS web projects has shown promising results in achieving a detection of a subset of JS smells that were reported by JSNOSE with 92% precision, with no metrics tuning needed.

The remainder of this paper is structured as follows. Section 2 provides the background required to understand our approach and the challenges in detecting code-smells in JS. In Sect. 3, we describe our approach and show how we deployed a GP to tune metrics that will be used for the smells detection. Section 4 presents and discusses the results obtained by comparing our approach with JSNOSE. Related work is discussed in Sect. 5, while in Sect. 6 we conclude and suggest future research directions.

2   Background and Problem Statement

After nearly two decades since code smells were introduced by Fowler [6], there is no consensus on how to standardize the definition of code smells. Several studies have been characterizing smells by their symptoms at the source code level that are be measured by structural metrics [14] or using history of code changes [15] or even using textual information extracted from the code base internal and external documentation [16]. It is to note that dynamic analysis was not solicited in the detection process mainly due to its complexity and also because static analysis offers a rich catalog of metrics that be used to create detection rules. However, this does not apply to JS. JS revolution in the last decade was driven by the dynamic manipulation of the Document Object Model (DOM) and XML objects under several web protocols [17]. The tremendous growth of JS web application has negatively impacted their maintenance especially with the propagation of the JS technology to become the leading language for servers and web databases [18]. In this context, Mesbah et al. [13] discovered the existence of traditional code smells in JS and clustered them into "classic" smells that are derived from the literature and "JS-specific" smells that identify exclusive bad programming patterns in JS. Since we aim at using the knowledge from existing smells detection literature, this paper will only focus on detecting the first type of the smells. Table 1 summarizes the code smells detected by JSNOSE and studied in this work.

Table 1. Detection Rules for JS code smells [13].

Code smell	Level	Detection rule	Structural metrics
Many global variables	File	GLB > 10	GLB: Number of global variables
Large object	Object	LOC > 750 OR NOP > 20	NOP: Number of properties
			LOC: Lines of code
Lazy object	Object	NOP < 3	MLOC: Method lines of code
Long method	Method	MLOC > 50	PAR: Number of parameters
Long parameter list	Method	PAR > 5	BUR: Base-Object usage ratio
Refused Bequest	Object	BUR < 1/3 AND NOP > 2	NOC: Number of cases
Switch statement	Method	NOC > 3	

Although JSNOSE has given promising results, it suffers from scalability issues as the application of the above-mentioned rules requires the manual calibration of thresholds which tends to be subjective, human intensive and error prone. Furthermore, previous detection studies resulted in several approximations of each smell in terms a set of metrics that be deployed to its identification and addressing this limitation by asking the developers to redefine their own rules is difficult as it needs an extensive knowledge about analysis and requires qualitative validation.

Recent studies [19, 20] have been investigating how developers rely on OO methodology when designing their JS code-base and have demonstrated the existence of OO-like structures and code-elements in JS [21]. Therefore, the main contribution of this paper is driven by the following research question: How to consider the existing knowledge in detecting bad programming practices in OO languages in the detection similar practices in JS. A straightforward approach would be to deploy existing detection techniques, defined for OO, to JS, but the detection process relies essentially on a profound static analysis that allows the definition of smells using a rich set of structural metrics, which are limited in the context of JS. Our contribution relies essentially on exploiting the similarity between JS and Java in order to identify smelly JS elements if they are similar to smelly Java elements. Also, we propose to address the above-mentioned limitations of JSNOSE by automatically generating thresholds for detection rules. Moreover, the base of smells examples can be generated using any developer-preferred existing detection tool in order to tune the rules to detect similar-smells in JS.

3 Approach Overview

The general workflow of this approach is decomposed into 4 main stages as shown Fig. 1. The 4 stages are described in this Section.

(1) **JS entities enumeration.** Our approach, built upon JSNOSE, inputting the web app, containing JS files, to the crawler. Once JS files extracted and parsed, the set of extracted JS Entities, called JSE, (e.g., objects, properties) is sent to the Similarity Calculator.

(2) **Similar Elements extraction.** This module takes as input JS entities and code elements from existing software systems. The purpose of this process is to extract code elements that are mostly similar in terms of structural properties, this set of similar extracted elements is labeled SEE. To avoid the exhaustive comparison between JS entities with all the code elements from the code base, which can become easily large, we apply an initial matching between them as follows [19] (Table 2):

Table 2. Initial mapping between JS entities and code elements

Code element	JS entity
Class	File/Object
Attribute	Property
Method	Function/Inner function

Then for each pair of entity/code element, we calculate their structural similarity. We consider this process similar to structural code clone detection and we extend this existing metric-based technique [22] that identifies exact elements by loosening this exactitude to a certain threshold. Let MX = $<m1(X), ..., mn(X)>$ be the set of metrics characterizing the entity X; $mi(X)$ ($i = 1 ... n$) stands for the i-th software metric chosen to describe X, and n is a fixed number metrics describing the entities. Any other entity Y is considered similar to X with threshold α *iff*:

$$Sim(X, Y) = \sum_{i=1}^{n} |m_i(X) - m_i(y)| < \sum_{i=1}^{n} \alpha_i \tag{1}$$

In order to automatically approximate α for each metrics, we use the box-plot technique to select near lower bound of the values space. Using these values, for each JS entity a subset of code elements will be traced.

(3) **Metrics thresholds calibration.** The purpose of this step is to update the thresholds of JS detection rules. To do so, we first extract the smelly elements, called SmellyE, from SEE. The detection of those elements can be done with any state-of-art detection tool, in this study we used infusion to detect smelly elements in our base of example projects. Also, this detection process may be done prior to running the calibration algorithm for performance purposes. Once the set of SmellyE is known, for each smell type a detection rule is generated. Therefore, for each generated rule, the metrics used by JSNOSE undergo the calibration process by inputting them in a tree structure. the tuning process aims in tuning metrics thresholds in order to maximize the number of detected smells in SmellyE, this way, the tuned rule can be used later on to detect smells in JS.

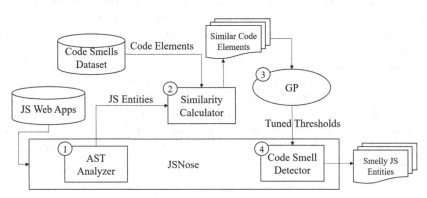

Fig. 1. Approach overview.

Solution Representation. Since our aim is to only tune thresholds for given rules, the individual initial setup was seeded with JSNose built in rules.

Solution Evaluation. The GP Initially takes as input the list of code elements, which were previously selected based on their similarity with a given JS entity. Initially, the calibrator tests whether a subset of elements contain smells. If the elements are smell free then the subset will be discarded and no calibration needed. Otherwise, the code smell types will be sorted based on their occurrence and the most occurring smell type triggers the GP's evolutionary process of tuning its metrics' thresholds. The fitness function used evolves the rule towards maximizing the detection of the infected elements in SmellyE, the set of identified smells is labeled DSmellyE.

Solution Evolution. Since the rules structure was not to change, the crossover was not solicited. Also, the uniform subtree mutation [23] was constrained to act exclusively on nodes with values and the function was only allowed to update the value by randomly adding or subtracting a randomly selected number between 0 and 1. After several generations, once the stopping criterion is met, the best solution i.e., a rule with the best detection ranking is then sent to back to JSNose to be used for the detection process. The following table gives a summary of the terminals used in the GP algorithm (Table 3).

Table 3. GP Terminology.

Term	Definition
JSE	Set of JS extracted entities, subject to smell investigation
SEE	Set of extracted elements from existing projects as they exhibit a strong structural similarity with the elements in JSE
SmellyE	Subset of JSE that are infected with code smells
DSmellyE	Subset of SmellyE that were identified by the detection rule

The following pseudo-code highlights the adaptation of GP for the problem of detection rules generation.

Algorithm1. Metrics calibration using GP for each smell type

Input: Subset of JSE, infected with code smells (SmellyE)
Input: Metrics (R)
Output: Detection rule
1: Create a random Population (P) of Individuals (I)
2: Randomly create a rule using metrics I ← rule(R)
3: repeat
4:    for all I ∈ P do
5:            DSmellyE ← I.executeRule(SmellyE)
6:            I.fitness ← DSmellyE ∩ SmellyE
7:    end for
8:    BestIndividual ← Rank(P, BestIndividual)
9:    P ← reproducePopulation(P)
10:
11:    generation←generation+1;
12: until generation = maxGeneration
13: return BestIndividual

---

(4) **Code Smells Detection.** The GP returns an updated detection rule, for any smell type that was known in the subset of code elements. This rule is then executed to report any JS entities that their properties do not violate the updated metrics thresholds.

4   Initial Evaluation Study

4.1   Research Questions

We defined two research questions to address in our experiments.

RQ1: What is the detection performance of the auto-tuned rules in the detection of several JS smell types?

RQ2: What is the impact of the base of examples' size on the finding code elements with similar properties to the JS entities and how similar are the tuned rules to the ones defined by JSNose?

To answer RQ1, we assess the performance of our detection process by its ability to replicate the detected smells by JSNOSE for the same given projects. To do so, we run JSNose to re-generate the code smells that we consider as expected. Then we run our approach to generating our suggested smells. These expected and suggested smells are used to calculate the precision and recall as follows:

$$PR_{precision} = \frac{|\text{ suggested smells} \cap \text{ expected smells}|}{|\text{suggested smells}|} \in [0,1] \quad RC_{recall} = \frac{|\text{ suggested smells} \cap \text{expected smells}|}{|\text{expected smells}|} \in [0,1] \quad (2)$$

For RQ2 we want to study the impact of varying the size of the dataset on the performance of the similarity process. We also illustrate the results by manually verifying a set of the reported JS entities.

4.2   Experimental Setting

To build our dataset of example, we randomly sampled 100 small to early medium open source projects. We limited the size of our projects files based on our initial observation that the average size of the JS projects is small. The sampled projects were 61 Java Projects and 39 C++ projects, this helps in diversifying the set of examples especially that C++ is not purely object oriented. To detect smells within the dataset, we used two state-of-art code smell detectors namely InCode [14] and PMD [24]. To reduce the cost of parsing several projects, we performed the detection process prior to running the GP and saved the results (Code elements, their metrics and the list of infected ones) on separate log files[1]. We tried selecting the projects previously used in JSNose as the JS smells were manually validated on that study. We couldn't locate two of the projects. It is also to note that the TinyMCE project is still under continuous development and its size has increased compared to when it was tested using the original experiment of JSNose. Since the previously used releases were not mentioned and the number of added smells is relatively low, we included it in our benchmark (Table 4).

---

[1] For replication purposes, the dataset and tools used are located in: https://github.com/mkaouer/Code-Smells-Detection-in-JavaScript.

Table 4. Projects constituting the benchmark for our approach.

Systems	Number of JS files	JS LOC	Number of infected JS entities
PeriodicTable	1	71	23
CollegeVis	1	177	53
ChessGame	2	198	64
Tunnel	0	234	54
GhostBusters	0	278	49
FractalViewer	8	1245	212
PhotoGallery	5	1535	221
TinySiteCMS	13	2496	172
TinyMCE	191	26908	59

During this study, we use the same parameter setting for all executions of the GP. The parameter setting is specified in Table 5.

Table 5. Parameter tuning for GP.

GP parameter	Values
Population size/Max tree depth	50/2
Selection/Survival/K	Roulette-Wheel/K-Tournament/2
Mutation/Mutation rate/Range	Uniform-Sub-tree/0.1/[0…1]
Max iterations	1000/2500/5000

4.3 Results and Discussions

As an answer to RQ1, Table 6 reports the results of the empirical qualitative evaluation of the tuned detection rules in terms of precision and recall.

It is observed in Table 6 that our GP algorithm was able in most cases to replicate the results of JSNose. For reporting a high number of global variables, GP and JSNose performed the same except for *PeriodicTable* project, which GP's acceptance threshold was lower than JSNose. Since Global variables are highly discouraged especially in OO programs, having 6 global variables in *PeriodicTable* was considered high. For the large object defect, it is to note that, JSNose has not reported any instance for the *GhostBusters* and *PhotoGallery* project which was not the case for GP, since, in relational programming, several classes and files have the blob behavior, it is most likely to find several functions condensed in one entity and this increases the chance of detecting them as large entities. For the lazy object, GP has missed several smells that were reported by JSNose mainly in projects with limited size. However, in larger projects, GP reported more smells than JSNose. Both algorithms have almost agreed on the long method, long parameter list and refused bequest smells, this was expected especially that the definition of these smells that was adopted by JSNose matches the exact same rules used by InCode [14] since the authors of JSNose tuned the exact subtree, previously proposed by the authors of InCode. It can be also seen that; in general, the recall was usually lower than the precision for the small-sized JS projects while the precision was mostly lower for

Table 6. Median values of precision and recall for the JS code smells in 9 JS web projects over 31 runs. Differences are highlighted

Software	Many global variables		Large object		Lazy object		Long method		Long parameter list		Refused Bequest		Switch statement		Median per Project	
	GP (+/-)	JSNose (+/-)	PRE (%)	REC (%)	PRE (%)	REC (%)	PRE (%)	REC (%)	PRE (%)	REC (%)	PRE (%)	REC (%)	PRE (%)	REC (%)	PRE (%)	REC (%)
PeriodicTable	+	-	1	0.25	1	0.40	1	1	1	1	1	1	1	1	1	0.77
CollegeVis	+	+	1	1	1	0.37	1	0.5	1	1	1	1	1	1	1	0.81
ChessGame	+	+	1	0.77	1	0.55	1	1	1	1	1	1	1	1	1	0.88
Tunnel	+	+	1	1	1	0.59	1	1	1	1	1	1	1	1	1	0.93
GhostBusters	-	-	0	0	1	0.65	1	1	1	0.33	1	1	1	1	0.83	0.66
FractalViewer	+	+	1	0.71	1	1	0.83	1	1	0.80	1	0.93	1	1	0.97	0.90
PhotoGallery	+	+	0	0	1	1	1	1	1	1	1	1	1	1	0.83	0.83
TinySiteCMS	+	+	1	0.77	0.86	1	1	1	0.51	1	1	1	1	1	0.89	0.96
TinyMCE	-	-	0.60	1	0.78	1	1	1	0.44	1	1	0.77	1	0.66	0.80	0.94
Median per Smell	N/A	N/A	0.73	0.61	0.96	0.72	0.98	0.94	0.88	0.90	1	0.93	1	0.96	0.92	0.85

the projects which were larger like *TinySiteCMS* and *TinyMCE*. This induces that GP tends to be stricter on smaller projects while its rules become less selective. To better understand if this is due to the random sampling of the projects or due to the number of similar code elements that were selected during the training of GP rules, we conducted thought of tuning the rules with only smells that existed different releases within the same project. During multiple releases of a software, several features are added, bugs are fixed and refactorings conducted, this induces several changes in the software structure and any smell that would survive throughout these changes can be considered persistent. To do so, we picked, for each project, 4 previous releases and we conducted the same static analysis to generate all the structural metrics and we analyzed them with PMD and infusion, then we ruled out all the smells that didn't exist throughout the total of 5 releases. Then we re-conducted threshold of our rules. The following Fig. 2 shows the comparison of tuning with one release for each project (GP1R) with the one with 5 releases (GP5R).

As observed in Fig. 2, GP5R has increased the recall score of rules with multiples metrics (e.g., lazy object, refused bequest) and this can be explained by the fact that tuning the threshold with fewer but persistent smells makes the detection harder and fewer fittest rules evolve during the GP. On the other hand, the precision of GP5R for refused bequest has reduced.

For **RQ2**, Fig. 3 shows that the number of existing projects in this study has provided enough elements that are structurally similar to the JS elements under analysis. In general, it was easier to quickly find functions with equivalent size and number of parameters and the similarity has converged into an acceptable range earlier compared to the objects and files; it was harder to find similar classes in terms of number of lines of code and number of properties and functions, especially that the JS projects sizes were

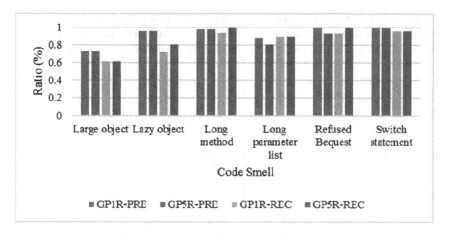

Fig. 2. Median values of precision and recall of GP1R and GP5R for the JS code smells in 9 JS web projects over 31 runs.

relatively small and so is for the projects that were also small and thus the number of classes was limited per project.

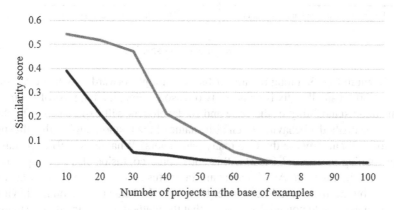

Fig. 3. Impact of the number of projects on the similarity between JS entities and code elements.

To illustrate the similarity between JS smells and the ones in the base of examples we extracted some JS smell instances and an equivalent selected code element from the base of examples with a smell instance.

As shown in Fig. 4, an object to be instantiated can be exceedingly large and often the object has many properties and functions that distinguish it as a code smell. Notice how it is logical to group the properties that are defined by lines 2 to 6. They are fundamental to the image entity. Lines 7 through 18 are really about effects, and so it may make sense to encapsulate these properties into their own object, perhaps called *Image-Effects*, and then include the object as a dependency within *Image*. As the code stands in the figure, the Image object is concerned about the properties of a text that the user may add while editing. Good software engineering practices suggest to separate concerns, and so it would also make sense to also encapsulate text properties into their own object. This smell is similar to the blob classes which are characterized by being data-driven highly cohesive and standalone objects (no inheritance and rare coupling).

```
function Image(id, fileName, url, height, width) {
    this.id = id;
    this.fileName = fileName;
    this.url = url;
    this.height = height;
    this.width = width;
    this.filter = null;
    this.rVal = 0;
    this.gVal = 0;
    this.bVal = 0;
    this.hue = 0;
    this.saturation = 0;
    this.contrast = 0;
    this.exposure = 0;
    this.shadow = 0;
    this.isBW = false;
    this.vignette = 0;
    this.vibrance = 0;
    this.userText = null;
    this.textColor = 'black';
    this.textRotation = 0;
    this.textSize = 'small';
    this.rotation = 0;
    this.zoomLevel = 0;

    this.doubleSize = function() {
        var aspectRatio = 0;

        aspectRatio = this.width / this.height;
        if(this.width > this.height) {
            this.width = this.width * 2;
            this.height = this.width / aspectRatio;
        } else {
```

Large object detected in PhotoGallery

```
public class TourOperator {
    public static final String _ID = "model.TourOperator";
    public static final String _TOUR_OPERATOR_ID = "tour_operator_id";
    public static final String _NAME = "name";
    public static final String _ADDRESS = "address";
    public static final String _PHONE = "phone";
    public static final String _FAX = "fax";
    public static final String _EMAIL = "email";
    public static final String _CONTACT = "contact";
    public static final String _LODGING_AVAILABLE = "lodging_available";
    public static final String _DB_PRIMARY_KEY = _TOUR_OPERATOR_ID;
    public static final Table _DB_TABLE = new Table("tour_operator");
    private int tour_operator_id = -1;
    private String name = null;
    private String address = null;
    private String phone = null;
    private String fax = null;
    private String email = null;
    private String contact = null;
    private Boolean lodging_available = false;
    public TourOperator(int tour_operator_id, String name, String address,
    public TourOperator(String name, String address, String phone, String
    public String getAddress() {
    public void setAddress(String address) {
    public String getContact() {
    public void setContact(String contact) {
    public String getEmail() {
    public void setEmail(String email) {
    public String getFax() {
    public void setFax(String fax) {
    public Boolean getLodging_available() {
    public void setLodging_available(Boolean lodging_available) {
    public String getName() {
    public void setName(String name) {
    public String getPhone() {
    public void setPhone(String phone) {
    public int getTour_operator_id() {
    public void setTour_operator_id(int tour_operator_id) {
    public String toString() {
```

Blob class detected in JVacation

Fig. 4. JS Large object smell.

As shown in Fig. 5, a long parameter list is a straightforward to detect code smell, it is an important smell to fix because of two reasons. First, the long list of parameters hurts the understandability of the code and so developers will experience difficulty in capturing the method's behavior. Even if the name of the method implies that the image will be rotated, but why are there so many parameters? What does *makeCopy* have to do with rotating an image? Clearly, this adds some confusion if a developer is not familiar with the function. And it can result in confusion even to someone who wrote the method but needs to revisit it in order to modify the behavior. Secondly, having so many parameters could potentially indicate that the method has assumed more than one responsibility as it has evolved over time. It is often simpler, and easier for developers to quickly add another parameter, and then create a 'special case', or a typical branch of execution for the respective arguments in order to tailor the method to new requirements. This is where smells become introduced over the lifetime of an application in either JS or any other language. Having such a long list of parameters like in the constructor in Fig. 5 makes its invocation difficult as well.

```
function rotateImage(imgUrl, height, width, x, y, isLandscape, currentOrientation, zoomState, hasUserText, makeCopy = false) {
```

```
public TourOperator(int tour_operator_id, String name, String address, String phone, String fax, String email, String contact, Boolean lodging_available) {
```

Fig. 5. Long parameter list smell seen in JS function *rotateImage* and Java constructor *TourOperator*

Refused Bequest in an object-oriented language such as Java refers to any class that extends some parent/base class but does neither use or override a reasonable amount of the base class's behavior nor uses a reasonable amount of its properties. In JavaScript, the concept is slightly different but it can still be applied. JavaScript is class-free but it uses prototype-based inheritance. That is, object A can share properties from another object, B, the prototype. As shown in this figure, there is a JSON object created called *photo*. That object has some simple information about the image's owner, a date, as well as data about how the photo was developed. Another object is created that uses this *photo* object as its prototype, meaning it has access and shares the same properties like *stopBathTime*. However, the *Instagram* object adds a new member to itself, *filter*, and only uses one of the original properties from the photo object. The *Instagram* objects use of the photo object's properties does not justify its extension. Similarly, *DBConnector* class extends *DBFactory* but defines its own attribute and two functions without really using any of the properties of its parent class. Both situations can be detected through a low value of the base-object usage ratio metric (Fig. 6).

```
var photo = { date: "11.22.1999", owner: "Craig", exposureTime: 0.25, developerBathTime: 10, stopBathTime: 30, fixerBathTime: 1};

var instagramPhoto = Object.Create(photo);
instagramPhoto.filter = "1977";
var newText = instagramPhoto.owner + " used the " + instagramPhoto.filter + " filter.";
document.getElementById('newPhotoCaption12').innerHTML(newText);

public class DBConnector extends DBFactory {

    private Connection connection = null;
    // open db-connection
    public DBConnector() {
    // close db-connection
    public void close() {
```

Fig. 6. Refused bequest smell seen in JS function *Instagram* and Java class *DBConnector*

5 Related Work

The detection of code smells on software systems has been the subject of several studies over the past decade since their first introduction by Fowler and Beck [6]. They described 22 code smells as structural code flaws that may decrease the overall software quality and serve as indicators of software vulnerabilities. To cope with these smells, Fowler has introduced a set of 72 Refactoring operations to fix code smells and thus improving the system overall design. The detection process can either be manual, semi-automated or fully automated. Van Emden and Moonen developed one of the first automated code-smell detection tools for Java programs [25]. Mäntylä et al. [26] provided an initial formalization of the code smells, in terms of metrics, based on analyzing Fowler's smells description, they studied the correlation between the smells and provided a classification according to their similarity. Marinescu et al. [27] presented an automated framework for smells identification using detection strategies which are defined by metric-based rules. Moha et al. [28] presented a semi-automated technique called DECOR. This framework allows subjects to manually suggest their own defects through their description with domain specific language, then the framework automatically searches for smells and visually reports any finding. Most of the above-mentioned work focus mainly on smells specification in order to automate their detection without taking the developer's opinion in the detection process. To better incorporate the developer's preference,

Kessentini et al. [29] suggested a by-Example approach that uses a base of previously detected code smells as a base of examples to generate user-oriented detection rules. This work was extended [30] to reduce the effort of the detection and correction process. The main limitation of the by-Example approach is the requirement of a large base of examples (manually detected and validated code smells) for each code smell type, this work does not rely on the use of a manually validated database of JS code smells examples, instead, any project can be used as a training through the automated generation of its smells instances using any detection tool.

6   Threats to Validity

In our experiments, we raise multiple construct threats that are related to the random sampling of the projects that belong to the base of examples, we mitigated this threat by selecting projects from two languages that both support object oriented concepts and their size was proportional to the size range of the JS projects. Also, the types of smells that exist in the base of examples represents another threat. We have used two state of the art and very popular detection tools that are known for their accuracy and also they are being cited by the authors of JSNOSE. We take into account the internal threats to validity in the use of stochastic algorithms since our experimental study is performed based on 31 independent simulation runs for each problem instance and the obtained results are statistically analyzed by using the Wilcoxon rank sum test with a 95% confidence level ($\alpha = 5\%$). Another threat is raised through the lack of metrics that may better capture the structure and properties of elements. As part of our future work, we are investigating the use of dynamic analysis to capture the call graphs of objects and records their afferent and efferent communications to be able to approximate their coupling and cohesion scores.

7   Conclusion and Future Work

The paper introduces a novel detection of the JS code-smells using classic smelly examples that are extracted from existing C++ and Java projects. The purpose of this paper was to automate the tuning of JS detection rules in order to avoid human intervention and to also take achieve example-like detection that benefits from the maturity of existing studies. This tuning has required the extension of a specific similarity function to identify structurally similar entities between JS and the elements extracted from the base of examples. The tuning process was done by GP that has taken as input the JS detection rules that have been evolving to detect the expected smells in the extracted subset of elements. The evaluation of this work has shown promising results that have proven the capability of our approach to replicate the results of JSNose with 92% precision.

We are planning as future work to extend the base of code smells and identify popular method-level defects such as feature envy and shotgun surgery, to do so, it is necessary to extend the base of metrics used to define the rules as measures like coupling, cohesion and complexity are mandatory to accurately detect those smells. This will require further investigation on how to measure these metrics on JS dynamic environment. We also plan on extending the evaluation to incorporate front end and back end JS projects.

References

1. Richards, G., Lebresne, S., Burg, B., Vitek, J.: An analysis of the dynamic behavior of JavaScript programs. In: Proceedings of the 31st ACM SIGPLAN Conference on Programming Language Design and Implementation, PLDI 2010, Toronto, Ontario, Canada, pp. 1–12 (2010)
2. Richards, G., Hammer, C., Burg, B., Vitek, J.: The eval that men do. In: Mezini, M. (ed.) ECOOP 2011. LNCS, vol. 6813, pp. 52–78. Springer, Heidelberg (2011). doi: 10.1007/978-3-642-22655-7_4
3. Ratanaworabhan, P., Livshits, B., Zorn, B.G.: JSMeter: comparing the behavior of JavaScript benchmarks with real web applications. In: WebApps 2010, vol. 10, p. 3 (2010)
4. Nikiforakis, N., Invernizzi, L., Kapravelos, A., Van Acker, S., Joosen, W., Kruegel, C., Piessens, F., Vigna, G.: You are what you include: large-scale evaluation of remote JavaScript inclusions. In: Proceedings of the 2012 ACM Conference on Computer and Communications Security, CCS 2012, Raleigh, North Carolina, USA, pp. 736–747 (2012)
5. Guarnieri, S., Pistoia, M., Tripp, O., Dolby, J., Teilhet, S., Berg, R.: Saving the world wide web from vulnerable JavaScript. In: Proceedings of the 2011 International Symposium on Software Testing and Analysis, ISSTA 2011, Toronto, Ontario, Canada, pp. 177–187 (2011)
6. Fowler, M., Beck, K., Brant, J., Opdyke, W., Roberts, D.: Refactoring: improving the design of existing programs. Addison-Wesley Longman Publishing Co., Inc., Boston (1999)
7. Madsen, M., Tip, F., Andreasen, E., Sen, K., Møller, A.: Feedback-directed instrumentation for deployed JavaScript applications. In: Proceedings of the 38th International Conference on Software Engineering, ICSE 2016, Austin, Texas, pp. 899–910 (2016)
8. Crockford, D.: JSLint: The javascript code quality tool, 95 (2011). http://www.jslint.com
9. Kovalyov, A., Kluge, W., Perez, J.: JSHint, a JavaScript code quality tool (2010)
10. Pradel, M., Schuh, P., Sen, K.: TypeDevil: Dynamic type inconsistency analysis for JavaScript. In: Proceedings of the 37th International Conference on Software Engineering, ICSE 2015, Florence, Italy, pp. 314–324 (2015)
11. Raychev, V., Vechev, M., Sridharan, M.: Effective race detection for event-driven programs. In: Proceedings of the 2013 ACM SIGPLAN International Conference, OOPSLA 2013, Indianapolis, Indiana, USA, pp. 151–166 (2013)
12. Mesbah, A., Prasad, M.R.: Automated cross-browser compatibility testing. In: Proceedings of the 33rd International Conference on Software Engineering, ICSE 2011, Waikiki, Honolulu, HI, USA, pp. 561–570 (2011)
13. Fard, A.M., Mesbah, A.: JSNOSE: detecting JavaScript code smells. In: Proceedings of the 13th IEEE International Conference on Source Code Analysis and Manipulation, SCAM 2013, pp. 116–125 (2013)
14. Marinescu, R., Ganea, G., Verebi, I.: inCode: continuous quality assessment and improvement. In: Proceedings of the 14th European Conference on Software Maintenance and Reengineering, pp. 274–275 (2010)
15. Palomba, F., Bavota, G., Di Penta, M., Oliveto, R., De Lucia, A., Poshyvanyk, D.: Detecting bad smells in source code using change history information. In: 2013 IEEE/ACM 28th International Conference on Automated Software Engineering (2013)

16. Palomba, F.: Textual analysis for code smell detection. In: Proceedings of the 37th International Conference on Software Engineering, ICSE 2015, Florence, Italy, pp. 769–771 (2015)
17. Garrett, J.J.: Ajax: a new approach to web applications (2005)
18. Cornelissen, B., Zaidman, A., Van Deursen, A., Moonen, L., Koschke, R.: A systematic survey of program comprehension through dynamic analysis. IEEE Transactions on Software Engineering 35(5), 684–702
19. Silva, L.H., Ramos, M., Valente, M.T., Bergel, A., Anquetil, N.: Does JavaScript software embrace classes? In: Proceedings of the 22nd International Conference on Software Analysis, Evolution and Reengineering (SANER), pp. 73–82 (2015)
20. Mendes, T., Valente, M.T., Hora, A.: Identifying utility functions in Java and JavaScript. In: 2016 X Brazilian Symposium on Software Components, Architectures and Reuse (SBCARS), 19–20 September 2016, pp. 121–130 (2016)
21. Humberto Silva, L., Hovadick, D., Tulio Valente, M., Bergel, A., Anquetil, N., Etien, A.: JSClassFinder: a tool to detect class-like structures in JavaScript. arXiv preprint arXiv: 1602.05891 (2016)
22. Merlo, E., Antoniol, G., Di Penta, M., Rollo, V.F.: Linear complexity object-oriented similarity for clone detection and software evolution analyses. In: Proceedings of IEEE 20th International Conference on Software Maintenance, ICSM 2004, pp. 412–416 (2004)
23. Van Belle, T., Ackley, D.H.: Uniform subtree mutation, pp. 152–161 (2002)
24. http://pmd.sourceforge.net/snapshot/. Accessed 17 July 2016
25. Van Emden, E., Moonen, L.: Java quality assurance by detecting code smells. In: Proceedings of the 9th Working Conference on Reverse Engineering (WCRE 2002), Washington, DC, USA, pp. 97–106 (2002)
26. Mäntylä, M., Vanhanen, J., Lassenius, C.: A taxonomy and an initial empirical study of bad smells in code. Proceedings of the International Conference on Software Maintenance, ICSM **2003**, 381–384 (2003)
27. Marinescu, R.: Detection strategies: metrics-based rules for detecting design flaws, pp. 350–359 (2004)
28. Moha, N., Gueheneuc, Y.-G., Duchien, L., Le Meur, A.-F.: DECOR: a method for the specification and detection of code and design smells. IEEE Trans. Software Eng. **36**(1), 20–36 (2010)
29. Kessentini, M., Kessentini, W., Sahraoui, H., Boukadoum, M., Ouni, A.: Design defects detection and correction by example. In: Proceedings of the 19th IEEE International Conference on Program Comprehension (ICPC 2011), 22–24 June 2011, pp. 81–90 (2011)
30. Ouni, A., Kessentini, M., Sahraoui, H., Boukadoum, M.: Maintainability defects detection and correction: a multi-objective approach. Automated Software Engineering **20**(1), 47–79 (2012)

Deep Parameter Tuning of Concurrent Divide and Conquer Algorithms in Akka

David R. White[1], Leonid Joffe[1], Edward Bowles[2], and Jerry Swan[2(✉)]

[1] CREST, University College London, Malet Place, London WC1E 6BT, UK
{david.r.white,leonid.joffe.14}@ucl.ac.uk
[2] Computer Science, University of York, Deramore Lane, York YO10 5GH, UK
{eab530,jerry.swan}@york.ac.uk

Abstract. Akka is a widely-used high-performance and distributed computing toolkit for fine-grained concurrency, written in Scala for the Java Virtual Machine. Although Akka elegantly simplifies the process of building complex parallel software, many crucial decisions that affect system performance are deferred to the user. Employing the method of Deep Parameter Tuning to extract embedded 'magic numbers' from source code, we use the CMA-ES evolutionary computation algorithm to optimise the concurrent implementation of three widely-used divide-and-conquer algorithms within the Akka toolkit: Quicksort, Strassen's matrix multiplication, and the Fast Fourier Transform.

Keywords: Genetic improvement · Concurrency · Scala · JVM · Akka · Deep parameter tuning · Divide and Conquer · FFT · Matrix multiplication · Quicksort

1 Introduction

Support for concurrency is an important requirement when developing software for modern multicore systems, but the cognitive and development-time overheads of creating and manually-configuring concurrent and parallel systems are high [7]. In mediation of this difficulty, frameworks offering powerful concurrency support are now routinely used. Akka is the *de facto* standard for concurrency in Java and Scala; the strengths of Akka's concurrency model include:

- Immutability: the absence of mutable data eliminates many race conditions.
- Lightweight: many hundreds of processes can share a thread.
- Fault Tolerance: via the 'let it crash' philosophy popularised by Erlang [4].

In this paper, we define a generic template for divide and conquer algorithms in Akka and use it to express concurrent versions of three well-known and ubiquitous algorithms: the Fast Fourier Transform (FFT) [8], quicksort [14], and Strassen's matrix multiplication [21]. We then apply the method of Deep Parameter Tuning (DPT) [26] to optimise these algorithms for execution time.

© Springer International Publishing AG 2017
G. Squillero and K. Sim (Eds.): EvoApplications 2017, Part II, LNCS 10200, pp. 35–48, 2017.
DOI: 10.1007/978-3-319-55792-2_3

2   Algorithms

Here we provide brief descriptions of the algorithms under optimisation, all of which are widely used and applicable to a large range of different problem areas.

2.1   Fast Fourier Transform

The FFT is an algorithm for computing the Discrete Fourier Transform (DFT) or its inverse of a sequence of complex numbers. The FFT is ubiquitous in signal and image processing and analysis, in order to refocus images, remove pattern noise, recover unclear images, pattern recurrence etc. [19]. The naïve approach uses a series of multiplications and additions of sinusoidal waves, resulting in $\mathcal{O}(n^2)$ complexity. In contrast, the FFT achieves $O(n \log n)$ complexity by decomposing the DFT into even and odd components, calculating their transforms and then fusing them back together. This asymptotic complexity is also beneficial in polynomial arithmetic where it is often preferred over the Karatsuba [15] or naïve) algorithms of $O(n^{\log 3})$ and $O(n^2)$ complexities respectively. There are different variants of the FFT, but all utilise the same properties of the DFT—periodicity and complex conjugate symmetry. The version implemented here is due to Cooley and Tukey [9].

2.2   Quicksort

Quicksort is a divide and conquer sorting algorithm [14], and is popular due to its average case time complexity of $\mathcal{O}(n \log(n))$. A heuristically-selected element is chosen as a *pivot point*, and the sequence is partitioned such that all of the elements in one subsequence are 'less than' the value of the element in the pivot position, and all the elements in the other subsequence are 'greater than' it. The sorting process is then recursively applied to the subsequences. The sequential performance of the algorithm is in practice heavily-dependent on the choice of pivot point, but due to its recursive nature, it is naturally suited to parallelisation. Previous work optimising quicksort for energy consumption used Genetic Programming to obtain an improved pivot function [23].

2.3   Strassen's Matrix Multiplication

Strassen's algorithm [21] is a divide and conquer approach that reduces the complexity of matrix multiplication from $\mathcal{O}(n^3)$ to $\mathcal{O}(n^{2.8074})$. Asymptotically faster algorithms exist, but are rarely used since their high constant factor makes them impractical. The gain in Strassen's algorithm is achieved by reducing the number of recursive calls. Although this comes at a greater storage cost, the trade-off is often preferable.

3   Implementation

We now describe the implementation details of our chosen algorithms within the Akka toolkit, give a little background on the Akka Dispatcher, and describe the optimisation framework that performs Deep Parameter Tuning (DPT).

3.1   Akka Message Dispatcher

Our algorithm implementations rely upon concurrency support from Akka. One of the essential building blocks of Akka concurrency is the `Future`, a widely-used notion in functional programming that acts as a kind of 'container'[1] for holding the eventual result of some concurrent operation. For example, an object of type `Future[Double]` will eventually yield a `Double` value. Our implementations use `Futures` to queue units of work as the problem is recursively subdivided.

Whilst the implementations themselves determine the division of the problem into subproblems represented as `Futures`, the details of how their concurrent execution is managed are deferred to Akka. The specific choice of concurrency policy to be used by Akka is encapsulated by an `ExecutionContext`. The `ExecutionContext` dispatcher manages the dispatch of threads used to execute `Futures`. We use the default dispatcher, known as the "fork-join-executor", which gives "excellent performance in most cases."[2] The fork-join executor has two integer parameters that are discovered by our Deep Parameter Tuning mechanism and exposed to the optimisation process:

1. *Parallelism Factor*—the number of threads to use relative to the number of physical cores on the machine.
2. *Throughput*—the fairness of resource sharing between threads.

3.2   Benchmark Implementation

Listing 1 shows our implementation of a `DivideAndConquer` template (c.f. [25]), which defines `concurrent`, an algorithm template that invokes the abstract methods `shouldDivide`, `sequential`, `divide`, and `merge`. These methods are subsequently defined in subclasses corresponding to each of our examples: FFT, `Quicksort`, and `Strassen`. The implementation of `concurrent` uses the Akka toolkit to represent an 'inversion of control' of the well-known recursion pattern of divide and conquer, with the divided arguments evaluated concurrently via a `Future`.

The results obtained via the completed `Futures` are then merged according to the subclass method implementation. Listing 2 gives the corresponding subclass implementation for `Quicksort`: a hard-coded `Threshold` parameter determines the point below which the sequential algorithm should be used—the implementations of `Strassen` and FFT also make equivalent use of a `Threshold` parameter. The implementations of `divide` and `merge` can be seen to have a direct correspondence with the implementation of `sequential`. Listing 3 gives the unit test for `Quicksort`, which asserts that both the sequential and concurrent implementations correctly sort randomly-generated test data.

Our implementation of Strassen's algorithm utilises an additional tunable `Leaf` parameter, which determines whether the matrices should be recursively split further (down to a size of 1x1), or naïvely multiplied. As with the `Threshold` parameter, this decision is independent from Akka.

---

[1] Strictly, a monad.
[2] http://doc.akka.io/docs/akka/current/scala/dispatchers.html

```scala
trait DivideAndConquer[Args,Result] {

  // Implemented by subclasses:

  def shouldDivide(args: Args): Boolean
  def sequential(args: Args): Result
  def divide(args: Args): Seq[Args]
  def merge(results: Seq[Future[Result]])
      (implicit ec: ExecutionContext): Future[Result]

  /////////////////////////

  final def concurrent(args: Args): Future[Result] = {
    if( !shouldDivide(args) )
      Future.successful(sequential(args))
    else {
      val futures = divide(args).map { Future( concurrent(_) ) }
      Future.sequence(futures).flatMap { merge(_) }
    }
  }
}
```

Listing 1. Generic concurrent divide and conquer for Akka

3.3 DPT Implementation

Deep Parameter Tuning [26] is a heuristic optimisation method that parses source code in order to identify performance-critical parameters that are not exposed via any external interface. The goal is to find 'magic numbers' or other variables that do not modify the semantics of the program, but are critical factors in determining non-functional properties. Here we implement such an approach in order to optimise the execution time of our algorithm implementations, by tuning parameters specific to the algorithms themselves along with those used by the Akka dispatcher to manage concurrent execution.

We implement a Deep Parameter Tuner (DPT) in Scala. Its top-level operation is as follows:

1. Parse the Scala source code of the application to be optimised: FFT.scala, Quicksort.scala, and Strassen.scala. Construct an abstract syntax tree.
2. Extract all embedded 'magic numbers', in this case, restricted to integer literals, by operating on the abstract syntax tree [22].
3. Perform a heuristic search over a parameter vector obtained from the extracted literals.

It should be emphasised that the DPT tool is agnostic about the nature of the program it is optimising.

```scala
class Quicksort
extends DivideAndConquer[List[Int],List[Int]] {

  val Threshold = 100
  val Throughput = 10
  val ParallelismFactor = 3

  val threadDispatcher =
      configureAkka(Throughput,ParallelismFactor)

  /////////////////////////

  override def shouldDivide(data: List[Int]): Boolean =
      data.length > Threshold

  // well-known recursive implementation:
  override def sequential(data: List[Int]): List[Int] = {
    if( data.isEmpty ) {
      data
    } else {
      val pivot = data.head
      val (left, right) = data.tail partition (_ < pivot)
      sequential(left) ++ (pivot :: sequential(right))
    }
  }

  override def divide(data: List[Int]): Seq[List[Int]] = {
      val pivot = data.head
      val (left,right) = data.tail partition(_ < pivot)
      Seq( left, List(pivot), right )
  }

  override def merge(data: Seq[Future[List[Int]]]):
      Future[List[Int]] = {
    Future.sequence( data ).map { l =>
        l.head ++ l.tail.head ++ l.tail.tail.head
    }
  }
}
```

Listing 2. Quicksort via concurrent Divide and Conquer framework

```
class TestQuicksort {
  @Test
  def test: Unit = {

    implicit val executionContext: ExecutionContext =
      ActorSystem().dispatcher

    val ArraySize = 1600000
    val testData = List.fill(ArraySize)(randomInt)

    val result1 = Quicksort.sequential(testData)
    val result2 = Quicksort.concurrent(testData)
    assertTrue(isSorted(result1))
    assertTrue(isPermutation(testData,result1))
    assertEquals(result1, result2)
  }
}
```

Listing 3. Unit Test for Quicksort

The search mechanism used for parameter optimisation is CMA-ES [11], a well-known evolutionary search mechanism that guides the search process via an adaptive approximation to the second derivative of the fitness function. The fitness function supplied to CMA-ES performs wall-clock timing of a modified version of the original source code, in which the magic numbers in the source are replaced by the corresponding values of a candidate solution, with vector elements rounded to the nearest integer. The modified source code is then compiled by the Scala compiler and executed via the appropriate test harness (e.g. as per Listing 3 for Quicksort), which helps ensure correctness of the modified code. The evaluation of the fitness function is repeated 10 times, and the median value taken, in order to reduce the impact of nondeterminism on the optimisation process.

To summarise, for a candidate solution vector $\bar{v}$ consisting of the proposed literals, the associated fitness function $f(\bar{v})$ to be minimised is given by:

$$f(\bar{v}) = \begin{cases} \infty, \text{if the test case fails} \\ \text{otherwise, the median time in seconds to run the test case} \end{cases}$$

4 Empirical Evaluation

We evaluated DPT on our three algorithm implementations, to assess the efficacy of DPT in reducing execution time. We compared the optimised results to a set of default parameters, and also compared DPT with a random search strategy to confirm that the evolutionary search is exploiting information in the search space. For each algorithm, we ran DPT and Random Search 10 times each.

All experiments were run on the same machine, which was a Windows 10 machine using a i7-2670QM processor with four physical cores at 2.20 GHz and 8 GB RAM. Due to ten repetitions per fitness evaluation, and the repeated runs for statistical testing, the main experiments took several days to complete.

4.1 Tuned Parameters

We evaluated DPT on our three algorithms, with the goal of reducing execution time by modifying performance-critical parameters in the source code, namely:

1. The size *Threshold* at which the algorithms terminates recursion and uses a sequential method instead.
2. The *Leaf* setting, a parameter specific to the Strassen example, which similarly controls recursive behaviour.
3. Akka's *Parallelism Factor*, the number of threads to use relative to the number of physical cores on the machine.
4. Akka's *Throughput* setting, which controls the fairness of resource sharing between threads.

These parameters were automatically extracted from the source code by our DPT tool. In general, there is no guarantee that such parameters will not affect the semantics of a program, a problem that can be mitigated by empirical evaluation using unit tests, and by manual inspection of the results. We implemented suitable unit tests and, once satisfied that the parameters did not impact the semantics of the code, we omitted the execution of those tests during the optimisation process to improve efficiency. Post-optimisation, we validated the results against unseen data, and our confidence is further increased through out knowledge of Akka and the system itself.

We selected a set of default parameter settings, to act as a starting point for the CMA-ES search, and also as a baseline for comparison with the optimised settings. These default parameter settings were chosen based partly on Akka documentation, but also through human judgement: the effectiveness of any settings are dependent on both the program implementation and host machine. The defaults are given in Table 1.

Table 1. Default parameter settings for each Algorithm

Algorithm	Input size	Threshold	Leaf	Parallelism factor	Throughput
FFT	524288	100	N/A	3	100
Quicksort	1000000	100	N/A	3	100
Strassen	800	200	10	3	99

4.2   Test Data

Each algorithm accepts a numerical vector as input. The size of this vector was selected for each algorithm to ensure its execution time ran for less than 10 s using our test machine when using the default parameter settings. The FFT algorithm implementation requires an input size that is a power of two. The input sizes for each algorithm are given in Table 1.

4.3   Sample Size

The inherent nondeterminism of concurrent execution creates a noisy fitness function, which can be exacerbated by the exploration of parameter settings that, for example, reduce the fairness of scheduling threads. After some exploratory data analysis, we chose 10 repetitions to form the basis of our fitness evaluation; we use the median of 10 measurements when evaluating the execution time of a given candidate solution. This is an imperfect measure, as it still means that a solution may be regarded by the search as superior only due to variance in execution time measurement. We evaluate the outputs of the optimisation separately when comparing against the baseline parameter settings.

4.4   CMA-ES Configuration

The CMA-ES implementation used was from Apache Commons Math [12], using its default parameter settings[3], with an initial sigma one order of magnitude greater than the default parameters. We execute the search for 100 steps, each consisting of the 10 executions of the program with a candidate solution of parameter settings. We take the final output of the search, in the form of the best parameters found for each benchmark.

4.5   Results

CMA-ES vs Default Parameters. We executed ten runs of the CMA-ES search for each algorithm. Given the noise inherent in measuring concurrency performance, we wish avoid reporting the behaviour of a possible outlier. As a conservative measure of success, we therefore select the optimised parameters produced by the sixth best result, i.e. an approximation of the median, and compared the resulting performance to the default parameter settings for that algorithm. The parameter settings from that result are provided in Table 2. We took 30 measurements of execution time and report the median in Table 3. We then compared the two sets of measurements for a significant difference using a Mann-Whitney U-Test, and calculated the Vargha-Delaney $\hat{A}_{12}$ measure to quantify effect size. The timing information gathered using the default parameters was tested for normality using the Shapiro-Wilk test, and the test statistic

---

[3] https://commons.apache.org/proper/commons-math/javadocs/api-3.6.1/index.html.

Table 2. Default Parameters compared to Optimised Parameter Settings from sixth best result found by CMA-ES

	Algorithm	Threshold	Leaf	Parallelism factor	Throughput
Default	FFT	100	N/A	3	100
	Quicksort	100	N/A	3	100
	Strassen	200	10	3	99
CMA-ES	FFT	1325	N/A	86	735
	Quicksort	2078	N/A	43	277
	Strassen	217	187	48	730

Table 3. Median execution time (ET) over 30 runs for default parameter settings and a representative solution found by CMA-ES. Figures to 2 d.p.

Algorithm	Default (s)	Optimised (s)	P Value	$\hat{A}_{12}$
FFT	9.16	3.67	2.87e−11	0.0
Quicksort	3.43	1.93	2.87e−11	0.0
Strassen	3.75	0.47	2.87e−11	0.0

was found to be less than the critical value for the Strassen and Quicksort benchmarks, meaning that we cannot assume a normal distribution of timing values. The Shapiro-Wilk test was chosen as the number of samples is sufficiently small to avoid biases. The Mann-Whitney U test was chosen as we cannot be sure as to the distribution of timing values and as such a parametric test would be inappropriate. Similarly, the Vargha-Delaney measure of effect size was chosen as it too is distribution-agnostic while also being able to handle inputs in the form of real numbers, as opposed to integers.

CMA-ES clearly made a very significant improvement to execution time, even when we only consider a representative, rather than best, result. The improvements in execution time are all significant at the $p < 0.0167$ level (a 0.05 p value Bonferroni-corrected to reflect our three separate benchmarks), and also have the strongest possible effect size. Examining the median execution times, we see an *order of magnitude* improvement for Strassen, and the execution time for FFT is more than halved.

CMA-ES vs Random Search. In order to demonstrate that CMA-ES produced these results through the exploitation of information within the search space, we implemented a simple random search algorithm as a baseline, and compared the distribution of optimised execution times against that found by CMA-ES over the ten runs. A summary of the results for each benchmark are given in Table 4, and boxplots are given in Fig. 1.

Whilst random search was able to make some improvements to execution time, they appear small in comparison to the performance of CMA-ES. We

Table 4. Optimised execution time statistics from CMA-ES and Random Search. Figures to 2 d.p.

	Algorithm	Min (s)	Max (s)	Median (s)
CMA-ES	FFT	3.54	3.97	3.84
	Quicksort	1.79	2.19	1.91
	Strassen	0.44	0.53	0.48
Random Search	FFT	8.85	8.96	8.92
	Quicksort	3.08	3.57	3.29
	Strassen	3.70	3.75	3.74

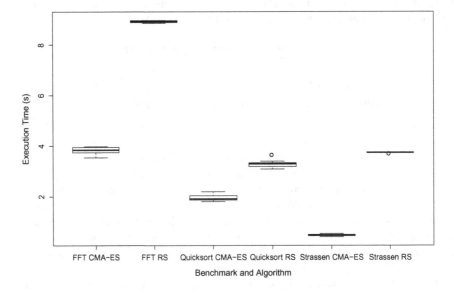

Fig. 1. Execution Times found by CMA-ES and Random Search (RS)

performed a Mann-Whitney U test and calculated the Vargha-Delaney $\hat{A}_{12}$ statistic for the comparison on each benchmark. While the timings resulting from the random search optimisation technique are normally distributed, given that we only have ten samples, we felt that a nonparametric test was safer, and continuing to use the Mann-Whitney U test maintained consistency with our previous experiments. The results are given in Table 5. All tests are significant at the $p < 0.05$ level, and the effect is as strong as possible for FFT and Strassen, whilst still strong for Quicksort. This supports our alternative hypothesis, that is CMA-ES outperforms random search; there exists information in the parameter space that CMA-ES can exploit to tune concurrent performance.

Table 5. Results for Mann-Whitney U Test and Vargha-Delaney Effect Size comparison between CMA-ES and Random Search. Figures to 2 d.p.

Benchmark	p-value	$\hat{A}_{12}$
FFT	2.80e−6	0.0
Quicksort	0.0095	0.223
Strassen	1.57e−4	0.0

4.6 Threats to Validity

As observed above, wall-clock measurements of concurrent systems are inherently noisy. We have attempted to mitigate against this by using the largest input sizes that still allow learning to take place within a reasonable amount of time, and by taking the median of 10 execution time measurements as our fitness function. The underlying idea is that with larger input sizes, asymptotic behaviour will dominate over 'constant-of-proportionality' effects such as startup-transients caused by Just-In-Time compilation. In addition, we only time the method call to the benchmark itself, excluding JVM startup overhead.

5 Related Work

Beginning with early work on compiler optimisation [3], there is an extensive body of work applying semantics-preserving transformations to improve the non-functional properties (NFPs) of software. Recent work in this area includes Kocsis et al. [16], which yield a 10,000-fold speedup of database queries on terabyte datasets within the Apache Spark analytics framework by eliminating redundant database joins and other transformations. Kocsis et al. also automatically repaired 451 systematic errors in the implementation of the Apache Hadoop HPC framework [17], whilst simultaneously significantly improving performance.

In addition to the work improving Quicksort for energy efficiency mentioned in Sect. 2, Burles et al. [6], also obtained a 24% improvement in energy consumption by optimising a single widely-used class, IMMUTABLEMULTIMAP, in Google's GUAVA collection library. They used a Genetic Algorithm and constrained the search space via the behavioural contracts of Object-Orientation. Recent work that explicitly addresses parallelism includes refactoring Haskell programs via rewrite rules [5].

Within the last decade there has been increasing interest in the use of stochastic search techniques to optimise NFPs [24], often described as "Genetic Improvement", relying on Genetic Programming as an optimisation method. Early work on execution time optimisation using search focused on obtaining patches to source code [1,13]. More recently, Baudry and Yeboah-Antwi produced ECSELR, a framework for *in-situ* runtime optimisation and slimming of software systems, which can optimize and trade-off functional and non-functional properties [27]. Goa et al. used a Genetic Algorithm to optimise webservice composition, with a focus on quality of service [10]. Calderón Trilla et al. also combined search with static analysis [7] to find *worthwhile parallelism*, i.e. semantics-preserving transformations that produce parallelism of meaningful granularity.

In contrast to the optimization of pre-existing software, Agapitos and Lucas used Genetic Algorithms to evolve sorting functions whose time complexity was measured experimentally [2]. Vasicek and Mrazek used Cartesian Genetic Programming to trade the solution quality of median-finding algorithms against NFPs such as power efficiency and execution time within embedded systems [18].

6 Conclusion

We applied the method of deep parameter tuning to extract and optimise literal values from the source code of concurrent versions of three well-known algorithms: FFT, quicksort, and Strassen's matrix multiplication, which make use of the Akka concurrency toolkit. We find that a DPT system based on the CMA-ES evolutionary algorithm achieves significant acceleration of all benchmarks, halving the execution time of FFT and producing an order of magnitude speed-up of Strassen's algorithm.

One of the major challenges in this work was the noisy execution time due to the inherent nondeterminism of the concurrent algorithms. Whilst CMA-ES did produce good results, exploratory measurements suggest that finding a gradient in the search space is quite difficult. Algorithms more suited to noisy fitness functions may find further improvements.

The execution time of the benchmarks varied according to the architecture of the host machine: thus for best results it is likely that a certain amount of re-tuning would be required for a given machine. Recently, Sohn et al. [20] demonstrated the feasibility of *amortised optimisation*, that is searching the parameter space at runtime. Applying amortised optimisation to recursive concurrent software may serve as the next challenge for developing this technique.

References

1. Ackling, T., Alexander, B., Grunert, I.: Evolving patches for software repair. In: GECCO 2011 Proceedings (2011)
2. Agapitos, A., Lucas, S.M.: Evolving efficient recursive sorting algorithms. In: 2006 IEEE International Conference on Evolutionary Computation Proceedings (2006)
3. Aho, A.V., Sethi, R., Ullman, J.D.: Compilers: Principles, Techniques, and Tools. Addison-Wesley Longman Publishing Co., Inc., Boston (1986)
4. Armstrong, J.: A history of Erlang. In: Proceedings of the Third ACM SIGPLAN Conference on History of Programming Languages. HOPL III (2007)
5. Brown, C.M., Hammond, K., Loidl, H.: Paraforming: forming parallel haskell programs using Novel Refactoring Techniques. In: Trends in Functional Programming (2011)
6. Burles, N., Bowles, E., Brownlee, A.E.I., Kocsis, Z.A., Swan, J., Veerapen, N.: Object-oriented genetic improvement for improved energy consumption in Google Guava. In: Barros, M., Labiche, Y. (eds.) SSBSE 2015. LNCS, vol. 9275, pp. 255–261. Springer, Cham (2015). doi:10.1007/978-3-319-22183-0_20

7. Calderón Trilla, J.M., Poulding, S., Runciman, C.: Weaving parallel threads. In: Barros, M., Labiche, Y. (eds.) SSBSE 2015. LNCS, vol. 9275, pp. 62–76. Springer, Cham (2015). doi:10.1007/978-3-319-22183-0_5

8. Cooley, J.W., Tukey, J.W.: An algorithm for the machine calculation of complex Fourier series. Math. Comput. **19**, 297–301 (1965)

9. Cooley, J.W., Tukey, J.W.: An algorithm for the machine calculation of complex Fourier series. Math. Comput. **19**(90), 297–301 (1965)

10. Gao, Z., Jian, C., Qiu, X., Meng, L.: QoE/QoS driven simulated annealing-based genetic algorithm for web services selection. J. China Univ. Posts Telecommun. **16**, 102–107 (2009)

11. Hansen, N., Ostermeier, A.: Adapting arbitrary normal mutation distributions in evolution strategies: the covariance matrix adaptation. In: Proceedings of IEEE International Conference on Evolutionary Computation (1996)

12. Hansen, N., Ostermeier, A.: Completely derandomized self-adaptation in evolution strategies. Evol. Comput. **9**(2), 159–195 (2001)

13. Harman, M., Langdon, W.B., Jia, Y., White, D.R., Arcuri, A., Clark, J.A.: The GISMOE challenge: constructing the pareto program surface using genetic programming to find better programs (keynote paper). In: Proceedings of the 27th IEEE/ACM International Conference on Automated Software Engineering, ASE 2012, pp. 1–14. ACM, New York (2012)

14. Hoare, C.A.R.: Algorithm 64: quicksort. Commun. ACM **4**(7), 321–322 (1961)

15. Karatsuba, A.A.: The complexity of computations. Proc. Steklov Inst. Math. Interperiodica Transl. **211**, 169–183 (1995)

16. Kocsis, Z.A., Drake, J.H., Carson, D., Swan, J.: Automatic improvement of apache spark queries using semantics-preserving program reduction. In: Proceedings of the 2016 on Genetic and Evolutionary Computation Conference Companion, GECCO 2016 Companion, pp. 1141–1146. ACM, New York (2016)

17. Kocsis, Z.A., Neumann, G., Swan, J., Epitropakis, M.G., Brownlee, A.E.I., Haraldsson, S.O., Bowles, E.: Repairing and Optimizing Hadoop hashCode Implementations (2014)

18. Mrazek, V., Vasicek, Z., Sekanina, L.: Evolutionary approximation of software for embedded systems: median function. In: Proceedings of the Companion Publication of the 2015 Annual Conference on Genetic and Evolutionary Computation (2015)

19. Rockmore, D.N.: The FFT: an algorithm the whole family can use. Comput. Sci. Eng. **2**(1), 60–64 (2000)

20. Sohn, J., Lee, S., Yoo, S.: Amortised deep parameter optimisation of GPGPU work group size for OpenCV. In: Sarro, F., Deb, K. (eds.) SSBSE 2016. LNCS, vol. 9962, pp. 211–217. Springer, Cham (2016). doi:10.1007/978-3-319-47106-8_14

21. Strassen, V.: Gaussian elimination is not optimal. Numerische Mathematik **13**(4), 354–356 (1969)

22. Swan, J., Epitropakis, M.G., Woodward, J.R.: Gen-O-Fix: An embeddable framework for Dynamic Adaptive Genetic Improvement Programming. Technical report CSM-195, Computing Science and Mathematics, University of Stirling (2014)

23. Swan, J., Burles, N.: TEMPLAR – a framework for template-method hyperheuristics. In: Machado, P., Heywood, M.I., McDermott, J., Castelli, M., García-Sánchez, P., Burelli, P., Risi, S., Sim, K. (eds.) EuroGP 2015. LNCS, vol. 9025, pp. 205–216. Springer, Cham (2015). doi:10.1007/978-3-319-16501-1_17

24. White, D.R., Clark, J., Jacob, J., Poulding, S.M.: Searching for resource-efficient programs: low-power pseudorandom number generators. In: GECCO 2008 Proceedings (2008)

25. Woodward, J.R., Swan, J.: Template method hyper-heuristics. In: Proceedings of the Companion Publication of the 2014 Annual Conference on Genetic and Evolutionary Computation, GECCO Comp 2014 (2014)
26. Wu, F., Weimer, W., Harman, M., Jia, Y., Krinke, J.: Deep parameter optimisation. In: GECCO Proceedings (2015)
27. Yeboah-Antwi, K., Baudry, B.: Embedding adaptivity in software systems using the ECSELR framework. In: Proceedings of the Companion Publication of the 2015 Annual Conference on Genetic and Evolutionary Computation, GECCO Companion 2015 (2015)

Focusing Learning-Based Testing Away from Known Weaknesses

Christian Fleischer and Jörg Denzinger[✉]

Department of Computer Science, University of Calgary, Calgary, Canada
{crfleisc,denzinge}@ucalgary.ca

Abstract. We present an extension to learning-based testing of systems for adversary-induced weaknesses that addresses the problem of repeated generation of known weaknesses. Our approach adds to the normally used fitness measure a component that computes the similarity of a test to known tests that revealed a weakness and uses this similarity to penalize new tests. We instantiated this idea to the testing of ad-hoc wireless networks using the IACL approach, more precisely to applications in precision agriculture, and our experiments show that our modification results in finding substantially different tests from the test(s) that we want to avoid.

1 Introduction

In the last decade, search-based software engineering has shown substantial success in supporting various kinds of testing of systems (see, for example, [1,2]). But in this time we also have seen an increased need to test distributed applications, especially for potential abuses by adversarial users with all kinds of agendas. While there are also approaches for supporting these kinds of testing problems using evolutionary learning to identify possible weaknesses (see [3–5]), a problem limiting the use of these testing approaches is that repeated runs of the testing systems often do not result in identifying many possible weaknesses without fixing previously found weaknesses first. Naturally, due to the use of random factors in the search, not every run of such a testing system will have the same result, but depending on how strongly the used fitness function identifies a particular weakness of the tested system, many runs can identify the same weakness over and over again. And, after a risk analysis, a found weakness might be deemed as unnecessary (or too expensive) to fix and then naturally the testing system needs to be made aware that this particular test is not considered a weakness anymore.

In this paper, we present an approach that solves this problem of learning-based testing. The basic idea is to enhance the used fitness function to allow specifying previously found weaknesses of the tested system and to penalize individuals created by the evolutionary search based on their similarity to these specified weaknesses (in the form of individuals from previous runs). Due to this intended use of the similarity it concentrates on the difference in the effects an

© Springer International Publishing AG 2017
G. Squillero and K. Sim (Eds.): EvoApplications 2017, Part II, LNCS 10200, pp. 49–65, 2017.
DOI: 10.1007/978-3-319-55792-2_4

attack has on the tested system, considering both the components of the tested system and its environment. We instantiated this general idea for the IACL approach to test ad-hoc wireless networks that was presented in [5,6].

Our evaluation of the improved testing system showed that our method finds rather different solutions (with respect to the behavior of the tested system) when given a single source solution to avoid. Iterating the process, i.e. adding the newly created best solution to the set of solutions to avoid, also rather consistently creates solutions that differ from all solutions that should be avoided.

The paper is organized as follows: After this introduction, in Sect. 2 we present the basic IACL approach. Following that, in Sect. 3, we present our modification of IACL that allows it to focus away from already known weaknesses. In Sect. 4, we describe the instantiation of IACL and our modification to the application area of precision agriculture. Section 5 presents the experimental evaluation using the instantiation. In Sect. 6, we relate our work to the known literature and Sect. 7 concludes with some remarks on future work.

2   The IACL Approach

Incremental Adaptive Corrective Learning (IACL, see [5]) is a search-based testing method for ad-hoc wireless networks. In the following, we will present how we model a particular test as an individual, then briefly describe the evolutionary learning method that zooms in more and more on tests fulfilling a given test goal and then describe how a given test is evaluated, including how we correct an individual in order to not obviously violate network protocol requirements.

2.1   General Set-up

An ad-hoc wireless network consists of a collection of mobile wireless nodes (also called agents) within a geographic area. They exchange messages following several network protocols that specify requirements for these messages. Usually these requirements include obligations which result in additional messages being spread through the network.

A particular test of an application of such a wireless network requires defining a scenario, which describes the geographical area of the network and behaviors for each of the nodes. These behaviors can be subdivided into its movements during a given period of time and its communications during that period of time. More formally, a scenario $S = (geo, t_{max}, vel_{max}, M, C)$ consists of the geographical area geo, the length t_{max} of the test run, the maximal velocity vel_{max} of any node, the set M of protocols used and the set C of so-called customer nodes that are acting within the network.

A particular test adds to S a set A of attack agents (nodes) that are also acting within the given scenario. Nodes in both A and S perform actions out of two sets Mov and $Comm$ and their behavior is characterized by an action sequence for each of them. The set Mov of movement actions consists of actions either of the form $spos$ or $v = (t, head, vel)$ where $spos$ is a starting position for the node. v is a movement change action, where t is a real number, $0 \leq t \leq t_{max}$, *head* is a natural number, $0 \leq head \leq 359$, giving a direction heading and *vel* is a real number, $0 \leq vel \leq vel_{max}$, giving a velocity, altogether indicating a change in direction and velocity at a given point in time. The set *Comm* has elements of 5 different forms: $c \in Comm = s|p|in|dr|mo$, where $s = (t, dest, data)$ is a data initiation action, indicating that the node should initiate the procedure necessary to send *data* to *dest* at time index t. $p = (t, target)$ is a so-called protocol action, which is the result of obligations a node has due to the actions of other nodes. *target* is the protocol-induced message sent at t. s- and p-actions are sufficient to describe the communications of customer nodes.

The other types of actions are used by attack agents to compromise the network. $in = (t, target)$ represents an *insertion action* where the agent should insert the packet specified in *target* into the network at time t. *Drop actions*, $d = (t, template)$, indicate to an agent that it should ignore a protocol-induced obligation of the form *template*, which should be sent at t. Finally, *modification actions*, $mo = (t, t_{actual}, template, target)$, indicate to an agent that a protocol-induced packet, *template*, normally sent at t should be modified by replacing it with *target* and sending it at t_{actual}.

In our testing system we are searching for a particular test for a given scenario, which means that we are looking for action sequences for the attack agents. We will use AS^i_{cust} to refer to the action sequence of customer node i and AS^j_{att} for the sequence of attack agent j. In general, for a node j an action sequence has the form $a^j_1, \ldots, a^j_n$.

2.2   The IACL Main Loop

As usual for an evolutionary algorithm, the main loop of IACL creates generations of individuals that each represents a test, more precisely action sequences for the attack agents in A. In order to deal with the very large set of possible individuals, IACL starts with a small number of attack agents (two) and increases the number over time (hence the incremental in the name). Whenever a new attack agent is added, the search first concentrates on the new agent to adapt its behavior to the behaviors of the already existing agents.

More precisely, IACL first creates n_{pop} tests with two attack agents and action sequences consisting just of a starting position for these agents. After evaluating these tests (which usually results in them being altered, see next subsection) using a given fitness function that reflects the test goal(s), we keep the n_{surv} best tests and replace all other tests with new ones created by applying various genetic operators (for more information on the operators, see [7]). This process of creating new generations is repeated ng_{GL_1} times but may be stopped early, if for n_{Stall} iterations the fitness of the best test does not improve.

After this first general learning phase, the method loops through the following routine (we describe the i-th loop of n_{max}). First, an attack agent is added, resulting in adding an action sequence for this agent to each test that consists just of a start position. In an adaptive learning phase AL_i we create new sets of tests like described above ng_{AL_i} times but apply genetic operators only to the action sequence of the new attack agent (with the same condition for stalling as above). Then we have a general learning phase GL_i for ng_{GL_i} generations (with the same stalling condition) in which the genetic operators now target the action sequences of all attack agents.

2.3   Evaluating (and Correcting) an Individual

In general, an individual (i.e. a test) is evaluated by running it, together with the given scenario, in a simulation and collecting information metrics that are used by the fitness function(s). But, due to the various requirements of the used network protocols, a newly created individual usually is easily identifiable as not conforming with the requirements by the customer nodes, which naturally is not what an adversary in control of attack agents would do. Therefore, in order to test for realistic attacks, we correct the individuals while doing the simulation. The performed corrections aim at fixing only unintended problems of an individual, while preserving the intentional violations of the requirements that were introduced in ancestors of an individual (or in the creation of the individual itself) and that are not easily detectable by non-attack nodes in the network.

With IACL, at the start of the simulation, each agent/node is placed at the starting position *spos* of its action sequence. Using the time indexes of each action in each sequence we move the simulation of the test represented by the individual forward. If we take the attack agent j and assume that $a_1^j, \ldots, a_{i-1}^j$ are the actions in its action sequence that have already been performed and further assume that the time index for action a_i^j has arrived, then there are the following three major cases (with some sub-cases) to consider:

Case 1: no protocol-induced obligation (due to receiving a message or another stimulus) needs to be fulfilled:
If $a_i^j \in Mov$, then j simply performs a_i^j and AS_{att}^j remains unchanged. If $a_i^j \in Comm$ we have the following sub-cases, depending on the form of a_i^j.

- form s: agent j starts the execution of the action according to the protocols in place and AS_{att}^j remains unchanged
- form in: j transmits the packet indicated in *in* and AS_{att}^j remains unchanged
- form mo or dr: AS_{att}^j needs to be corrected, since there is no packet to modify or drop. a_i^j is therefore removed from AS_{att}^j
- form p: a_i^j is an artifact from a previous test idea which is no longer required. a_i^j is removed from AS_{att}^j, node j moves ahead to a_{i+1}^j and the simulation continues.

Case 2: there is a protocol-induced obligation (requiring to send a packet):
As before, if $a_i^j \in Mov$, then j performs a_i^j, but j then also performs the protocol-induced obligation. And this protocol-induced obligation is inserted into AS_{att}^j as a_{i+1}^j as a p action. j moves ahead to a_{i+2}^j in AS_{att}^j and the simulation continues. If $a_i^j \in Comm$ then we do the following, depending on the form of a_i^j:

- form s or in: node j performs a_i^j and then the protocol-induced action is inserted into AS_{att}^j as a_{i+1}^j. j moves ahead to a_{i+2}^j (if it exists) and the test continues.
- form mo or dr: the agent checks to see if the packet listed in the *template* area of a_i^j matches the protocol-induced action that the agent is required to take. Matching involves the agent checking to see if the packets in a_i^j's template area and the protocol-induced action are of the same type, and that their fields contain the same information. If the packets match, then the protocol-induced obligation is not performed, and instead a_i^j is executed (this is an intentional break of the obligation). If the packets do not match, then there has been a change in the network's behaviour (compared to a previous test) that caused a_i^j to be invalid. a_i^j is replaced in AS_{att}^j with a p action corresponding to the actual protocol-induced obligation, the agent then fulfills this obligation and the simulation continues.
- form p: If the network-induced obligation matches (see above) the target area of a_i^j, then the agent fulfills the obligation and the test continues. If it does not match, then a_i^j is replaced with a new p action reflecting the actual protocol-induced obligation required of the agent, the agent fulfills the obligation and the simulation continues.

Case 3: the test has reached a point where the node j has a new network-induced obligation to fulfill but it has no element a_i^j at the current time index:
In this case, the agent examines its AS_{att}^j in order to find a_{ins}^j and a_{ins+1}^j, where the time index of a_{ins}^j is earlier than the current time index and a_{ins+1}^j's time index is greater than the current time index. A new p action corresponding to the network-induced obligation is created and inserted into AS_{att}^j between a_{ins}^j and a_{ins+1}^j and the simulation continues.

While the above is the behavior of an attack agent the procedure is the same for customer nodes, except that customer nodes naturally do not use in, mo or dr actions.

2.4 Other IACL Components

The two remaining components of IACL not explained so far are the set of genetic operators and the fitness function(s). Due to the complexity of network protocols, a large number of genetic operators are needed, together with a strategy on how to decide what operators should be applied when. Each field in a packet is the target of at least one mutation operator, but for quite a number of fields there are more such operators (using knowledge about the role of the field in the protocol). Other mutations insert actions into action sequences or change communication actions into drop actions. It is also possible to fragment messages (via such a mutation operator). Additionally, there are crossover operators that apply to different levels of a test, switching parts of sequences between different agents within the same test, between agents in different tests, or switching whole attack sequences between tests. A detailed description of the various operators and how they are controlled is given in [7].

Naturally, the chosen fitness function is very important for finding tests that fulfill a test goal, i.e. tests that find a particular kind of weakness of the tested system. While usually there is an obvious metric that measures the fulfillment of a particular goal by a test (resp. its simulation), as [6] (and for a totally different kind of system [4]) showed, additional metrics are needed to guide a learning-based testing system toward tests that fulfill the given goal. To deal with this need for combining metrics and the fact that different test goals require different metric combinations [5,6] used fitness functions that essentially computed the weighted Euclidean distance between the position of an individual in the n-dimensional space created by n metrics and a so-called goal point in the same space which represents the "optimal" combination of metric values for the test goal. While there are some rather general metrics, many of the metrics are application- and some test goal-dependent.

3   Modifying IACL to Avoid Known Solutions

Since evolutionary algorithms at their core are optimization methods, it is not exactly surprising that performing several runs of such an algorithm for a given problem instance does not always result in producing different solutions. In fact, some proponents of other optimization methods consider the fact that two runs are not always producing the same result a weakness of evolutionary methods. But from the perspective of security testing, getting the same solutions in several runs naturally represents a weakness because resources are essentially "wasted". And the longer a run takes to produce solutions, the more serious the problem becomes.

While tricks like varying parameters between runs might reduce this problem, they offer no guarantee that runs might not still produce the same solutions, even if there are other solutions of interest. Our solution approach to this problem is to modify the used fitness function with a component that penalizes solutions based on their similarity to previously found solutions.

More precisely, given a basic fitness function fit_{base} and a set $Sol = \{sol_1, ..., sol_k\}$ of known solutions, we evaluate an individual ind using the function fit_{no-sim} defined as follows:

$$fit_{no-sim}(ind, Sol) = fit_{base}(ind) + sim_{Set}(ind, Sol) * fit_{base}(ind) * w_{sim} \quad (1)$$

(this assumes that fit_{base} is intended to be minimized.) w_{sim} is a parameter that determines the influence that similarity to known solutions has on the evaluation of an individual. sim_{Set} should combine the similarities sim of ind to each of the elements of Sol. Obviously, there are several possible ways to achieve this. We used the following definition:

$$sim_{Set}(ind, Sol) = 1/k * \sum_{i=1}^{k} sim(ind, sol_i) \quad (2)$$

While the previous definitions were not IACL specific, defining sim naturally has to reflect that IACL has the attack agents test a scenario happening in an environment and a system consisting of customer agents. Therefore, like fit_{base}, sim combines several measures from two groups, namely measures comparing events related to the environment and events that happen to customer agents. Assuming that ind is already corrected (as described in Sect. 2.3), the second group of events can be evaluated by just looking at actions/messages recorded for them, while the first group requires analyzing the simulations of both individuals.

Both groups of events potentially contain several different types of events. Two individuals can be compared based on the number of occurrences of the event, as well as the differences in times that those events occur between the two individuals. In fact, we combine these two ideas for most of our measures that we combine to create sim.

More precisely, a dual event similarity ev_{sim} is defined as

$$ev_{sim}(ind_1, ind_2) = \sum_{ag \in Ag} occ_{ev}(ind_1, ind_2, ag) * time_{ev}(ind_1, ind_2, ag) * w_{ev}(ag)$$

(3)

where Ag is either A or C (although we use in our instantiation only agents from C), occ_{ev} is the difference of the number of occurrences of the event in the action sequence for agent ag in the two individuals. $time_{ev}$ is the minimal sum of time differences between assigned events between the two action sequences for ag of all possible assignments of events of the type in ind_1 to events in ind_2 such that sequence is preserved (and the assignment's length is the smaller of the numbers of occurrences of the event type in the two action sequences for ag) divided by t_{max} and subtracted from 1. Note that by making w_{ev} potentially different for different agents we can focus on particular agents by providing them with a higher weight.

A small conceptual example for the computation of ev_{sim} is the following. Let us assume that ind_1 has created the action sequences $((a_{11}, a_{12}, b_{13}), (c_{21}, d_{22}))$ for two customer nodes and ind_2 has created $((a'_{11}, b'_{12}), (c'_{21}, d'_{22}))$ (for the same nodes) with a_{11}, a_{12}, a'_{11} being of the same event type and a_{11} happening at time 2, a_{12} at time 4 and a'_{11} happening at time 5 (and $t_{max} = 10$). If our event is occurrences of actions of type a, then for the second agent occ_{ev} is 0 and consequently $time_{ev}$ is also 0. For the first agent we have two possible assignments of a-events between the two individuals, namely a'_{11} to a_{11} and a'_{11} to a_{12}. Since the time difference for the first assignment is the sum consisting of 3 and for the second assignment is 1, the second assignment determines $time_{ev}$ as $1 - 1 \div 10$, which together with the occurrence difference of 1 produces as ev_{sim}-value 0.9 (assuming that w_{ev} for the first agent is also 1).

We combine a set of event similarities (which can be dual as defined above, but also computed differently, see the next section) $ev_{sim,1},...,ev_{sim,l}$ by summing their evaluations up:

$$sim(ind_1, ind_2) = \sum_{j=1}^{l} ev_{sim,j}(ind_1, ind_2)$$

(4)

Note that due to the various weight parameters, the maximal similarity, i.e. between identical solutions, is usually not equal to 1 (which obviously is not a requirement for our application).

4 Instantiation to Precision Agriculture

For our evaluation of the proposed modification of the fitness computation in IACL from Sect. 3 we have chosen the same application as in [5], namely precision agriculture. The idea behind this application area is to use wireless sensor networks monitoring growing conditions in a field together with actuators that can influence these growing conditions (like watering an area of the field) and that are also parts of the wireless network. By so automating the care for crops the aim is to reduce the amount of manual labour of farmhands and the overall operating costs. Since all nodes require batteries for operation, one test goal determines if it is possible to deplete these batteries much faster than normal, so that the intended gains are negated. Naturally, another test goal is to make sure that the right actuators act correctly in all conditions.

The simulation uses as M the Internet Protocol (IP, [8]), the User Datagram Protocol (UDP, [9]), Ad-hoc On-demand Distance Vector Algorithm (AODV, [10]) for message routing and an improvised agriculture network application layer protocol (IAP) as defined in [5]. This means that *template* and *target* from Sect. 2.1 have the form $(IP, UDP, Payload)$, where IP and UDP represent all the fields that these protocols require and *Payload* contains as possible packets all the packets from AODV and the *watering trigger* and *watering request* packets from IAP. We will refer to the packets from IAP as DATA packets (or messages or actions). Among the packets from AODV are the route request (RREQ), route reply (RREP) and route error packets (RERR), which are used to find routes between two agents (RREQ to start the search, RREP to report the results of the search) and to indicate that a route is not valid anymore (RERR). In order to use these protocols, an agent needs to keep a so-called routing table that aims to represent the knowledge of how to reach a particular agent. An invalid routing table usually results in a lot of messages that try to make it valid again.

For fit_{base} we use, as in [5], as metrics the power consumption of the whole network determined by counting the number of transmissions made, the distribution of this power consumption over the course of the simulation, the number of nodes that have exhausted their power supply before the end of the simulation, the number of sensor nodes that have moisture levels below the acceptable threshold at the end of the simulation and how long each sensor node had a moisture level below the lowest level measured in the network with no attack agents present.

For constructing sim_{Set}, we used the following dual event similarities. The event similarities in the group of events happening in the environment are measuring the events that the soil moisture dropped below a given measure ($sim_{ev,moi}$, we measure moisture, as in fit_{base}, where the sensor nodes are located, so that this could also be considered as a measure in the second group but conceptually we could do this measurement everywhere in the simulated environment). Events about the customer nodes are a customer node sending a RREQ message ($sim_{ev,rreq}$), a RREP message ($sim_{ev,rrep}$), a RERR message ($sim_{ev,rerr}$) or a DATA message ($sim_{ev,sdata}$) and the events that a customer node received a DATA message ($sim_{ev,rdata}$)[1].

Additionally, we used $sim_{ev,en}$ which is the difference in the total amount of energy used throughout the two simulations (which is obviously in the group of events related to the customer nodes) weighted by a $w_{ev,en}$ and $sim_{ev,t-out}$ which is the time difference between the two simulations when a customer node runs out of power (summed-up over all customer nodes, with the end of the simulation being the used time if a node did not run out of energy, weighted by $w_{ev,t-out}$).

Similar to some of the measures in the dual event similarities, we have an additional event similarity $sim_{ev,maxseq}$ that is applied to the customer nodes. For a node, we abstract and filter the action sequences in both individuals to only containing the message types RREQ, RREP, RERR and DATA. We then determine the length of the largest subsequence of those types that both sequences have in common. $sim_{ev,maxseq}$ is this number weighted by a $w_{ev,maxseq}$ for this node.

Finally, event similarity measure $sim_{ev,alltime}$ also looks at the nodes and the times of events (actions) for a node. It sums up the difference of the times the first action is taken, the difference of the times the second action is taken and so on until we run out of actions in one of the action sequences. And the sum for a node ag is weighted by a $w_{ev,alltime}(ag)$.

Note that looking only at the message/packet/action types from the AODV and IAP protocols is justified for this application, since these types reflect the fact that we have wireless networks (with moving agents) and the goals of the application. The application is also highlighted by not just looking at events sending messages but also events representing the reception of a message. While $sim_{ev,en}$ and $sim_{ev,t-out}$ obviously represent looking at the test goals for this application, $sim_{ev,maxseq}$ and $sim_{ev,alltime}$ are rather strong generalizations and therefore represent also a strong push away from already known solutions (provided that their associated weights are not neutralizing them). As our experiments in the next section show, these event similarities are useful.

5 Experimental Evaluation

To evaluate our modification of the fitness computation to focus on avoiding known solutions (i.e. weaknesses) while naturally still trying to find weaknesses, we have chosen a test scenario S that offers a lot of possibilities for an adversary to exploit. We have already provided M. geo is 10000 by 10000. t_{max} for the

---

[1] These kinds of events could also be applied to attack agents which would create a third group of events. As our experiments show, concentrating on environment and customer agents is enough for our application, but other applications and other testing methods might require this third group.

Table 1. Average results for focused runs with single source

Source	Focused runs				
Sol. nr.	fit_{base}	av. fit_{base}	av. sim_{Set}	av. nr. of gen.	av. run time (in min.)
1	16660.53	16875.55	0.34	90.2	96.9
2	16690.00	16515.56	0.30	119.4	87.4
3	16310.53	16355.63	0.32	84.6	125.3
4	17615.92	17227.34	0.28	83.4	55.3
5	16507.93	17121.76	0.32	25.1	49.0

Table 2. Variance of fit_{base} and sim_{Set} for focused runs with single source

Source	Focused runs				
Sol. nr.	fit_{base}	min fit_{base}	max fit_{base}	sim_{Set} for min	sim_{Set} for max
1	16660.53	16439.35	17295.63	0.32	0.28
2	16690.00	16136.41	17238.95	0.25	0.29
3	16310.53	16079.28	16947.55	0.30	0.34
4	17615.92	16905.89	17306.03	0.35	0.26
5	16507.93	16695.84	17306.60	0.35	0.27

scenario is 1000 time units and vel_{max} (for the attack agents) is also 1000 (which is the distance travelled in 10 time units). The customer nodes are a master node placed at (4500, 4000), an actuator node that waters the field at (5000, 4500) and 3 sensor nodes placed at (5000, 5300), (5000, 6100), and (5000, 6900). All these nodes do not move. The communication range is 850. Each node has a battery capacity of 150 and without attack agents the nodes will use between 50 and 75 energy units (to deal with the requests for watering due to having the field dry out over time; we did not have rain in this scenario). Since we wanted to test the ability of our approach to avoid a particular solution we needed to be able to create several source solutions for the scenario (without too many runs of the IACL system without the modification) and therefore we allowed 7 attack agents (which provides enough opportunities for finding tests that reveal weaknesses).

For the various parameters of IACL we used the following values: $n_{pop} = 30$, $n_{surv} = 9$, $n_{Stall} = 20$, $ng_{AL_i} = 75$ and $ng_{GL_i} = 75$. The weights in our modification of the fitness computation were set as $w_{sim} = 0.1$, for all agents ag we used $w_{ev,moi}(ag) = 2/1800$, $w_{ev,rreq}(ag) = 11/1800$, $w_{ev,rrep}(ag) = 3.6/1800$, $w_{ev,rerr}(ag) = 3.6/1800$, $w_{ev,sdata}(ag) = 3.6/1800$, $w_{ev,rdata}(ag) = 3.6/1800$, $w_{ev,maxseq}(ag) = 3/180$ and $w_{ev,alltime}(ag) = 2/180$, and finally we used $w_{ev,en} = 11/1800$ and $w_{ev,t-out} = 11/1800$.

To get some initial solutions to avoid and to establish a baseline, we performed around 50 runs of the original version of our IACL instantiation. The biggest similarity sim_{Set} for two of those solutions was 0.55, the minimal similarity was 0.34 and the average similarity between two of these solutions was 0.43. Of all these solutions, we selected the two with the least similarity and then additionally three that had the least similarity to all already selected ones (named 1 to 5) for our first experimental series. For each of these solutions we ran the modified version 10 times. The results of these experiments are reported in Tables 1 and 2. As Table 1 shows, the average base fitness of the focused runs by our modified system is not much worse than the base fitness of the source solution to be avoided. In fact, already the average base fitness of the 10 focused runs to source solutions 2 and 4 is better than the base fitness of the source solutions. Consequently, the best of the 10 focused runs for these source solutions have solutions that are substantially better than the source solution. Even more, the best runs for source solutions 1 and 3 are also better (see Table 2). Looking at the worst runs, they are worse than the source solutions they avoided (except for source solution 4), with a maximal base fitness difference of 800. Given that the base fitness values are over 16000 and that by avoiding solutions worse solutions are to be expected, this result is definitely not bad.

Looking more closely at the values of our similarity measure, we see in Table 1 that the average sim_{Set}-values are between 0.28 and 0.34 indicating that we are better, i.e. less similar, that what our baseline achieved. Table 1 shows that the similarity of the best solutions in the 10 runs for each source solution is not always lower than for the worst solution. While this is not unexpected (given that solutions found while avoiding a source solution can be better with regards to fit_{base}), a question that these tables cannot answer is whether our proposed similarity measure really is allowing us to find different weaknesses than those revealed by the respective source solutions. To look into this, we observed the behaviors of all agents in the simulations of the source solutions and the best solutions in each of the focused runs and found that these behaviors were rather different (although between focused runs we naturally saw some rather similar ones).

More precisely, in source solution 1, the attack agents send false route requests from customer nodes for other attack agents and one attacker also sends irrelevant information to the master node. And another attacker sends data to a fictitious attack agent. This results in essentially bombarding all customer nodes with messages that they have to route, which resulted in very quick battery depletion for all but the master node and serious network congestion in general. The best focused run for this source solution has the attackers moving a lot through the field, with one attacker dropping many requests it receives while sending requests as if it is the master node and then sending requests for the master node (totally confusing the routing tables of all agents getting these requests). This attacker also does a lot of modifying of messages it receives. Overall, this solution focuses on disrupting the routing tables of the customer nodes, which leads to preventing the sensor nodes from informing the master and actuator node about the need to water the field which then causes the field to go without water for most of the simulation. This is very different from the source solution.

Source solution 2 has the attackers hitting all customer nodes with a sudden burst of nearly constant RREQ messages for around 10 time units, which results in depleting their batteries. The best solution of a focused run makes extensive use of the possibility to fragment messages (on the level of the UDP protocol) and the attack agents especially target the first sensor node (which is the connection between sensor nodes and the other nodes in this scenario) resulting in depleting this node's battery even quicker than the batteries of the nodes in the source solution. Again, this is very different from the source attack.

Source solution 3 shows a more drawn out version of the behavior seen in source solution 2, having attack agents producing messages that the customer nodes will in the end reject but that require the use of energy. The attack agents also impersonate the master node and immediately after move around which all results in a very congested network. As a result, we see initially too infrequent watering (while the batteries are still working) and no watering starting when the batteries are depleted. As in source solution 1, the master node's battery maintains power the longest. The best solution of the focused runs is very similar to the best solution of the focused runs for source solution 2, attacking the first sensor node and due to that, interrupting rather quickly the legitimate communication within the network (and leading to watering issues relatively early). Again, both attacks are highlighting different weaknesses of the scenario.

In source solution 4, different attack agents use different strategies, with one agent introducing many watering requests and impersonating the master node, while the other agents move around a lot and drop messages while sending RREQ messages. This results in a little more build-up until the batteries of the actuator node and the sensor nodes are depleted and also the moisture levels are bad later than for the other source solutions (which results in this solution having the lowest fit_{base}-value of all source solutions and allowing for all focused runs to it to have better best solutions). The best solution from the focused runs has the attack agents not attack the battery power of the actuator node at all and only the battery of the first sensor node is depleted at all in the simulation. The key problem produced by this solution is insufficient moisture levels and this is achieved by only two attack agents that compromise the routing tables of the sensor nodes. One of the agents is essentially zipping around the sensor nodes (at full speed) sending a lot of message requests with the other agent making sure that all of these requests reach at least one customer node.

Finally, in source solution 5, one attack agent sends a lot of watering requests directly to the master node which results in depleting the battery of the actuator node rather quickly which then leads to insufficient moisture in the field. The other attackers work on depleting the batteries on 2 sensor nodes via having them relay messages between themselves. In contrast to that, the best solution from the focused runs does not target the actuator battery at all. Like the best solution of a focused run for source solution 2, the first sensor node is the main target for battery depletion, but this happens later in this simulation. Soil moisture is problematic earlier due to attack agents invalidating routing tables and creating network congestion.

Table 3. Experiments with iterated focused runs

Example1			Example2		
Iteration	fit_{base}	sim_{Set}	Iteration	fit_{base}	sim_{Set}
Initial source	16310.53	–	Initial Source	17283.23	–
After 1st it.	16601.95	0.39	After 1st it.	16640.69	0.39
After 2nd it.	16717.64	0.30	After 2nd it.	15997.61	0.29
After 3rd it.	16926.88	0.34	After 3rd it.	16682.59	0.41
After 4th it.	16849.59	0.37	After 4th it.	16500.23	0.35
After 5th it.	16553.99	0.34	After 5th it.	16082.90	0.29

As these high-level descriptions show, when avoiding a given source solution our method creates very different attacks, showing that our similarity measure really achieves what we want it to do.

We also performed experiments to see the performance of iteratively applying our modification, i.e. we choose a source solution, run our modified version of IACL, add the best solution from this run to the set *Sol*, run our modified version again and so on for 5 iterations of the modified system. Table 3 reports on two such experiments with the best source solution from the previous experimental series (3 from the previous tables, here Example1) and a not so good source not used so far (Example2). As the table shows, we are still getting solutions with rather good fit_{base}-values. In fact, the second iteration for Example2 has the best fit_{base}-value we observed in all of our experiments. Just looking at the sequence of fit_{base} or the sequence of sim_{Set} does not reveal any general trends except that we get good solutions and that the average similarity between solutions is less than what we saw in the baseline experiments, which is exactly what we wanted to achieve.

But, as with the previous experimental series, a look at the behaviors created in the simulations is of more interest. We have already described the weakness produced by the source for Example1. In the first iteration, the best found solution has 4 attack agents contribute in depleting first the actuator nodes battery and later the sensor nodes' batteries. The best solution of the second round also has mostly 4 attack agents being responsible for depleting the battery of one of the sensor nodes halfway through the simulation but the main effect of the attack agents' behavior is to avoid the field getting watered by intercepting watering requests and moving around a lot. The solution found in the third iteration has 6 attack agents contributing to first depleting the first sensor node and then the actuator node by targeting them with a lot of network traffic. This includes one agent who heavily fragments the messages from other agents. In the fourth iteration, 6 attack agents contribute, again, by attacking the batteries of the first and second sensor node using modifications of the messages of the master node (resulting in checksum errors and the requests not being accepted). Finally, in the last iteration, all attackers contribute to achieving the attack. In contrast to the other solutions, this solution does not attack the batteries but blocks any watering from happening relatively early in the simulation by modifying all messages from the master node to the actuator node and making them invalid. We see also a lot of fragmenting of messages, although this does not result in the depletion of any of the batteries.

In Example2, the initial source solution has 5 attack agents contributing by depleting the actuator node's battery around halfway through the simulation. The methods used are impersonating other agents, moving around to invalidate the routing tables and sending watering requests. In the first iteration, the attack also has 5 attackers contributing in depleting the batteries of the first and second sensor node early in the simulation. The used methods are moving around while sending messages and impersonating customer agents. In the second iteration, 6 attack agents contribute to the achieved effect, which is to block all watering requests the master sends to the actuator node. In fact, not a single watering by the actuator occurs in the whole simulation which explains the good fit_{base}-value. The third iteration's solution only needs 5 attack agents, again. It depletes the batteries of the first and second sensor node which makes the environmental effects rather similar to the solution from the first iteration, but the used methods to achieve this are rather different, namely faking data fragmentation (i.e. sending a packet that claims that it has more fragments coming, which never happens). This creates difference, but not as much as for many of the other iterations, which is reflected by the rather high sim_{Set}-value (compared to other iterations). The fourth iteration has all 7 attackers contributing to the effects of the attack. The battery of the actuator node is the target and it is depleted early in the simulation. The behaviors of the attackers include all kinds of bad behavior without any clear pattern except for the result for the actuator. The final iteration manages to block all watering requests, but in contrast to the second iteration, this is achieved by depleting the battery of the first sensor just before it would send a watering request and naturally that means also that the requests from the other sensor nodes are not relayed. In the simulation for this solution, the master and actuator node end up with higher battery charges than they have in the simulation without the attackers present.

These two examples show, again, that our similarity measure is achieving its aim, namely creating different attacks to a scenario when used to produce a penalty for being too similar to known solutions. Attacks that have similar elements are producing higher similarity values as intended (and are mostly avoided). It also seems that in order to have a low similarity to the already known attacks, involving more attack agents to create more difficult attacks is a trend.

6   Related Work

As mentioned in Sect. 3, focusing evolutionary algorithms away from a particular solution has not exactly been a focus of research. In fact, any interest in similarity of solutions is usually associated with additional interests, like improving migration in distributed GAs (see [11]) or keeping a higher diversity of solutions during the search (see [12]). In [11], similarity, respectively distance of solutions is used to improve the selection of solutions from a particular generation for sending them to other populations by other search agents. In [12] similarity, resp. again distance from each other, is added as an additional search objective. Both papers differ from our approach in that they are not using distance to given known solutions, but apply the distance/similarity to individuals created during the search. Also, they focus on similarity on the level of the structure of the individual (which for us would be the action sequences of the attack agents) and not on its evaluation.

If we broaden our look to approaches that try to focus evolutionary search outside of the standard focus on optimizing the given fitness measure, then there are also not many works. An exception is [13]. In contrast to our approach for guiding the search, [13] tries to achieve a focus by learning which genetic operators to choose (which the standard IACL already does, and which is not sufficient to solve our problem of avoiding known solutions).

If we look into software testing, then the area of search-based software engineering is looking into the creation of test cases (see [1] for an overview, but also [2]). Also some works in this area look into similarity, resp. difference, between and also within solutions. As with [11,12], these works define similarity on the structure of an individual and not on aspects of its evaluation. [14] uses a set of test cases as individuals and the difference of the elements of such a set to the other elements is measured and included in the fitness measure (essentially realizing a multi-objective optimization). Like our approach, [15] uses an already found solution, but not with the intend to avoid it but in order to use it to guide the search towards similar solutions, which is realized via the genetic operators.

Finally, with regard to using evolutionary learning for security testing or for testing wireless networks, there are no works involving previously found tests, and only a few works that are using learning techniques. In the already mentioned [16], as in other works of this group, evolutionary methods are used to find weaknesses in systems. KleeNet, [17] tries to discover bugs in wireless sensor network protocol stacks and network configurations automatically, but without involving adversaries, and consequently the misbehaviours are limited to packet loss, duplication and corruption. [18] uses evolutionary algorithms to search for network topologies that have a poor network performance when the network is subjected to automatically generated traffic. Although this work identifies such topologies, the protocols used by the network are not tested, in that no communication misbehaviours are allowed. The last two approaches might be able to make use of our improvement to IACL.

7   Conclusion and Future Work

We presented the idea of using similarity to known solutions in order to penalize individuals in a search run as a solution to the problem of having repeated runs of a learning-based testing system discovering the same solutions. We tested this idea with the IACL approach for testing ad-hoc wireless networks and instantiated the general method for an application in precision agriculture. Our experiments showed that we are indeed able to focus runs away from already known solutions, even in an iterated setting that adds solutions to the set of solutions to avoid over time.

Future work obviously should first evaluate our method for more applications of IACL (like the ones described in [6]) and then for other approaches to learning-based testing (like [3,4], as mentioned before).

References

1. McMinn, P.: Search-based software test data generation: a survey. Softw. Test. Verif. Reliab. **14**, 105–156 (2004)
2. Baars, A.I., Lakhotia, K., Vos, T.E.J., Wegener, J.: Search-based testing, the underlying engine of future internet testing. In: Proceedings of FedCSIS 2011, pp. 917–923. IEEE Press (2011)
3. Blackadar, M., Denzinger, J.: Behavior learning-based testing of starcraft competition entries. In: Proceedings of AIIDE 2011, pp. 116–121. AAAI Press (2011)
4. Hudson, J., Denzinger, J., Kasinger, H., Bauer, B.: Efficiency testing of self-adapting systems by learning of event sequences. In: Proceedings of ADAPTIVE 2010, pp. 200–205 (2010)
5. Bergmann, K.P., Denzinger, J.: Testing of precision agricultural networks for adversary-induced problems. In: Proceedings of GECCO 2013, pp. 1421–1428. IEEE Press (2013)
6. Bergmann, K.P., Denzinger, J.: Automated testing for cyber threats to ad-hoc wireless networks. In: Proceedings of CICS 2014, pp. 34–41. IEEE Press (2014)
7. Bergmann, K.P.: Vulnerability testing in wireless ad-hoc networks using incremental adaptive corrective learning. Ph.D. thesis, Department of Computer Science, University of Calgary (2014). http://theses.ucalgary.ca/bitstream/11023/1504/4/ucalgary_2014_bergmann_karel.pdf
8. Postel, J.: Internet Protocol, RFC 791 (Standard) (1981)
9. Postel, J.: User Datagram Protocol, RFC 768 (Standard) (1980)
10. Perkins, C., Belding-Royer, E., Das, S.: Ad hoc On-Demand Distance Vector (AODV) Routing, RFC 3561 (Experimental) (2003)
11. Denzinger, J., Kidney, J.: Improving migration by diversity. In: Proceedings of CEC 2003, pp. 700–707 (2003)
12. de Jong, E.D., Watson, R.A., Pollack, J.B.: Reducing bloat and promoting diversity using multi-objective methods. In: Proceedings of GECCO 2001, pp. 11–18 (2001)
13. Maturana, J., Saubion, F.: A compass to guide genetic algorithms. In: Rudolph, G., Jansen, T., Beume, N., Lucas, S., Poloni, C. (eds.) PPSN 2008. LNCS, vol. 5199, pp. 256–265. Springer, Heidelberg (2008). doi:10.1007/978-3-540-87700-4_26
14. Bueno, P.M.S., Jino, M., Wong, W.E.: Diversity oriented test data generation using metaheuristic search techniques. Inf. Sci. **259**, 490–509 (2014)
15. Yoo, S., Harman, M.: Test data regeneration: generating new test data from existing test data. J. Softw. Test. Verif. Reliab. **22**(3), 171–201 (2012)

16. Kayacik, H.G., Zincir-Heywood, A.N., Heywood, M.I.: Can a good offense be a good defense? Vulnerability testing of anomaly detectors through an artificial arms race. Soft Comput. **11**(7), 4366–4383 (2011)
17. Sasnauskas, R., Landsiedel, O., Alizai, M.H., Weise, C., Kowalewski, S., Wehrle, K.: Kleenet: discovering insidious interaction bugs in wireless sensor networks before deployment. In: Proceedings of IPSN 2010, pp. 186–196 (2010)
18. Woehrle, M.: Search-based stress testing of wireless network protocol stacks. In: Proceedings of ICST 2012, pp. 794–803 (2012)

Polytypic Genetic Programming

Jerry Swan[1](✉), Krzysztof Krawiec[2], and Neil Ghani[3]

[1] Computer Science, University of York, Deramore Lane, York YO10 5GH, UK
jerry.swan@york.ac.uk
[2] Institute of Computing Science,
Poznan University of Technology, 60-965 Poznań, Poland
krzysztof.krawiec@cs.put.poznan.pl
[3] Department of Computer and Information Sciences, University of Strathclyde,
Glasgow G1 1XH, Scotland
ng@cis.strath.ac.uk

Abstract. Program synthesis via heuristic search often requires a great deal of 'boilerplate' code to adapt program APIs to the search mechanism. In addition, the majority of existing approaches are not type-safe: i.e. they can fail at runtime because the search mechanisms lack the strict type information often available to the compiler. In this article, we describe POLYTOPE, a Scala framework that uses *polytypic programming*, a relatively recent advance in program abstraction. POLYTOPE requires a minimum of boilerplate code and supports a form of strong-typing in which type rules are automatically enforced by the compiler, even for search operations such as mutation which are applied at runtime. By operating directly on language-native expressions, it provides an embeddable optimization procedure for existing code. We give a tutorial example of the specific polytypic approach we adopt and compare both runtime efficiency and required lines of code against the well-known EpochX GP framework, showing comparable performance in the former and the complete elimination of boilerplate for the latter.

Keywords: Polytypic programming · Datatype generic programming · Genetic programming · Functional programming · Scala

1 Introduction

For over 20 years, Genetic Programming (GP) has been applied to a wide variety of program induction tasks, yielding an impressive list of (often human-competitive) results [1]. Most such endeavours require the domain-specific code, expressed in some *host language* (e.g. Java™ in the case of the popular ECJ GP framework [2]), to be *manipulable* by some search mechanism (e.g. an evolutionary algorithm in the case of GP). Technically, this is often achieved by mapping the host language API of interest to individual functions in the GP instruction set. For instance, in order to manipulate programs which use the API of a computer vision library (e.g., OpenCV [3], as in the GP/GI work of

© Springer International Publishing AG 2017
G. Squillero and K. Sim (Eds.): EvoApplications 2017, Part II, LNCS 10200, pp. 66–81, 2017.
DOI: 10.1007/978-3-319-55792-2_5

[4–6]), one could provide adaptor code for each API call of interest. This task is nowadays greatly facilitated by availability of a rich choice of domain-agnostic software packages (ECJ [2], EpochX [7] and DEAP [8] to name a few), which offer a extensive support for the representations and operators of GP.

However, tailoring a domain-agnostic search framework to a problem/domain comes at price: the GP instructions in question have to be implemented according to the contracts mandated by a given framework. In the prevailing object-oriented paradigm, this requires extending certain framework classes (representing programs, instructions, data etc.). In common domains (e.g. numeric and Boolean regression), this can be achieved at relatively low human effort. Otherwise, one is forced to realize the instructions as 'wrappers' that delegate the actual execution to the host language, which results in substantial amounts of boilerplate code, i.e. code which does little other than act as adaptor, but which is sufficiently different on a per-API basis that conventional automation approaches (e.g. C++ style macros) are insufficient. For example, Listing 1 shows some of the EpochX code required for Boolean expressions. Moreover, producing and maintaining such code may become particularly labour-intensive if a non-trivial grammar and/or type system is required, which becomes a necessity when approaching real-world program synthesis problems.

The majority of Genetic Improvement (GI) work has been in an *offline* setting, i.e. taking source- or object- code as input and producing transformed code for subsequent compilation/execution. However, the desire for systems which can respond adaptively to dynamic environments [9] has motivated a trend towards online approaches. Previous work on dynamic GI frameworks include GEN-O-FIX [10], TEMPLAR [11] and ECSELR [12]. GEN-O-FIX operates at runtime via reflection on the abstract syntax trees generated by the Scala compiler, which TEMPLAR is a wrapper for EpochX GP which makes it easy to generate the multiple variation points of a user-specified algorithm skeleton [13]. In the spirit of 'Embedded Dynamic Improvement' [14], both GEN-O-FIX and TEMPLAR can be configured via an embeddable callback mechanism which allows the training phase to take place either once, periodically or asynchronously. ECSELR extends the 'Java Agent' monitoring API to apply evolutionary operators to state snapshots of the JVM.

Despite recent work in GI (e.g. [4]), relatively little has been done to manipulate domain-specific functionality (as expressed in the host language) without the additional effort of re-presenting that knowledge in a form acceptable to the search framework. In this article, we describe POLYTOPE, an embeddable Scala framework *operating directly on the host language*. The main features of POLYTOPE are:

1. It allows the creation of manipulable (optimizable) expressions and programs with a minimum of boilerplate code.
2. It provides a strongly typed approach to GP [15], with typing rules automatically enforced *by the Scala compiler*. This is in direct contrast to other approaches, in which types must be cast/queried at runtime (see Listing 1).

3. Operates directly on language constructs, thereby easing the path to wider adoption of SBSE techniques by mainstream software developers.

The reader desiring an advance look at the resulting simplicity for the practitioner is referred to Listing 8. Crucially, the Boolean expression presented there is expressed in the host language and requires no knowledge that it is to be manipulated via POLYTOPE, nor does it depend on POLYTOPE in any sense typically considered in software engineering. Hence, it could have been equally well taken verbatim from an existing Scala library, without the intent of actually being manipulated by GP, GI or indeed any other synthesis approach. All the domain-specific knowledge (as implied by the grammatical structure of possible programs — see next section) that is necessary for forthcoming synthesis or improvement is automatically derived by building upon mechanisms available in standard Scala.

We proceed in Sect. 2 with the theoretical underpinnings of POLYTOPE, then experimentally compare its performance with a popular GP framework in Sect. 3, and discuss consequences and prospects in Sects. 4 and 5.

2   Background

GP can be considered to be constrained by the production rules of a user-specified grammar. For example, here is an EBNF for a grammar representing Boolean expressions:

```
<BoolEx>   ::= <Const> | <Var> | <AndEx>
                 | <OrEx> | <XorEx> | <NotEx> | <IfEx>
<Const>    ::= <True> |<False>
<Var>      ::= Var <Varname>
<Varname>  ::= string
<AndEx>    ::= And <BoolEx> <BoolEx>
<OrEx>     ::= Or <BoolEx> <BoolEx>
<XorEx>    ::= Xor <BoolEx> <BoolEx>
<NotEx>    ::= Not <BoolEx>
<IfEx>     ::= If <BoolEx> <BoolEx> <BoolEx>
```

In the expression trees are manipulated via traditional GP, the grammar is implicit and (as can be seen in Listing 1) describing the production rules for each entity in the grammar can require a lot of boilerplate code. In the case of Grammatical Evolution [16], the grammar rules are explicit, though they typically have some interpreted representation (e.g. as strings) which cannot be checked for validity at compile-time. In either case, the required type system must be implemented explicitly within a GP software framework, which often involves additional classes for representing particular types (cf. GPType class in ECJ [2]). This code often duplicates in part the type system of the underlying programming language, but with the attendant need for runtime type checking (again, Listing 1).

```
class AndNode extends Node {
  @Override
  public Object eval() {
    if(getChildren().length == 2) {
      Boolean b1 = (Boolean)getChild(0).eval();
      Boolean b2 = (Boolean)getChild(1).eval();
      return b1 && b2;
    }
    else throw new IllegalStateException();
  }

  @Override
  public Class<?>
  getReturnType(Class<?>... inputs) {
    return inputs.length == 2 ? Boolean.class : null;
  }
}

class OrNode extends Node {
  @Override
  public Object eval() {
    if(getChildren().length == 2) {
      Boolean b1 = (Boolean)getChild(0).eval();
      Boolean b2 = (Boolean)getChild(1).eval();
      return b1 || b2;
    }
    else throw new IllegalStateException();
  }

  @Override
  public Class<?>
  getReturnType(Class<?>... inputs) {
    return inputs.length == 2 ? Boolean.class : null;
  }
}

class ConstNode extends Node {
  public ConstNode(boolean value) { this.value = value; }
  @Override
  public Object eval() {
    if(getChildren().isEmpty)
      return value;
    else
      throw new IllegalStateException();
  }

  @Override
  public Class<?>
  getReturnType(Class<?>... inputs) {
    return inputs.isEmpty() ? Boolean.class : null;
  }
}
// Similarly for Var, Not, Xor and If.
```

Listing 1. Some of the boilerplate code required for Boolean expressions in EpochX

```
sealed trait Nat
case object Zero extends Nat
case class Succ(n: Nat) extends Nat
// Example use:
val three: Nat = Succ(Succ(Succ(Zero)))
```

Listing 2. Algebraic datatype for Peano arithmetic in Scala

In contrast, mainstream programming languages have progressively increased in their ability to abstract across datatypes. Starting in the 1960s with subtype polymorphism [17], it became possible to use inheritance to express common behaviours via the abstraction of a shared superclass. In the 1970s, parametric polymorphism was introduced [18], allowing the expression of functions and datatypes that do not require knowledge of the *type* of their arguments (e.g. a function to determine the length of a list is independent of the type of the elements it contains). More recently, there have been a number of developments in *polytypic programming*, whereby the specific *structure* of a datatype is abstracted away by one of a number of alternative generic mechanisms. These alternative approaches have a variety of names, e.g. *type-parametric programming* or *structural-/shape-/intensional- polymorphism*. In particular, the Haskell community tends to use the term *data-generic programming*, which should not be confused with the more populist notion of 'generic programming', since the latter refers only to parametric polymorphism.

Unlike parametric polymorphism whose strength derives from type agnosticism (e.g. as with the list length example above), polytypic programming captures a wide class of algorithms which are defined by interrogating the structure of the data type, e.g. so as to operate inductively upon it. Over the last 10 years or so, the functional programming community has shown particular interest in polytypic programming, originating a range of alternative approaches [19–23]. Algorithms which have been defined polytypically include equality tests, parsers and pretty printers.

3 The Polytope Framework

3.1 Polytypic Programming in Scala

Languages such as Scala and Haskell achieve considerable expressive power via their support for *Algebraic Data Types* (ADTs)[1], where the creation and manipulation of ADT expressions is ubiquitous programming practice. As shown in the example in Listing 2, ADT expressions are built-up via inductive construction, which, amongst other benefits, allows them to be conveniently manipulated via sophisticated statically-checked pattern matching. POLYTOPE combines polytypic programming with an embedded search procedure that makes it possible

---

[1] Not to be confused with the weaker notion of *abstract data types*.

to directly manipulate expressions of the host language (such as the last line of Listing 2) by an arbitrary combinatorial search mechanism, including GP. This in turn allows replacing the existing expressions with optimized equivalents (GI), or even synthesizing new expressions according to some specification or examples (GP). The polytypic approach we use here is essentially the Scala variant of Hinze's 'Generics for the Masses' [24] given by Oliveira and Gibbons [21], in which ADTs are converted to/from a universal representation.

In the following, we give a tutorial introduction to polytypic programming with a simple example, namely the polytypic calculation of size for a program tree[2]. This example is relevant to polytypic GP, as determining program size is an important part of GP workflow, allowing (for example) size-related feasibility checking. Other necessary functionality for GP, in particular mutation, is realized in a directly analogous fashion.

Boolean expressions can be represented in Scala by the ADT in Listing 3, which in the following is our example host language for either synthesis (GP) or modification (GI) of programs. We define literals of 'atomic' types such as int, char, double etc. to have a size of 1. Given these atomic building blocks, the polytypic approach allows us to inductively define size independantly of any specific ADT, so that the compiler can generate code for e.g. both size(Not(Const(true))) and size(Succ(Succ(Succ(Zero)))), yielding 3 and 4 respectively.

Since we wish to add this functionality in a non-intrusive manner, i.e. without requiring any change to the ADT we wish to operate on, we adopt the technique of *typeclasses*, well-known to the functional programming community. First developed in Haskell, this approach allows the *post-hoc* addition of functionality to any datatype. The essence of the approach is to provide a trait (for purposes of this article, equivalent to a Java interface) which defines the required methods, together with specialized subclasses for all types of interest.

Listing 4 shows the Size typeclass, together with specializations for atomic types. To make use of this functionality of POLYTOPE, one uses the statement import polytope.Size._ (Listing 8). In result of this, the functions defined in the Size object are brought into scope, and automatic promotion from some atomic type A to the corresponding imported specialization of $Size[A]$ is made possible via the use of the *implicit* keyword.

For this mechanism to be fully operational, apart from the specializations of Size for atomic types in Listing 4, it is also necessary to provide specializations for ADTs. Listing 5 shows how this *could* be done manually for the first few subclasses of Ex. In POLYTOPE, we achieve this automatically, and not just for Ex, but for any ADT. Confronting Listing 5 with Listing 3 reveals that there is a common pattern which is driven by the *shape* of the subclass constructor. Indeed, it is the ability to 'abstract over shape' that characterizes polytypic programming. In the following section, we explain how we employ this mechanism to automate creation of such specializations and avoid manually writing such boilerplate code as Listing 5.

---

[2] We focus on tree-based GP in this paper.

```
sealed trait BoolEx {
    def eval: Boolean
}

case class And(x: BoolEx, y: BoolEx) extends BoolEx {
    override def eval: Boolean = x.eval && y.eval
}

case class Or(x: BoolEx, y: BoolEx) extends BoolEx {
    override def eval: Boolean = x.eval || y.eval
}

case class Xor(x: BoolEx, y: BoolEx) extends BoolEx {
    override def eval: Boolean = x.eval ^^ y.eval
}

case class Not(x: BoolEx) extends BoolEx {
    override def eval: Boolean = !x.eval
}

case class If(cond: BoolEx, then: BoolEx, els: BoolEx) extends BoolEx {
    override def eval: Boolean = if cond.eval then.eval else els.eval
}

case class Const(override val eval: Boolean) extends BoolEx

case class Var(name: String) extends BoolEx{
    override def eval: Boolean = symbolTable.lookupVar(name)
}
```

Listing 3. Scala algebraic datatype for Boolean expressions

3.2 Product and Coproduct Types

Automatic specialization of ADT like the one exemplified in Listing 5 requires generic mechanisms for the decomposition, transformation and reassembly of ADTs. It turns out that it is possible to provide the remaining required specializations of Size (and other operations of interest for GP) for all ADTs in terms of a generic 'sum of products' representation [21]. This requires consideration of the elementary building blocks of ADTs, viz. *products* and *coproducts*[3]. The conversion of an ADT to and from this representation is described extensively by Hinze [24] and is beyond the scope of this article, but fortunately the Scala library Shapeless [25,26] provides complete support for this and a variety of other polytypic methods (e.g. [20]).

---

[3] The term 'coproduct' represents a generalized notion of 'sum' inherited from Category Theory.

```
trait Size[T] {
  def size(t: T): Int
}

object Size {
  def atomicSize[T] = new Size[T] {
    def size(t: T): Int = 1
  }

  implicit def intSize: Size[Int] = atomicSize
  implicit def booleanSize: Size[Boolean] = atomicSize
  implicit def charSize: Size[Char] = atomicSize
  // ... short, long, float etc.
  implicit def doubleSize: Size[Double] = atomicSize

  // syntactic sugar:
  def size[T](x: T)(implicit ev: Size[T]) = ev.size(x)
}
```

Listing 4. Size typeclass and specializations for atomic types

Products will already be familiar in the guise of tuples — the type of a tuple is the 'Cartesian product' of the types it contains. The Shapeless product type is HList, a heterogeneous list with compile-time knowledge of the different types of *each of its elements*. It is actually more general than a tuple, in that it supports an 'append' constructor '::'. Thus, a HList(2.3,"hello") would have type Int :: String :: HNil, where HNil represents the type-level analog of the well-known use of Nil as a list terminator. If a Double is appended, the resulting type would be Int :: String :: Double:: HNil. As seen in the above listings, an ADT consists of a collection of subclasses implementing a given trait. Each subclass has zero or more attributes and can therefore be generically represented as a HList of these attributes.

Regarding coproducts, each subclass in an ADT can be considered to represent a specific choice of construction step. They can therefore be represented by a disjoint union of subclass types. The canonical example of disjoint union in Scala or Haskell is the type Either[A, B], which contains an object known at compile-time to be of type A or else of type B. The corresponding 'shapeless' coproduct type for types A and B is denoted by A :+: B[4]. Hence the ADT Nat of Listing 2 can be generically represented as the type Zero :+: Succ :+: CNil, with CNil being the coproduct equivalent of HNil.

Specialization for generic product and coproduct types is defined inductively, starting with the base case, as represented by the types HNil and CNil respectively. The top two functions in Listing 6 show how this is done for product types, and the bottom two functions for coproduct types. The induction step is simplified via a

---

[4] Type constructors in Scala can be infix and composed of non-alphabetic characters.

```
implicit def constSize(implicit ev: Size[Boolean]) =
  new Size[Const] {
    def size(x: Const): Int = 1 + ev.size(x.value)
  }

implicit def andSize(implicit ev: Size[BoolEx]) =
  new Size[And] {
    def size(x: And): Int = 1 + ev.size(x.a) + ev.size(x.b)
  }

implicit def orSize(implicit ev: Size[BoolEx]) =
  new Size[Or] {
    def size(x: Or): Int = 1 + ev.size(x.a) + ev.size(x.b)
  }

// Similarly for other subclasses of BoolEx...
```

Listing 5. Manual specializations of Size for some subclasses of Ex. The equivalent functionality is achieved automatically in POLYTOPE.

recursive nesting technique: as is well-known, all n-tuples can be represented by recursive nesting of pairs, e.g. the triple (a, b, c) can be represented as $(a, (b, c))$. For purposes of building specializations one inductive step at a time, the tails of product and coproduct types are similarly nested. Determining the specialization for the nested tail T of the HList is dispatched to some other specialization of Size via the call to t.size(x.tail). Specialization for coproducts relies on analogous dispatching, where Inl and Inr denote left and right type-projections respectively, i.e. Inl(H :+: T) yields H, Inr(H :+: T) yields T.

The universal product and coproduct specializations in Listing 6, together with the support provided by Shapeless for conversion to/from this generic 'sum of products representation' [21] is all that is required to allow the compiler to synthesize code for size(x) for any ADT built up from the atomic specializations, automating so the functionality that would have to be otherwise implemented manually (Listing 5), for any host language expressed in standard Scala, including the example in 2, the Boolean domain in 3, and most of other common domains.

3.3   Initialization and Mutation

POLYTOPE employs the principles of polytypic programming in the design of all operators necessary to perform program synthesis or improvement, thereby allowing manipulation of arbitrary ADTs. In the current version, programs are stochastically initialized using the well-known 'full' method [27] and subtree-replacing mutation (a randomly selected subtree in a program is replaced by a random 'full' tree). The generic definitions for tree initialization and mutating

```
implicit val productBase = new Size[HNil] {
  def size(x: HNil): Int = 0
}

implicit def productInductionStep[H, T <: HList](
  implicit h: Size[H], t: Size[T]) =
    new Size[H : : T] {
      def size(x: H : : T) = {
        val hd = h.size(x.head)
        val tl = t.size(x.tail)
        hd + tl
      }
    }

implicit val coproductBase = new Size[CNil] {
  def size(x: CNil): Int = 0
}

implicit def coproductInductionStep[H, T <: Coproduct](
  implicit h: Size[H], t: Size[T]) =
    new Size[H :+: T] {
      def size(x: H :+: T): Int = x match {
        case Inl(l) => h.size(l)
        case Inr(r) => t.size(r)
      }
    }
```

Listing 6. Generic Size specialization for product and coproduct types

a subtree follow the same general pattern as the Size example. As can be seen in Listing 7 (which gives the SubtreeMutate typeclass and an example of the corresponding client code), the actual mutation is performed in the method mutateImpl. The implementation of this method is slightly more complex than the Size example, since it requires additional book-keeping to keep track of the node indexing. This is represented by the Either[T,Int] return type, in which the Int value represents the index of the node for subsequent consideration. The corresponding overridden versions for atomic, product and coproduct types are too lengthy for this article, but are implemented analogously. Similar remarks apply to the initialization operator. As in the case of Size, both mutation and initialization work for any domain-specific host language expressible in Scala.

3.4 Comparison of Lines of Code

For the Boolean domain considered here, the total required by EpochX 1.4.1 is 301 lines of code (LOC) (specifically that for the classes AndFunction,OrFunction, NotFunction,XorFunction,ImpliesFunction in the org.epochx.epox.bool package).

```
trait SubtreeMutate[T] {
  def mutate(t: T, index: Int): Option[T] =
    mutateImpl(t, index) match {
      case Left(t) => Some(t)
      case Right(newIndex) => None
    }

  protected def mutateImpl(t: T, index: Int): Either[T,Int] = ...
}

def mutate[T](x: T, rng: Random)(
  implicit m: SubtreeMutate[T], sz: Size[T]): T =
    ev.mutate(x,rng.nextInt(sz.size(Ex))).getOrElse(x)
}

// client code:
import Size._
import SubtreeMutate._

val ex = Not(Xor(Var("a"),Const(false)))
val mutated = mutate(ex)
```

Listing 7. Mutation typeclass and client code

We discount the EpochX code required for Const since it is provided by built-in support for ephemeral random constants. In contrast, POLYTOPE can operate directly on the 20 LOC given in the classes of Listing 3. However, the important thing to note is that the code of Listing 3 will in general be some arbitrarily complex API that has already been implemented and that we wish to manipulate via search.

4   Experiments

With POLYTOPE's generic initialization and mutation operators, we can apply search routines to obtain an instance of any ADT, optimized to some user-specified criterion. To this end, POLYTOPE provides an implementation of the well-known Evolution Strategies (ES) metaheuristic [28], specifically, Algorithms 18 and 19 from Luke [29].

POLYTOPE can either be applied to optimize existing code (i.e. an ADT expression) or else can synthesize an ADT from scratch. Listing 8 shows the client code required to obtain an optimized expression for Mux6, the well-known 6-input multiplexer problem [27], for both *ex-nihilo* synthesis (GP-style) and improvement of existing code (GI-style). In contrast to the boilerplate of Listing 1, the only client responsibility is the implementation of the fitness function (here, the normalized sum of the zero/one errors on all possible 2^6 fitness cases).

```
// client code
def mux6Fitness(x:BoolEx): Double = // error of x.eval on fitness cases...

def main(args: Array[String]) = {

    // bring implicit specializations into scope
    import polytope.Size._
    import polytope.FullInitializer._
    import polytope.SubtreeMutate._

    // 1. ex−nihilo synthesis
    val opt1 = polytope.optimize(mux6Fitness)
    println( opt1, opt1.eval )

    // 2. Improvement of some existing expression
    val ex = If(Or(Var("x"),False),
        And(Var("y"),Var("z")),
        Or(Not(Var("x")),True))

    val opt2 = polytope.optimize(mux6Fitness,ex)
    println( opt2, opt2.eval )
}
```

Listing 8. Client code for Mux6 problem. Note the 'last-minute' import of POLYTOPE.

To determine the performance relative to a traditional GP implementation, we compared our ES approach against EpochX on Mux6 over 30 runs with common parameters as given in Table 1. We compare against two variants of EpochX: EpochX-1 uses EpochX 'out of the box', i.e. with default parameters[5] (i.e. subtree crossover with probability 0.9, elitism count = 10, max tree depth = 17). EpochX-2 is intended to provide a more 'like for like' comparison with the current implementation of POLYTOPE, and therefore has no crossover and no upper bound on max-tree-depth. Although a lack of crossover is somewhat unusual in

Table 1. Parameters common to all Mux-6 experiments

Parameter	Value
Population-size	1,000
Max-generations	100
Max-initial-tree-depth	5
Tree-initialization-method	Full
Mutation-method	Subtree

---

[5] http://www.epochx.org/javadoc/1.4/.

Table 2. Results of Mux-6 experiment

Algorithm	Fitness	Time (s)	Generations	Time per individual (ms)	0/1 successrate
EpochX-1	0.00 ± 0.00	2.26 ± 0.95	17.10 ± 6.71	7.14 ± 1.17	100%
EpochX-2	0.06 ± 0.11	3.60 ± 2.01	62.40 ± 31.63	17.49 ± 4.74	7.3%
POLYTOPE	0.25 ± 0.14	7.26 ± 1.96	92.03 ± 18.77	13.29 ± 1.85	6.7%

GP (Cartesian GP being a notable exception [30]) it is not so common in GI (e.g. [31]). For the ES-specific parameters, we use a $(\lambda + \mu)$-ES we take λ to be population size and $\mu = \lambda/5$. A run is terminated once a correct program is found or 100 generations elapse, whichever comes first.

Experiments were run on a Windows 10 desktop PC with 8 GB of RAM and an Intel Core i5-3570 CPU @ 3.40 GHz. Table 2 shows the results of the experiments, giving averaged normalized fitness, execution time in seconds, number of generations at termination, processing time per individual (elapsed time divided by the number of generations), and 0/1 success rate (defined as '1 for the optimum output, else 0'), accompanied with 0.95-confidence intervals. The rates of convergence to the optimum make it clear that the absence of crossover is detrimental to solution quality. Comparing POLYTOPE with the EpochX-2 setup, the performance of the former can be explained in part by the fact that it lacks a bloat control method [32], which fails to impose selection pressure against large expressions and leads to trees which take longer to evaluate. However, the end-of-run fitness of POLYTOPE is not statistically significantly worse[6] than that of EpochX-2, and the 'zero or one' success rate is comparable.

Concerning the time for processing a program, POLYTOPE performs slightly better than the 'like for like' comparator EpochX-2, which might be explained by the amount of compile-time support afforded by our chosen polytypic approach. Since there are no theoretical obstacles to adding polytypic equivalents for crossover and bloat control to POLYTOPE, it would then be expected to behave comparably to (or even slightly better than) the 'out of the box' version of EpochX.

5   Discussion and Conclusion

We have described how polytypic programming (specifically Oliveira and Gibbons [21] variant of Hinze's 'Generics for the Masses' [24]) can be used to provide initialization and mutation operators for arbitrary datatypes, and have implemented POLYTOPE, a Scala framework which uses embedded optimization to perform synthesis and improvement of Scala code with minimal end-user effort.

Using POLYTOPE as a GP system frees the end-user from having to write the significant amounts of instruction-set specific code that is necessary when using most popular GP frameworks (Listing 1). Although previous work [10,33] has

---

[6] as determined by the nonparametric Wilcoxon Signed Rank test.

used runtime reflection as a means of reducing this burden, we describe how this can be via compile-time techniques. We explain how methods from polytypic programming can achieve this via the automatic and non-intrusive derivation of the grammatical structure of datatypes.

In addition to manipulating existing datatypes, POLYTOPE resembles GP in that it also supports *ex-nihilo* synthesis of expressions involving these datatypes. This is in contrast to some other GI frameworks [31,34] that manipulate programs by 'plastic surgery' (i.e. moving around pre-existing expressions modulo variable re-naming). With the historical emphasis on GI being 'offline, top-down', POLYTOPE can therefore be considered to occupy an intermediate position between traditional notions of GP and GI.

The current version of POLYTOPE lacks both crossover and any built-in mechanism for bloat control. The experiments in Sect. 4 show that that both are desirable. There is no intrinsic technical obstacle to the implementation of either and they are suitable subjects for further work. Regarding bloat-control, irrespective of the provision of a general mechanism for this, reducing expressions to some minimal-size form via domain-specific rewrite rules [35] can be implemented very naturally on ADTs using pattern-matching. Nevertheless, even without these extensions, we anticipate two distinguishing uses of POLYTOPE in its current form: as a 'rapid prototyping tool' for GP, in which development time is more of an issue than raw speed, and as a background optimization process in long-running systems, continuing to adapt to an operating environment that changes over time.

Acknowledgements. J. Swan would like to thank Miles Sabin and the contributors to the Scala 'shapeless' library. His work on this paper is funded by EPSRC grant EP/J017515/1 (DAASE). K. Krawiec acknowledges support from National Science Centre, Poland, grant 2014/15/B/ST6/05205.

References

1. Kannappan, K., Spector, L., Sipper, M., Helmuth, T., La Cava, W., Wisdom, J., Bernstein, O.: Analyzing a decade of human-competitive ("HUMIE") winners: what can we learn? In: Riolo, R., Worzel, W.P., Kotanchek, M. (eds.) Genetic Programming Theory and Practice XII. Genetic and Evolutionary Computation, pp. 149–166. Springer, Heidelberg (2015)
2. Luke, S.: The ECJ owner's manual (2010). http://www.cs.gmu.edu/~eclab/projects/ecj
3. Dawson-Howe, K.: A Practical Introduction to Computer Vision with OpenCV, 1st edn. Wiley Publishing, Chichester (2014)
4. Langdon, W.B., White, D.R., Harman, M., Jia, Y., Petke, J.: API-constrained genetic improvement. In: Sarro, F., Deb, K. (eds.) SSBSE 2016. LNCS, vol. 9962, pp. 224–230. Springer, Cham (2016). doi:10.1007/978-3-319-47106-8_16
5. Krawiec, K., Bhanu, B.: Visual learning by coevolutionary feature synthesis. IEEE Trans. Syst. Man and Cybern. Part B **35**(3), 409–425 (2005)

6. Harding, S., Leitner, J., Schmidhuber, J.: Cartesian genetic programming for image processing. In: Riolo, R., Vladislavleva, E., Ritchie, M.D., Moore, J.H. (eds.) Genetic Programming Theory and Practice X. Genetic and Evolutionary Computation. Springer, New York (2012)
7. Otero, F., Castle, T., Johnson, C.: EpochX: genetic programming in java with statistics and event monitoring. In: Proceedings of the 14th Annual Conference Companion on Genetic and Evolutionary Computation (GECCO 2012), pp. 93–100, New York, NY, USA. ACM (2012)
8. Fortin, F.-A., De Rainville, F.-M., Gardner, M.-A., Parizeau, M., Christian Gagné, D.: Evolutionary algorithms made easy. J. Mach. Learn. Res. **13**, 2171–2175 (2012)
9. Harman, M., Jia, Y., Langdon, W.B., Petke, J., Moghadam, I.H., Yoo, S., Fan, W.: Genetic improvement for adaptive software engineering (keynote). In: Proceedings of the 9th International Symposium on Software Engineering for Adaptive and Self-Managing Systems (SEAMS 2014), pp. 1–4, New York, NY, USA. ACM (2014)
10. Swan, J., Burles, N.: TEMPLAR – a framework for template-method hyper-heuristics. In: Machado, P., Heywood, M.I., McDermott, J., Castelli, M., García-Sánchez, P., Burelli, P., Risi, S., Sim, K. (eds.) EuroGP 2015. LNCS, vol. 9025, pp. 205–216. Springer, Cham (2015). doi:10.1007/978-3-319-16501-1_17
11. Swan, J., Epitropakis, M.G., Woodward, J.R.: Gen-O-Fix: an embeddable framework for dynamic adaptive genetic improvement programming. Technical report CSM-195, Computing Science and Mathematics, University of Stirling, Stirling FK9 4LA, Scotland, January 2014
12. Yeboah-Antwi, K., Baudry, B.: Embedding adaptivity in software systems using the ECSELR framework. In: Proceedings of the Companion Publication of the 2015 on Genetic and Evolutionary Computation Conference, pp. 839–844. ACM (2015)
13. Woodward, J.R., Swan, J.: Template method hyper-heuristics. In: Proceedings of the Companion Publication of the 2014 Annual Conference on Genetic and Evolutionary Computation (GECCO Comp 2014), pp. 1437–1438, New York, NY, USA. ACM (2014)
14. Burles, N., Swan, J., Bowles, E., Brownlee, A.E.I., Kocsis, Z.A., Veerapen, N.: Embedded dynamic improvement. In: Genetic and Evolutionary Computation Conference (GECCO 2015), Companion Material Proceedings, Madrid, Spain, 11–15 July 2015, pp. 831–832 (2015)
15. Montana, D.J.: Strongly typed genetic programming. Evol. Comput. **3**(2), 199–230 (1995)
16. Ryan, C., Collins, J.J., Neill, M.O.: Grammatical evolution: evolving programs for an arbitrary language. In: Banzhaf, W., Poli, R., Schoenauer, M., Fogarty, T.C. (eds.) EuroGP 1998. LNCS, vol. 1391, pp. 83–96. Springer, Heidelberg (1998). doi:10.1007/BFb0055930
17. Mitchell, J.C.: Concepts in Programming Languages. Cambridge University Press, Cambridge (2003)
18. Milner, R., Morris, L., Newey, M.: A logic for computable functions with reflexive and polymorphic types. In: Proceedings of the Conference on Proving and Improving Programs, Arc-et-Senans (1975)
19. Gibbons, J.: Datatype-generic programming. In: Backhouse, R., Gibbons, J., Hinze, R., Jeuring, J. (eds.) SSDGP 2006. LNCS, vol. 4719, pp. 1–71. Springer, Heidelberg (2007). doi:10.1007/978-3-540-76786-2_1
20. Lämmel, R., Jones, S.P.: Scrap your boilerplate: a practical design pattern for generic programming. In: Proceedings of the 2003 ACM SIGPLAN International Workshop on Types in Languages Design and Implementation (TLDI 2003), pp. 26–37, New York, NY, USA. ACM (2003)

21. Oliveira, B.C.d.S., Gibbons, J.: Scala for generic programmers: comparing haskell and scala support for generic programming. J. Funct. Program. **20**(3–4), 303–352 (2010)
22. Gibbons, J.: Origami programming. In: Gibbons, J., de Moor, O. (eds.) The Fun of Programming, Cornerstones in Computing, pp. 41–60. Palgrave, New York (2003)
23. Moors, A., Piessens, F., Joosen, W.: An object-oriented approach to datatype-generic programming. In: Proceedings of the 2006 ACM SIGPLAN Workshop on Generic Programming (WGP 2006), pp. 96–106, New York, NY, USA. ACM (2006)
24. Hinze, R.: Generics for the masses. J. Funct. Program. **16**(4–5), 451–483 (2006)
25. Sabin, M., et al.: Shapeless: generic programming for Scala, 2011–2016. http://github.com/milessabin/shapeless
26. Gurnell, D.: The type astronaut's guide to shapeless. Underscore consulting LLP (2016). http://underscore.io/books/shapeless-guide. ISBN 978-1-365-61352-4
27. Koza, J.R.: Genetic Programming: On the Programming of Computers by Means of Natural Selection. MIT Press, Cambridge (1992)
28. Rechenberg, I.: Evolutionsstrategie: optimierung technischer Systeme nach Prinzipien der biologischen Evolution. Number 15 in Problemata. Frommann-Holzboog, Stuttgart-Bad Cannstatt (1973)
29. Luke, S.: Essentials of Metaheuristics, 2nd edn. Lulu, Raleigh (2013). http://cs.gmu.edu/~sean/book/metaheuristics/
30. Miller, J.F., Thomson, P.: Cartesian genetic programming. In: Poli, R., Banzhaf, W., Langdon, W.B., Miller, J., Nordin, P., Fogarty, T.C. (eds.) EuroGP 2000. LNCS, vol. 1802, pp. 121–132. Springer, Heidelberg (2000). doi:10.1007/978-3-540-46239-2_9
31. Langdon, W.B., Harman, M.: Optimising existing software with genetic programming. IEEE Trans. Evol. Comput. **19**(1), 118–135 (2015)
32. Luke, S., Panait, L.: A comparison of bloat control methods for genetic programming. Evol. Comput. **14**(3), 309–344 (2006)
33. Keijzer, M., O'Reilly, U.-M., Lucas, S., Costa, E., Soule, T. (eds.): EuroGP 2004. LNCS, vol. 3003. Springer, Heidelberg (2004)
34. Le Goues, C., Nguyen, T.V., Forrest, S., Weimer, W.: GenProg: a generic method for automatic software repair. IEEE Trans. Softw. Eng. **38**(1), 54–72 (2012)
35. Swan, J., Kocsis, Z.A., Lisitsa, A.: The 'representative' metaheuristic design pattern. In: Proceedings of the Companion Publication of the 2014 Annual Conference on Genetic and Evolutionary Computation (GECCO Comp 2014), pp. 1435–1436, New York, NY, USA. ACM (2014)

Evolving Rules for Action Selection in Automated Testing via Genetic Programming - A First Approach

Anna I. Esparcia-Alcázar[✉], Francisco Almenar,
Urko Rueda, and Tanja E.J. Vos

Research Center on Software Production Methods (PROS),
Universitat Politècnica de València, Camino de Vera s/n, 46022 Valencia, Spain
{aesparcia,urueda,tvos}@pros.upv.es
http://www.testar.org

Abstract. Tools that perform automated software testing via the user interface rely on an action selection mechanism that at each step of the testing process decides what to do next. This mechanism is often based on random choice, a practice commonly referred to as *monkey testing*. In this work we evaluate a first approach to genetic programming (GP) for action selection that involves evolving IF-THEN-ELSE rules; we carry out experiments and compare the results with those obtained by random selection and also by $\mathcal{Q}$-learning, a reinforcement learning technique. Three applications are used as Software Under Test (SUT) in the experiments, two of which are proprietary desktop applications and the other one an open source web-based application. Statistical analysis is used to compare the three action selection techniques on the three SUTs; for this, a number of metrics are used that are valid even under the assumption that access to the source code is not available and testing is only possible via the GUI. Even at this preliminary stage, the analysis shows the potential of GP to evolve action selection mechanisms.

Keywords: Automated testing via the GUI · Action selection for testing · Testing metrics · Genetic Programming

1 Introduction

The relevance of testing a software application at the Graphical User Interface (GUI) level has often been stated due to several reasons, the main being that it implies taking the user's perspective and is thus the ultimate way of verifying a program's correct behaviour. Current GUIs can account for 45–60% of the source code [2] in any application and are often large and complex; hence, it is difficult to test applications thoroughly through their GUI, especially because GUIs are designed to be operated by humans, not machines. Furthermore, they are usually subject to frequent changes motivated by functionality updates, usability enhancements, changing requirements or altered contexts. Automating the

© Springer International Publishing AG 2017
G. Squillero and K. Sim (Eds.): EvoApplications 2017, Part II, LNCS 10200, pp. 82–95, 2017.
DOI: 10.1007/978-3-319-55792-2_6

process of testing via the GUI is therefore a crucial task in order to minimise time-consuming and tedious manual testing.

The existing literature in testing via the User Interface covers three approaches: *capture-and-replay* (C&R), which involves recording user interactions and converting them into a script that can be replayed repeatedly, *visual-based* which relies on image recognition techniques to visually interpret the images of the target UI [3], and *traversal-based*, which uses information from the GUI (GUI reflection) to *traverse* it [1], and can be used to check some general properties. Of the three, the latter group is considered the most resilient to changes in the SUT.

The designer of any automated tool for carrying out traversal-based testing is faced with a number of design choices. One of the most relevant is the decision of the action selection mechanism which, given the current state (or window) the system is in, involves answering the question "what do I do next?". Although most tools leave this to purely random choice (a procedure known as *monkey testing*), some authors have resorted to metaheuristics or machine learning techniques in order to decide what action to execute at each step of the testing sequence, such as Q-learning [7] and Ant Colony Optimisation [5]. Here we present a first approach to using Genetic Programming (GP) to evolve action selection rules in traversal-based software testing. There is a large body of work that shows the power of GP to evolve programs and functions and, more specifically, rules; on the other hand, GP has also previously been used in software testing, e.g. by [11,12] but, to the best of our knowledge, not to evolve action selection rules.

In our approach GP evolves a population of rules whose quality (or *fitness*) is evaluated by using each one of them as the action selection mechanism in a traversal-based software testing tool. In order to do this suitable metrics must be defined and a number of options are available in the literature. For instance, in [6] metrics are proposed for event driven software; [10] defines a coverage criteria for GUI testing, while in [4] the number of crashes of the SUT, the average time it takes to crash and the reproducibility of these crashes are used. In this work we will follow the approach taken by [7], who propose four metrics which are suitable for testing web applications, based on the assumption that source code is not available.

In order to carry out our study we chose three applications as the SUTs: the Odoo enterprise resource planning (ERP) system, a software testing tool called Testona and the PowerPoint presentation software. These are very different types of SUT: while Odoo is an open source web application, both Testona and Powerpoint are proprietary desktop applications. Statistical analysis was carried out on the results of the three action selection methods over the three SUTs.

The rest of this paper is structured as follows. Section 2 describes the action selection mechanism using genetic programming. Section 3 introduces the metrics used for quality assessment of the testing procedure. Section 4 summarises the experimental set up, the results obtained and the statistical analysis carried out;

it also highlights the problems encountered. Finally, in Sect. 5 we present some conclusions and outline areas for future work.

2   Genetic Programming for Action Selection in GUI-Based Automated Testing

Tree-based Genetic Programming is the original form of GP as introduced by Koza [8]. It involves the evolution of a population of individuals, or candidate solutions, that can be represented as expression trees, given suitable nodes (functions) and leaves (terminals) are defined for the problem at hand. In this work we represent individuals as IF-THEN-ELSE rules that, given the current state of the SUT, pick the next action to execute. An example rule would be something like this:

> **IF** *previousAction* **EQ** *typeInto*
> **AND** *nLeftClick* **LE** *nTypeInto*
> **PickAny** *typeInto*
> **ELSE**
> **PickAnyUnexecuted**

According to this rule, if the last executed action (*previousAction*) was entering text in a box (*typeInto*) and the number of clickable items (*nLeftClick*) is less than or equal to the number of text boxes (*nTypeInto*), then the next action will be typing text in any of the text boxes (**PickAny** *typeInto*); otherwise, a random action will be chosen that has not been executed before (**PickAnyUnexecuted**). Note that the text entered would be chosen at random.

The GP engine chosen was ponyGP[1] and the set up for the experiments is given in Table 1. The fitness of each individual was calculated by using it as the action selection rule for the traversal-based tool *TESTAR*[2]; metrics are collected in the process, one of which is used as the fitness value.

Figure 1 shows how the genetic programming process could be embedded within the testing tool (*TESTAR* here). The *live* version of *TESTAR* tests the SUT at hand using the best action selection rule found so far, while, in parallel, the evolutionary algorithm uses a *sandbox* version of *TESTAR* in order to evaluate the fitness of the new individuals. When a better individual is found, it is sent to the live *TESTAR*, that carries on testing using the new individual for action selection.

3   Testing Performance Metrics

As stated in Sect. 1, a number of metrics have been defined in the literature to assess the quality of the testing, e.g. those given by [10] or [4]. However, two main

---

[1] Developed by Erik Hemberg from the ALFA Group at MIT CSAIL http://groups. csail.mit.edu/EVO-DesignOpt/PonyGP/out/index.html.

[2] http://www.testar.org.

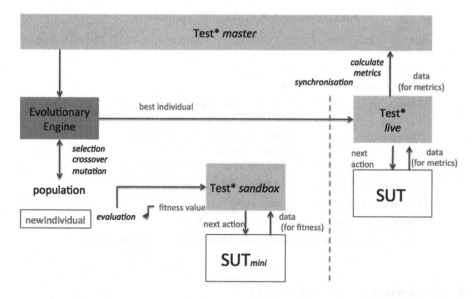

Fig. 1. The evolutionary process embedded within a traversal-based testing tool.

issues can be found with them: namely, that they either imply having access to the SUT source code (which is not always the case) or that they focus on errors encountered and reveal nothing about to what extent the SUT was explored (which is particularly relevant if no errors are detected). For these reasons, we decided on the following metrics, as defined by [7]:

- **Abstract states.** This metric refers to the number of different states, or windows in the GUI, that are visited in the course of an execution. An abstract state does not take into account modifications in parameters; for instance, a window containing a text box with the text "tomato" would be considered the same abstract state as the same window and text box containing the text "potato".
- **Longest path.** This is defined as the longest sequence of non-repeated consecutive states visited.
- **Minimum and maximum coverage per state.** The *state coverage* is defined as the rate of executed over total available actions in a given state/window; the metrics are the highest and lowest such values across all windows.

It is interesting to note that longest path and maximum coverage are in a way opposed metrics, one measuring exploration and the other exploitation of the SUT.

Table 1. Genetic programming parameters.

Feature	Value
Population size	20
Max tree size	20
Functions	Pick, PickAny, PickAnyUnexecuted, AND, OR, LE, EQ, NOT
Terminals	nActions, nTypeInto, nLeftClick, previousAction, RND, typeLeftClick, typeTypeInto, Any
Evolutionary operators	Mutation and crossover
Evolutionary method	Steady state
Selection method	Tournament of size 5
Termination criterion	Generating more than 30 different states

4   Experiments and Results

4.1   Procedure

We have taken a simplified approach which involves evolving action selection rules by genetic programming using PowerPoint as the *sandbox* SUT and then validating the best evolved rule by using it to test the three different SUTs described below. For the latter phase we carried out 30 runs of 1000 actions each. In this way we can ascertain how well the GP-evolved rule generalises to SUTs not encountered during evolution.

The best evolved rule was as follows:

> **IF** *nLeftClick* **LT** *nTypeInto*
> **PickAny** *leftClick*
> **ELSE**
> **PickAnyUnexecuted**

In order to carry out statistical comparisons, the validation process was repeated using random and Q-learning-based action selection. Q-learning [13] is a model-free reinforcement learning technique in which an agent, at a state s, must choose one among a set of actions A_s available at that state. By performing an action $a \in A_s$, the agent can move from state to state. Executing an action in a specific state provides the agent with a reward (a numerical score which measures the utility of executing a given action in a given state). The goal of the agent is to maximise its total reward, since it allows the algorithm to look ahead when choosing actions to execute. It does this by learning which action is optimal for each state. The action that is optimal for each state is the action that has the highest long-term reward. The choice of the algorithm's two parameters, maximum reward, R_{max} and discount γ, will promote exploration or exploitation of the search space. In our case we chose those that had provided best results in [7].

A summary of the experimental settings is given in Table 2.

Table 2. Experimental set up.

Set	Action selection algorithm	Parameters	Max. actions per run	Runs
Ev	GP-evolved rule	See Table 1	1000	30
Qlearning	Q-learning	$R_{max} = 9999999; \gamma = 0.95$	1000	30
RND	Random	N/A	1000	30

4.2 The Software Under Test (SUT)

We used three different applications in order to evaluate our action selection app-roach, namely Odoo, PowerPoint and Testona. **Odoo** is an open source Enterprise Resource Planning software consisting of several enterprise management applications; of these, we installed the mail, calendar, contacts, sales, inventory and project applications in order to test a wide number of options. **Power-Point** is a slide show presentation program part of the productivity software Microsoft Office. It is currently one of the most commonly used presentation programs available. **Testona** (formerly known as *Classification Tree Editor*) is a software testing tool that runs on Windows. It implements tree classification, which involves classifying the domain of the application under test and assigning tests to each of its leaves.

4.3 Statistical Analysis

We run the Kruskal-Wallis non parametric test, with $\alpha = 0.05$, on the results for the three action selection mechanisms. The test shows that all the metrics have significant differences among the sets. Running pair-wise comparisons by means of the Mann-Whitney-Wilcoxon test, provides the results shown in the boxplots contained in Figs. 2, 3, 4, 5 and 6; these results are ordered in Table 3, where the shaded column is the best option. It can be seen that the GP approach wins in the abstract states and longest path metrics for both Powerpoint and Odoo and comes second in Testona, where, surprisingly, random testing performs best (Fig. 7).

One metric we have not considered in the statistical analysis is the number of failures encountered, shown in Table 4. Here we can see that in general, the evolutionary approach finds the most real failures[3].

---

[3] Note that ascertaining whether these failures are associated to any defects is beyond the scope of the *TESTAR* tool.

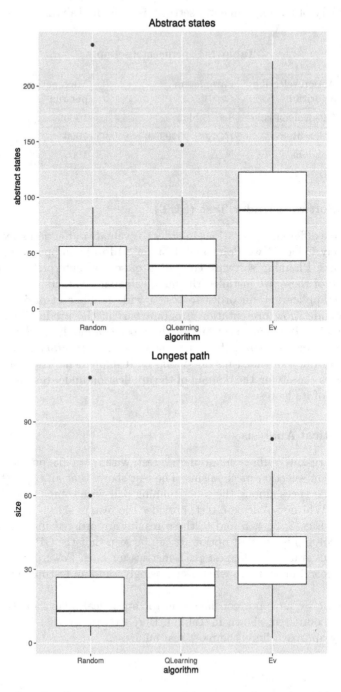

Fig. 2. Boxplots for the abstract states and longest path metrics with the results obtained for Odoo

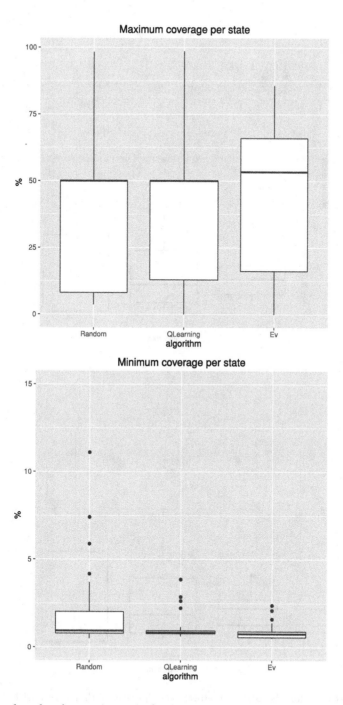

Fig. 3. Boxplots for the maximum and minimum coverage metrics with the results obtained for Odoo

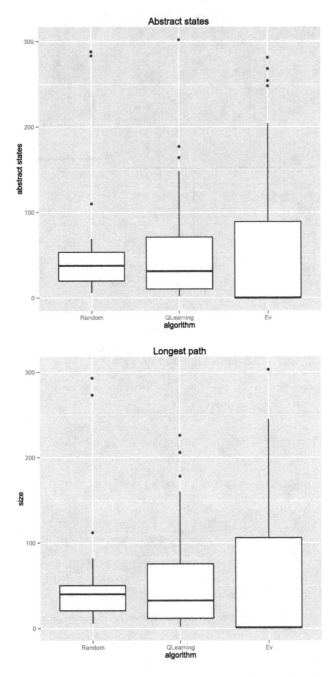

Fig. 4. Boxplots for the abstract states and longest path metrics with the results obtained for PowerPoint.

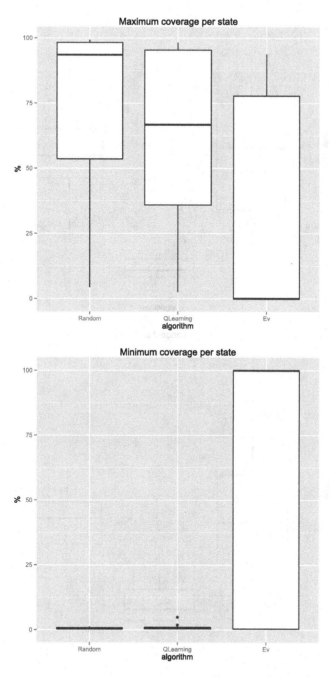

Fig. 5. Boxplots for the maximum and minimum coverage metrics with the results obtained for PowerPoint.

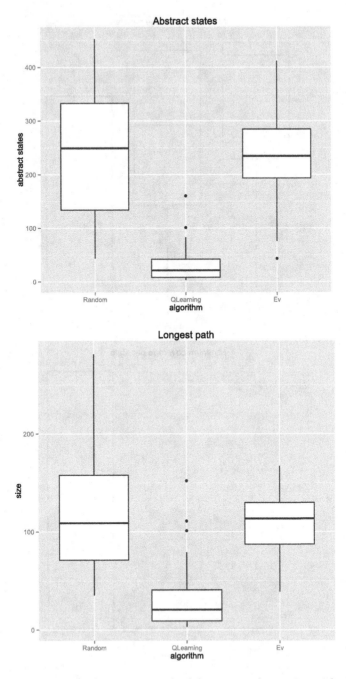

Fig. 6. Boxplots for the abstract states and longest path metrics with the results obtained for Testona.

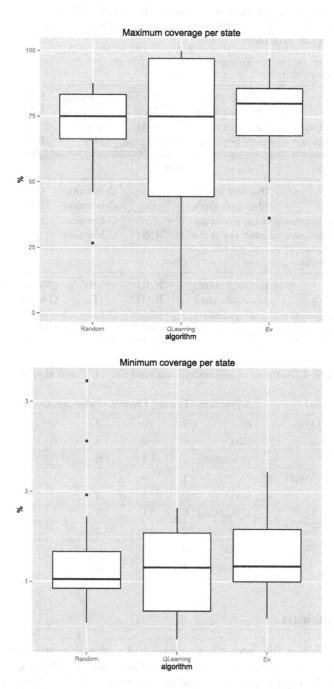

Fig. 7. Boxplots for the maximum and minimum coverage metrics with the results obtained for Testona.

Table 3. Results of the statistical comparison for all algorithms and metrics, in the three different SUTs. The shaded column represents the best choice, the remaining ones are in order of preference.

PowerPoint	Set		
Abstract states	Ev	Q-learning	RND
Longest path	Ev	Q-learning	RND
Maximum coverage per state	RND	Q-learning	Ev
Minimum coverage per state	Q-learning	Ev	RND

Odoo	Set		
Abstract states	Ev	Q-learning	RND
Longest path	Ev	Q-learning	RND
Maximum coverage per state	Ev	Q-learning	RND
Minimum coverage per state	RND	Q-learning	Ev

Testona	Set		
Abstract states	RND	Ev	Q-learning
Longest path	RND	Ev	Q-learning
Maximum coverage per state	Ev	Q-learning	RND
Minimum coverage per state	Ev	Q-learning	RND

Table 4. Number of failures encountered per SUT and algorithm.

SUT	Algorithm	Errors	Freezes	False positives
Odoo	Ev	**4**	0	2
	RND	0	0	4
	Q-learning	1	1	6
PowerPoint	Ev	**1**	0	5
	RND	0	1	2
	Q-learning	0	1	5
Testona	Ev	**2**	2	3
	RND	0	3	6
	Q-learning	1	1	3

5   Conclusions

We have shown here the successful application of a genetic programming-evolved action selection rule within an automated testing tool. The GP-evolved rule was also compared to Q-learning and random, or *monkey testing*. The performance was evaluated on three SUTs (PowerPoint, Odoo and Testona) and according to four metrics. Statistical analysis reveals the superiority of the GP approach in PowerPoint and Odoo, although not in Testona.

Further work will involve developing more complex rules by introducing new functions and terminals. A further step ahead will also involve eliminating the fitness function and guiding the evolution based on novelty only [9].

Acknowledgments. This work was partially funded by project **SHIP** (*SMEs and HEIs in Innovation Partnerships*, ref: EACEA/A2/UHB/CL 554187).

References

1. Aho, P., Menz, N., Rty, T.: Dynamic reverse engineering of GUI models for testing. In: Proceedings of the 2013 International Conference on Control, Decision and Information Technologies (CoDIT 2013), May 2013
2. Aho, P., Oliveira, R., Algroth, E., Vos, T.: Evolution of automated testing of software systems through graphical user interface. In: International Conference on Advances in Computation, Communications and Services, Valencia (2016)
3. Alegroth, E., Feldt, R., Ryrholm, L.: Visual GUI testing in practice: challenges, problems and limitations. Empirical Softw. Eng. **20**, 694–744 (2014)
4. Bauersfeld, S., Vos, T.E.J.: User interface level testing with TESTAR: what about more sophisticated action specification and selection? In: Post-proceedings of the Seventh Seminar on Advanced Techniques and Tools for Software Evolution, SAT-ToSE 2014, L'Aquila, Italy, 9–11 July 2014. pp. 60–78 (2014). http://ceur-ws.org/Vol-1354/paper-06.pdf
5. Bauersfeld, S., Wappler, S., Wegener, J.: A metaheuristic approach to test sequence generation for applications with a GUI. In: Cohen, M.B., Ó Cinnéide, M. (eds.) SSBSE 2011. LNCS, vol. 6956, pp. 173–187. Springer, Heidelberg (2011). doi:10.1007/978-3-642-23716-4_17
6. Chaudhary, N., Sangwan, O.: Metrics for event driven software. Int. J. Adv. Comput. Sci. Appl. (IJACSA) **7**(1), 85–89 (2016)
7. Esparcia-Alcázar, A.I., Almenar, F., Martínez, M., Rueda, U., Vos, T.E.: Q-learning strategies for action selection in the TESTAR automated testing tool. In: Proceedings of META 2016 6th International Conference on Metaheuristics and Nature Inspired Computing, pp. 174–180 (2016)
8. Koza, J.R.: Genetic Programming: On the Programming of Computers by Means of Natural Selection. MIT Press, Cambridge (1992). http://mitpress.mit.edu/books/genetic-programming
9. Lehman, J., Stanley, K.O.: Novelty search and the problem with objectives. In: Riolo, R., Vladislavleva, E., Moore, J.H. (eds.) Genetic Programming Theory and Practice IX. Genetic and Evolutionary Computation, pp. 37–56. Springer, New York (2011)
10. Memon, A.M., Soffa, M.L., Pollack, M.E.: Coverage criteria for GUI testing. In: Proceedings of ESEC/FSE 2001, pp. 256–267 (2001)
11. Seesing, A., Gross, H.G.: A genetic programming approach to automated test generation for object-oriented software. Int. Trans. Syst. Sci. Appl. **1**(2), 127–134 (2006)
12. Wappler, S., Wegener, J.: Evolutionary unit testing of object-oriented software using strongly-typed genetic programming. In: Proceedings of the 8th Annual Conference on Genetic and Evolutionary Computation, GECCO 2006, pp. 1925–1932. ACM, New York (2006). http://doi.acm.org/10.1145/1143997.1144317
13. Watkins, C.: Learning from Delayed Rewards. Ph.D. thesis, Cambridge University (1989)

EvoSTOC

A New Multi-swarm Particle Swarm Optimization for Robust Optimization Over Time

Danial Yazdani[1(✉)], Trung Thanh Nguyen[1], Juergen Branke[2], and Jin Wang[1]

[1] School of Engineering, Technology and Maritime Operations,
Liverpool Logistics, Offshore and Marine Research Institute,
Liverpool John Moores University, Liverpool, UK
D.yazdani@2016.ljmu.ac.uk, {T.T.Nguyen,J.Wang}@ljmu.ac.uk
[2] Warwich Business School, University of Warwick, Coventry, UK
Juergen.Branke@wbs.ac.uk

Abstract. Dynamic optimization problems (DOPs) are optimization problems that change over time, and most investigations in this area focus on tracking the moving optimum efficiently. However, continuously tracking a moving optimum is not practical in many real-world problems because changing solutions frequently is not possible or very costly. Recently, another practical way to tackle DOPs has been suggested: robust optimization over time (ROOT). In ROOT, the main goal is to find solutions that can remain acceptable over an extended period of time. In this paper, a new multi-swarm PSO algorithm is proposed in which different swarms track peaks and gather information about their behavior. This information is then used to make decisions about the next robust solution. The main goal of the proposed algorithm is to maximize the average number of environments during which the selected solutions' quality remains acceptable. The experimental results show that our proposed algorithm can perform significantly better than existing work in this aspect.

Keywords: Robust optimization over time · Robust optimization · Dynamic optimization · Benchmark problems · Tracking moving optima · Particle swarm optimization · Multi-swarm algorithm

1 Introduction

Many real-world optimization problems are dynamic and changing over time. Most of previous studies in this domain focus on tracking the moving optimum (TMO) [1]. However, this is not practical in many cases since changing solutions may be very costly, and changing the solution frequently is not possible. As a result, there is a gap between academic research and real-world scenarios in this domain.

Recently, a new approach for solving DOPs was proposed to address the above concern that aims at finding solutions that are robust over the course of time [2]. A robust solution is one that is not necessarily the best solution in the environment, but at least is acceptable. A found robust solution can be utilized until its quality degrades to an unacceptable level in the current environment.

© Springer International Publishing AG 2017
G. Squillero and K. Sim (Eds.): EvoApplications 2017, Part II, LNCS 10200, pp. 99–109, 2017.
DOI: 10.1007/978-3-319-55792-2_7

In case the current robust solution becomes unsatisfactory, a new robust solution must be chosen. Therefore, the task for addressing the DOPs in this approach is not to find the best solutions in each environment but to find robust solutions that can remain acceptable for a large number of environments. The process of finding such a sequence of robust solutions is referred to as robust optimization over time (ROOT) [2, 3].

In [2] ROOT was proposed as a new perspective on DOPs. In [4], a new framework for ROOT algorithms was proposed in which the algorithm searches for robust solutions by means of local fitness approximation and prediction. In this framework, an adapted radial-basis-function was used as the local approximator and an autoregressive model as the predictor. The metric in this framework uses the average of current fitness value of a solution, its p previous fitness values (by approximator) and its q future fitness values (by predictor) to search for robust solutions.

In [5], authors proposed two different robustness definitions and metrics, namely *survival time* and *average fitness*. The *survival time* is the maximum time interval in which the fitness of the robust solution remains acceptable, and the *average fitness* is the fitness value of the robust solution in a pre-defined time window. Then, two metrics and also performance indicators were defined based on these two definitions. In this framework, an autoregressive model is used as the predictor. In [12], a new multi-objective method was proposed to find robust solutions that can maximize both of *survival time* and *average fitness*.

In [6], some problem difficulties of ROOT were analyzed. Also, two different benchmark problems which one of them is specially designed for maximizing survival time and another benchmark is for maximizing average fitness, were proposed in [6].

In this paper, we propose a new algorithm for ROOT based on multi-swarm PSO. The main goal of this algorithm is to maximize the average number of environments that the robust solutions remain acceptable *i.e.*, we focus on the *survival time* definition of ROOT [5, 6]. The procedure of the proposed algorithm in finding robust solutions differs from previous works in several aspects. First, we have a multi-swarm PSO [8] that is responsible for not only finding and tracking optima as usual but also for gathering some information about peaks. Second, different to [4, 5], the fitness function for our proposed algorithm is the normal fitness function of the problem without involving any estimator. The proposed algorithm checks the robust solution at the end of each environment and if its fitness value is not acceptable, then a new robust solution is chosen. Third, for choosing a robust solution, the algorithm uses the gathered information to choose the most reliable *Gbest* [13] among PSO swarms as a position for the next robust solution. The results based on the average number of environments that robust solutions can remain acceptable show that the performance of our algorithm is substantially better than previous works in this domain.

The remainder of this paper is structured as follows. Section 2 presents the proposed algorithm. In Sect. 3, a new generic performance indicator is presented for ROOT and the experimental result, analysis and comparison with previous works are shown in this section. In the final section, we summarize the main findings and suggest directions for future work.

2   A New PSO Algorithm for Robust Optimization Over Time

In this section, a new algorithm based on Multi-swarm PSO [8] is proposed for ROOT. In the proposed algorithm, Multi-swarm PSO behaves in a similar way to previous multi-swarm algorithms proposed to track a moving optimum, *i.e.,* our algorithm tries to find all peaks and track them after each environmental change. However, while tracking peaks, our algorithm gathers information about the behavior of all peaks. Then, our algorithm uses this information to choose a robust solution on peaks that have the most suitable characteristics based on the aim to maximize the number of environments that a robust solution remains acceptable.

From another point of view, our algorithm predicts the robustness of solutions based on this information. In order to highlight the difference of our algorithm with previous works [4, 5], it is worth mentioning that in the previous frameworks, specific estimators were adopted and used in order to search for robust solutions. In addition, the fitness function for algorithms was based on average of these estimated values. But, our algorithm is different in that we use the normal fitness function for dynamic optimization and use information the algorithm has gathered to make decisions about which peak is the best for choosing a robust solution. So, in the proposed algorithm we do not use any specific estimator and the algorithm relies on previous behavior of peaks in order to predict future of candidate robust solutions on them.

In the proposed algorithm, there is a *Finder_swarm* that is responsible for searching for uncovered peaks. Additionally, there are *Tracker_swarms* that have two main tasks, namely tracking peaks and gathering information about the behavior of their covered peak. Each Tracker_swarm stores in its memory the difference between fitness value of the best found position in each environment with its fitness value after environmental change. The average of these values (named *Fit_drop*) shows how much the fitness value of points close to the top of the peak is expected to change after an environmental change. In addition, each *Tracker_swarm* stores the Euclidean distance between its *Gbest* at the end of successive environments, and the average of these distances reflect the *shift_severity* of each peak.

At the beginning, there is only one *Finder_swarm* in the problem space. After it converges to a peak [8], a new Tracker_swarm is created in place of the *Finder_swarm*, and the *Finder_swarm* is re-initialized to continue its global search for finding another possibly uncovered peak. On the other hand, the Tracker_swarm performs a local search for exploiting its peak and aims to reach the top of it.

In the proposed algorithm, exclusion mechanism [7] is used to avoid covering each peak by more than one *Tracker_swarm*. If the *Finder_swarm* converges to a covered peak (if the Euclidean distance between *Gbest* of Finder_swarm with *Gbest* of each *Tracker_swarm* is less than r_{excl} [8]), it will be re-initialized. Moreover, if the Euclidean distance between *Gbest* of two *Tracker_swarms* is less than a value r_{excl}, then the older swarm is kept because of its valuable memory and the other one is removed. However, if the *Gbest* fitness value of the newer swarm is better than that of the older one, the better *Gbest* information is copied to the older Tracker_swarm. Moreover, if both *Tracker_swarms* are of the same age, the one with better *Gbest* is kept.

Multi_swarm PSO for ROOT
1:    Initialize Finder_ swarm
2:    repeat:
3:        Re-evaluate Gbest Positions for change detection
4:        If the environmental change is detected then
5:            Update Fit_Drop
6:            If f (Robust_solution   ) $< \delta$
7:                Choose the next Robust_Solution based on Eq.1
8:            End if
9:            Re-evaluate Pbest positions in Finder_swarm
10:           Update Shift _severity   for each covered peak
11:           Re_diversify all Tracker_swarms
12:       End if
13:       Execute an iteration of PSO on Finder_swarm
14:       Execute Exclusion   mechanism on Finder_swarm
15:       If the Finder_swarm   is converged then
16:           create a new Tracker_swarm
17:           Re-initialize Finder_swarm
18:       End if
19:       Execute an iteration of PSO on all   Tracker_swarms
20:       Execute Exclusion mechanism on each pair of Tracker_swarms
21:   until stopping criterion is met

Fig. 1. The pseudocode of the proposed algorithm.

For change detection, the algorithm re-evaluates all *Gbest* positions of all *Tracker_swarms* in each iteration and if any obtained fitness value is different from the saved ones, then a change in the environment is detected. After change detection, first of all, all *Tracker_swarms* store the difference of the new fitness values of their *Gbest* with their saved value to obtain *Fit_drop*. After this, all *Pbest* positions [13] in *Finder_swarm* re-evaluate and a re-diversification mechanism [8] is done by all *Tracker_swarms* based on obtained *Shift_Severity* value for each peak.

In the proposed algorithm, robust solutions are chosen from the best found positions by all *Tracker_swarms* according to a decision making process based on current fitness value as well as *Fit_drop*. For making a decision about the current robust solution, its quality is checked at the end of each environment based on a user-defined lower bound threshold δ [5, 6]. Having this type of threshold is realistic in many real-world problems where there is a specification indicating the acceptability of a solution. If the fitness value of the robust solution is better than δ, then it is deemed acceptable and the robust solution is kept for at least another environment, otherwise the algorithm must choose a new robust solution.

The next robust solution will be a *Gbest* position of one of the *Tracker_swarms*. The best location for the next robust solution is a peak with the highest fitness value and lowest *Fit_drop*. In the proposed algorithm, the next robust solution position is placed on the *Gbest* of a *Tracker_swarm* which is chosen by Eq. 1:

$$C = argmax_{i=1}^{i=S}\left(f\left(Gbest_i\right) - Fit\_Drop_i\right) \tag{1}$$

where S is the number of *Tracker_swarms*, $f(Gbest_i)$ is the *Gbest* fitness value of the ith *Tracker_swarm*, C is the index of a *Tracker_swarm* in which the next robust solution is located. This equation suggests how much the fitness value of a peak solution is dropped in the next environment, based on the difference between it's the current fitness value and the past behavior (*Fit_drop*). The equation allows choosing a robust solution that may likely keep its quality for a greater number of changing environments.

The pseudo code of the proposed algorithm is shown in Fig. 1.

3   Experimental Results and Their Analysis

In this section, the proposed algorithm is tested on a modified version of the Moving Peak Benchmark [9] (mMPB) [5] in which each peak has its own *height_severity* and *width_severity*. The mMPB is described in Eq. 2.

$$F_t\left(\vec{X}\right) = max_{i=1}^{i=m}\left\{H_t^i - W_t^i * \vec{X} - \overrightarrow{C_{t2}^i}\right\} \tag{2}$$

where m is number of peaks, $\vec{X}$ is a solution in the problem space, and H_t^i, W_t^i and $\overrightarrow{C_t^i}$ are the height, width and center of ith peak in the tth environment, respectively. The height, width and center of a peak change in each environment as follows:

$$H^i_{t+1} = H^i_t + height\_severity^i * N(0.1) \tag{3}$$

$$W^i_{t+1} = W^i_t + width\_severity^i * N(0.1) \tag{4}$$

$$\vec{C}^i_{t+1} = \vec{C}^i_t + \vec{V}^i_{t+1} \tag{5}$$

$$\vec{V}^i_{t+1} = Shift\_severity * \frac{(1-\lambda)*\vec{r}+\lambda*\vec{V}^i_t}{(1-\lambda)*\vec{r}+\lambda*\vec{V}^i_t} \tag{6}$$

where $N(0,1)$ represents a random number drawn from Gaussian distribution with zero mean and one variance. The parameter setting of mMPB is shown in Table 1 based on [5].

Table 1. Parameter setting of the modified MPB

Parameter	Value
Number of peaks, M	5
Change frequency	2500
Shift severity, s	1
Height severity	Randomized in range [1.0,10.0]
Width severity	Randomized in range [0.1,1.0]
Peaks shape	Cone
Number of dimensions, D	2
Correlation Coefficient, λ	0
Peaks location range	[0–50]
Peak height	[30.0–70.0]
Peak width	[1–12]
Initial height value	50.0
Initial width value	6.0
Number of Environments	150

In the proposed algorithm, the problem is solved by multi_swarm PSO as a maximization problem. Our algorithm tries to track moving peaks and gathers information about them. Additionally, it uses this information as well as *Gbest* fitness values of *Tracker_swarms* for choosing the next robust solution in its decision making process. The main goal of this process is that the chosen robust solutions keeps their quality above the threshold δ over a larger number of environments. As a result, the average number of environments that each robust solution remains acceptable is used as a performance measure as follows:

$$Average\ Survival\ time = \frac{Number\ of\ Environments}{Number\ of\ Robust\ Solutions} \tag{7}$$

where *number of environments* shows how many times the environment changes, and *number of robust solutions* indicates the number of times that the algorithm changed the robust solution because the existing robust solutions no longer remains acceptable.

Therefore, higher values of *Average Survival time* show better results and the best situation happens when the first robust solution remains acceptable for all environments.

It is worth mentioning that, in [5], Fu *et al.* proposed a performance measure based on average of *survival time* which was calculated by Eq. 8:

$$F^s(x,t,\delta) = \begin{cases} 0, & \text{iff}(x,\alpha(t)) < \delta \\ max\{l | t \le i \le t + l : f(x,\alpha(i)) \ge \delta\}, & \text{else} \end{cases} \tag{8}$$

where F^s is maximal time interval starting from time t until $t + l$ in which the fitness value of solution x remains above δ. The average of F^s was used as the performance measure which the result is the same with Eq. 7. However, we preferred to use Eq. 7 as performance indicator, because in our proposed algorithm, we do not use the *survival time* metric like in [5]. Furthermore, in [4], Jin *et al.* introduced different performance measures including the robustness rate as Eq. 9:

$$RobustnessRate = 1 - \frac{NumberofRobustSolutions - 1}{NumberofEnvironments - 1} \tag{9}$$

The parameter used in both Eqs. 7 and 9 are the same and the main idea of both of them is measuring *average survival time* based on the length of robust solution sequence. However, the outcome of Eq. 7 is more suited to the main goal of ROOT, *i.e.*, maximizing the number of environments a robust solution can keep its quality above the threshold.

The parameter setting of the proposed algorithm is shown in Table 2. Experiments are done on the mMPB with a parameter setting shown in Table 1 with different values of δ (40, 45 and 50). Results are obtained from 30 executions of the proposed algorithm and each execution continues for 150 environmental changes (375,000 function evaluations).

Table 2. Parameter values of the proposed algorithm

Parameters	Initial value
c1, c2	2.05 [10]
χ	0.729843788 [10]
Trackers' Population Size	5
Finder's Population Size	10
P	1[8]
Q	1[8]
Conv_limit	1[8]
K	10[8]
δ	40,45,50
Environment number	150
Stop criterion	Max number of function evaluations

Table 3 shows the experimental result of the proposed algorithm. In Table 3, *Offline_error* [11] shows the performance of Multi_swarm PSO. Additionally, RS_error shows the average error of robust solutions in all environments and *RS_Fit* shows the average fitness value of robust solutions in all environments. Also the numbers in parentheses are *standard_error*.

Table 3. Results of the proposed algorithm on mMPB with $\delta = 40$, 45, and 50.

δ	Offline_error (std_error)	RS_error (std_error)	RS_Fit (std_error)	Average Survival time (Eq. 7) (std_error)
40	0.0210 (0.0037)	9.3154 (0.2588)	53.1573 (0.2845)	8.3488 (0.6331)
45	0.0214 (0.0043)	6.9659 (0.2267)	55.8288 (0.2078)	6.8309 (0.6571)
50	0.0218 (0.0055)	5.2021 (0.1488)	58.1354 (0.1426)	4.2483 (0.1849)

The main goal of the proposed algorithm is to increase *Average survival time, i.e.,* to decrease the number of times that the algorithm needs to change the robust solution because of a lack of quality as determined by δ. As expected, a lower δ allows a robust solution to survive longer.

The value of *offline_error* is almost the same for all experiments because the problem is the same from the point of view of DOP and the results show that the accuracy of multi_swarm PSO for finding and tracking peaks is acceptable. This is important because the performance of choosing robust solutions is totally dependent on the performance of multi_swarm PSO in finding and tracking moving peaks. The average error of robust solutions decreases when δ increases because the proposed algorithm tried to keep fitness value of robust solutions above δ and change them if their fitness value came under δ. As a result, with higher values of δ, fitness values of acceptable robust solution increases, and the error decreases. Therefore, when δ increases, the average fitness value of robust solutions increases, at the expense of requiring more changes. Figure 2 illustrates the average fitness of the best found position by multi_swarm PSO in each environment by TMO as well as robust solutions' fitness values.

To compare the result of proposed algorithm with that of previous works in the field of ROOT, in [12], the number of robust solutions for the proposed Multi_objective ROOT algorithm and the ROOT algorithm from [5] are reported. Since the experiments in [12] were done on the same benchmark and for the same number of environments as this paper, the *Average Survival time* of existing works i.e. works in [5, 12] can be calculated by Eq. 7 and compared with our algorithm. It is worth mentioning that since in some papers such as [4, 6], the benchmark problem is different with the one that we used in this paper, so we cannot use their reported results for our comparisons and comparing the result of our algorithm with of them will be done in future works. The best *Average Survival time* with $\delta = 40$, 45 and 50 of Guo's algorithm [12], and the average of reported values in [12] for Fu's Algorithm [5], and our proposed algorithm are shown in Table 4. The results in Table 4 show that our proposed algorithm can perform significantly better than compared works in term of *Average Survival time*. Note

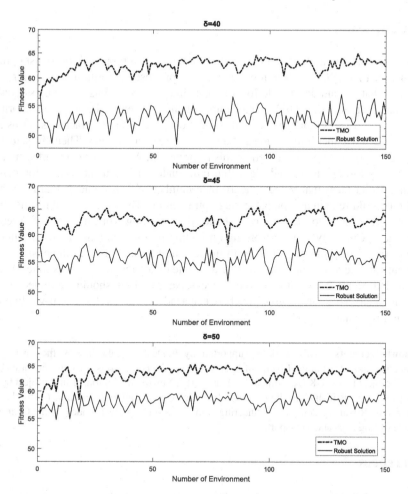

Fig. 2. Average fitness values of the best TMO and robust solutions found by multi_swarm PSO.

that Table 4 does not have comparisons on *standard error* or *standard deviation*, because these figures were not provided in [12] for Guo's and Fu's algorithms.

Table 4. The Average Robustness obtained by the three algorithms on mMPB.

δ	Average Robustness		
	Fu's Algorithm [5]	Guo's Algorithm [5]	Proposed Algorithm
40	2.30	2.67	**8.35**
45	1.91	2.08	**6.83**
50	1.53	1.61	**4.25**

4 Conclusion

In this paper, a new multi-swarm PSO algorithm has been proposed for robust optimization over time (ROOT). The main goal of the proposed algorithm is finding robust solutions that remain acceptable for a longer time, *i.e.,* solutions with fitness quality above an acceptance threshold over a number of environments. The proposed algorithm differs from previous work to find ROOT solutions. We use PSO Tracker_swarms that track peaks and gather information about how they react to changes. Then, the selection of the next robust solution is based on this information. As a performance measure, we use an easy-to-implement and algorithm-independent performance indicator named Average Robustness that reflects the average number of environments that the robust solutions could remain acceptable during optimization. The experimental results show that our proposed algorithm performs better than existing work in terms of Average Robustness. Currently, we are working on finding robust solutions based on different characteristics of peaks for DOPs with higher number of peaks and dimensions, and different specifications. In addition, new dynamic characteristics such as time-linkage [14] and distance constrains between successive solutions should be added to the problem to close the current gaps [15] between academic research and real-world problems in this domain.

Acknowledgements. This work is supported by a Dean Scholarship by the Faculty of Engineering and Technology, Liverpool John Moores University, and is partially supported by a T-TRIG project by the UK Department for Transport, a Newton Institutional Links project by the UK BEIS via the British Council, a Newton Research Collaboration Programme (3) by the UK BEIS via the Royal Academy of Engineering, and a Seed-corn project funded by the Chartered Institute of Logistics and Transport.

References

1. Nguyen, T.T., Yang, S., Branke, J.: Evolutionary dynamic optimization: a survey of the state of the art. Swarm Evol. Comput. **6**, 1–24 (2012)
2. Yu, X., Jin, Y., Tang, K., Yao, X.: Robust optimization over time – a new perspective on dynamic. In: IEEE Congress on Evolutionary Computation, pp. 1–6 (2010)
3. Fu, H., Sendhoff, B., Tang, K., Yao, X.: Characterizing environmental changes in robust optimization over time. In: IEEE Congress on Evolutionary Computation, pp. 1–8 (2012)
4. Jin, Y., Tang, K., Yu, X., Sendhoff, B., Yao, X.: A framework for finding robust optimal solutions over time. Memetic Comput. **5**(1), 3–18 (2013)
5. Fu, H., Sendhoff, B., Tang, K., Yao, X.: Finding robust solutions to dynamic optimization problems. In: Esparcia-Alcázar, A.I. (ed.) EvoApplications 2013. LNCS, vol. 7835, pp. 616–625. Springer, Heidelberg (2013). doi:10.1007/978-3-642-37192-9_62
6. Fu, H., Sendhoff, B., Tang, K., Yao, X.: Robust optimization over time: problem difficulties and benchmark problems. IEEE Trans. Evol. Comput. **19**(5), 731–745 (2015)
7. Blackwell, T., Branke, J.: Multiswarms, exclusion, and anti-convergence in dynamic environments. IEEE Trans. Evol. Comput. **10**(4), 459–472 (2006)

8. Yazdani, D., Nasiri, B., Sepas-Moghaddam, A., Meybodi, M.R.: A novel multi-swarm algorithm for optimization in dynamic environments based on particle swarm optimization. Appl. Soft Comput. **13**(4), 2144–2158 (2013)
9. Branke, J.: Memory enhanced evolutionary algorithms for changing optimization problems. In: IEEE Congress on Evolutionary Computation, pp. 1875–1882 (1999)
10. Eberhart, R.C., Shi, Y.: Comparing inertia weights and constriction factors in particle swarm optimization. IEEE Congress Evolut. Comput. **1**, 84–88 (2001)
11. Yang, S., Li, C.: A clustering particle swarm optimizer for locating and tracking multiple optima in dynamic environments. IEEE Trans. Evol. Comput. **14**(6), 959–974 (2010)
12. Guo, Y., Chen, M., Fu, H., Liu, Y.: Find robust solutions over time by two-layer multi-objective optimization method. IEEE Congress on Evolutionary Computation, pp. 1528–1535 (2014)
13. Kennedy, J., Eberhart, R.: Particle swarm optimization. IEEE International Conference on Neural Networks, vol. 4, pp. 1942–1948 (1995)
14. Nguyen, T.T., Yao, X.: Dynamic time-linkage problems revisited. In: Giacobini, M., Brabazon, A., Cagnoni, S., Caro, Gianni, A., Ekárt, A., Esparcia-Alcázar, A.I., Farooq, M., Fink, A., Machado, P. (eds.) EvoWorkshops 2009. LNCS, vol. 5484, pp. 735–744. Springer, Heidelberg (2009). doi:10.1007/978-3-642-01129-0_83
15. Nguyen, T.T.: Continuous dynamic optimisation using evolutionary algorithms. Ph.D. thesis, University of Birmingham (2011)

The Static and Stochastic VRP with Time Windows and both Random Customers and Reveal Times

Michael Saint-Guillain[1,2]([✉]), Christine Solnon[2], and Yves Deville[1]

[1] ICTEAM, Université catholique de Louvain,
Louvain-la-Neuve, Belgium
michael.saint@uclouvain.be
[2] LIRIS, Institut National des Sciences Appliquées de Lyon,
Villeurbanne, France

Abstract. Static and stochastic vehicle routing problems (SS-VRP) aim at modeling and solving real life problems by considering uncertainty on the data. In particular, customer data may not be known with certainty. Before the beginning of the day, probability distributions on customer data are used to compute a first-stage solution that optimizes an expected cost. Customer data are revealed online, while the solution is executed, and a recourse strategy is applied on the first-stage solution to quickly adapt it. Existing SS-VRP variants usually make a strong assumption on the time at which a stochastic customer reveals its data (*e.g.*, when a vehicle arrives at the corresponding location). We introduce a new SS-VRP where customer reveal times are stochastic. We define first-stage solutions and a recourse strategy for this new problem. A key point is to introduce waiting locations that are used in the first stage-solution to wait for the realization of customer stochastic data. We show how to compute the expected cost of a first-stage solution in pseudo polynomial time, in the particular case where the vehicles are not constrained by a maximal capacity. We also introduce a local search-based approach for optimizing the first-stage solution, and introduce a *scale* parameter to tune the precision and cost of the expected cost computation. Experimental results on small to large instances demonstrate its efficiency and flexibility.

1 Introduction

The Vehicle Routing Problem (VRP) aims at modeling and solving a real life common operational problem, in which a set of customers must be visited using a fleet of vehicles. Each customer comes with a certain demand. In the VRP with Time Windows (VRPTW), each customer must be visited within a given time window. A feasible solution of the VRPTW is a set of vehicle routes, such that every customer is visited exactly once during its time window and that sum of the demands along each route does not exceed the corresponding vehicle's capacity.

© Springer International Publishing AG 2017
G. Squillero and K. Sim (Eds.): EvoApplications 2017, Part II, LNCS 10200, pp. 110–127, 2017.
DOI: 10.1007/978-3-319-55792-2_8

The objective is then to find an optimal feasible solution, where optimality is usually defined in terms of travel distances.

The classical deterministic VRP(TW) assumes that customer data are known with certainty before the computation of the solution. Contrary to standard academic formulations, real world applications usually have missing part of the problem data when computing a solution. For instance, only a subset of the customer demands may be known before online execution. Missing demands hence arrive in a dynamic fashion, while vehicles are on their route. In such a context, a solution should contain operational decisions that deal with current known demands, but should also anticipate potential unknown demands. Albeit uncertainty may be considered for various attributes of the VRP (*e.g.*, travel times), we focus on situations where the customer data are unknown a priori, and we assume that we have some probabilistic knowledge on missing data (*e.g.*, probability distributions computed from historical data). This probabilistic knowledge is used to compute a first-stage solution which is adapted online when random variables are realized. Two different kinds of adaptations may be considered: *Dynamic and Stochastic VRPTW* (DS-VRPTW) and *Static and Stochastic VRPTW* (SS-VRPTW).

In the DS-VRPTW, the solution is re-optimized at each time-step, and this re-optimization involves solving an $\mathcal{NP}$-hard problem so that it is usually approximated with meta-heuristics as proposed, for example, in [1–3]. Note that the DS-VRPTW assumes a probabilistic knowledge on the potential requests. In contrary, in [4] for instance no prior knowledge is provided on the potential requests, which are then assumed to be uniformly distributed in the Euclidean plan.

In the SS-VRP(TW), no expensive reoptimization is allowed during online execution. When unknown information is revealed, the first stage solution is adapted online by applying a predefined recourse strategy whose time complexity is polynomial. In this case, the goal is to find a first stage solution that minimizes its total cost plus the *expected* extra cost caused by the recourse strategy. For example, in [5], the first stage solution is a set of vehicle tours which is computed offline with respect to probability distributions of customer demands. Real customer demands are revealed online, and two different recourse strategies are proposed: in the first one, each demand is assumed to be known when the vehicle arrives at the customer place, and if it is larger than or equal to the remaining capacity of the vehicle, then the first stage solution is adapted by adding a round trip to the depot to unload the vehicle; in the second recourse strategy, each demand is assumed to be known when leaving the previous customer and the recourse strategy is refined so that customers with null demands are skipped.

In this paper, we focus on the SS-VRPTW, and introduce a new variant where no strong assumption is made on the moment at which customer requests are revealed during the operations (contrary to most existing work that assume that customer requests are known either when arriving at the customer place, or when leaving the previous customer). In this new variant, called the *SS-VRPTW with random Customers and Reveal time* (SS-VRPTW-CR), the reveal times of customer requests are random variables. To handle uncertainty on reveal times, we introduce waiting locations when computing first-stage solutions: the routes computed offline visit waiting locations and a waiting time is associated with each waiting location. When a customer request is revealed, it is either accepted (if it is possible to serve it) or rejected. The recourse strategy then adapts routes so that all accepted requests are guaranteed to eventually be served. The goal is to compute the first-stage solution that minimizes the expected number of rejected requests.

Our motivating application is an on-demand health care service for elderly or disabled people. Health care services are provided directly at home by mobile medical units. Every person who's registered to the service can request a health care support at any moment of the day with the guarantee to be satisfied within a given time window. From historical data, we know, for each customer region and each time unit, the probability that a request appears. Given this stochastic knowledge, we compute a first-stage solution. When a request appears (online), the recourse strategy is used to decide whether the request is accepted or rejected and to adapt medical unit routes. When a request is rejected, the system must rely on an external service provider in order to satisfy it. Therefore, the goal is to minimize the expected number of rejected requests.

Organization. In Sect. 2, we review the existing studies on VRPs that imply stochastic customers. Section 3 formally defines the general SS-VRPTW-CR. Section 4 describes a recourse strategy for this problem. Section 5 shows how the expected number of rejected requests can be efficiently computed from a first stage solution and for a specific recourse strategy. Section 6 describes a local search-based approach for approximating an optimal first stage solution. Experimental results are analysed in Sect. 7. Further research directions are finally discussed in Sect. 8.

2   Related Work

The most studied cases in SS-VRPs are stochastic customers (presence of customers are random variables), stochastic demands (quantities required by customers are random variables), and stochastic times (travel and/or service times are random variables). Since the SS-VRPTW-CR belongs to the first case, we focus this review on customers uncertainty.

The Traveling Salesman Problem (TSP) is a special case of the VRP with only one uncapacitated vehicle. [6] introduced the TSP with stochastic Customers (SS-TSP-C), and provided mathematical formulations and a number of properties and bounds. In particular, he showed that an optimal solution for the deterministic problem can be arbitrarily bad in case of uncertainty. [7] developed the first exact solution method for the SS-TSP-C, using the integer L-shaped method [8] to solve instances up to 50 customers. Heuristics for the SS-TSP-C have then been proposed (e.g. [9–11]) as well as meta-heuristics such as simulated annealing [12] or ant colony optimization [13].

The first SS-VRP with stochastic Customers (SS-VRP-C) has been studied by [9] as a generalization of the SS-TSP-C. [14] compared different heuristics. [5] considered a VRP with stochastic Customers and Demands (SS-VRP-CD). A customer demand is assumed to be revealed either when the vehicle leaves the previous customer or when it arrives at the customer's own location. Two different recourse strategies are proposed. For both strategies, closed-form mathematical expressions are provided to compute the expected total distance, provided a first stage solution. [15,16] developed the first exact algorithm for solving the SS-VRP-CD for instances up to 70 customers, by means of an integer L-shaped method. [17] later proposed a tabu search to efficiently approximate the solution. Experimentations are reported on instances with up to 46 customers. [18] later developed an adaptive memory programming metaheuristic for the SS-VRP-C and assess it on benchmarks with up to 483 customers and 38 vehicles.

Particularly close to the SS-VRPTW-CR is the SS-TSP-C with Deadlines [19]. Unlike the SS-VRPTW-CR, the set of customers is revealed at the beginning of the operations. A recent literature review on SS-TSP-C may be found in [20].

[21] considered a variant of the SS-VRPTW-C, the Courier Delivery Problem with Uncertainty. Unlike the SS-VRPTW-CR, authors assume that customer presences are not revealed at some random moment during the operations, but all at once at the beginning of the day (that is, after computing the first stage solution).

3   Description of the SS-VRPTW-CR

Input Data. We consider a complete directed graph $G = (V, A)$ and a discrete time horizon $H = [1, h]$, where interval $[a, b]$ denotes the set of all integer values i such that $a \leq i \leq b$. To every arc $(i, j) \in A$ is associated a travel time (or distance) $d_{i,j} \in \mathbb{N}$. The set of vertices $V = \{0\} \cup W \cup C$ is composed of a depot 0, a set of m waiting locations $W = [1, m]$ and a set of n customer regions $C = [m + 1, m + n]$. We note $W_0 = W \cup \{0\}$ and $C_0 = C \cup \{0\}$. The fleet is composed of K uncapacitated vehicles.

We consider the set $R = C \times H$ of potential customer requests such that an element $(c, \Gamma) \in R$ represents a potential request revealed at time $\Gamma \in H$ for customer region c. To each potential request $r = (c, \Gamma) \in R$ is associated a deterministic demand $q_r \in [1, Q]$, a deterministic service duration $s_r \in H$ and deterministic time window $[e_r, l_r]$ with $\Gamma \leq e_r \leq l_r \leq h$. We note p_r the probability that r appears on vertex c at time Γ, and assume independence between request probabilities. Although our formalism imposes $\Gamma \geq 1$ for all potential requests, in practice a request may be known with certainty that is, with probability 1.

To simplify notations, a request $r = (c, \Gamma)$ can be written in place of its own region c. For instance, the distance $d_{v,c}$ can also be intuitively written $d_{v,r}$. Furthermore, we use Γ_r to denote the reveal time of a request $r \in R$ and c_r for its customer region.

First Stage Solution. The first-stage solution is computed offline, before the beginning of the time horizon. It consists in a set of K vehicle routes visiting a subset of the m waiting vertices, together with time variables denoted τ indicating how long a vehicle should wait on each vertex. More specifically, we denote (x, τ) a first stage solution to the SS-VRPTW-CR, where:

- $x = \{x_1, ..., x_K\}$ defines a set of K sequences of waiting vertices of W, such that each sequence x_k starts and ends with 0 and each vertex of W occurs at most once in x. We note $W^x \subseteq W$ the set of waiting vertices visited in x.
- $\tau : W^x \to H$ associates a waiting time $\tau_w \geq 1$ to every waiting vertex $w \in W^x$;
- Each sequence $\langle 0, w_1, ..., w_{m'}, 0 \rangle$ in x is such that the vehicle is back to the depot before the end of the day.

In other words, x defines a *Tour Orienteering Problem* (TOP, see [22]) to which each visited location is assigned a waiting time by τ. Given a first stage solution (x, τ), we define $on(w) = [\underline{on}(w), \overline{on}(w)]$ for each vertex $w \in W^x$ such that $\underline{on}(w)$ (resp. $\overline{on}(w)$) is the arrival (resp. departure) time on w. In a sequence $\langle 0, w_1, ..., w_{m'}, 0 \rangle$ in x, we then have $\underline{on}(w_i) = \overline{on}(w_{i-1}) + d_{w_{i-1}, w_i}$ and $\overline{on}(w_i) = \underline{on}(w_i) + \tau_{w_i}$ for $i \geq 1$ and assume both $\overline{on}(0) = 1$ and $\underline{on}(0) = \overline{on}(w_{m'}) + d_{w_{m'}, 0} \leq h$. Figure 1 (left) illustrates an example of first stage solution on a basic SS-VRPTW-CR instance.

Recourse Strategy and Second Stage Solution. A recourse strategy $\mathcal{R}$ states how a second stage solution is gradually constructed as requests are dynamically revealed. In this paragraph, we define the properties of a recourse strategy. An example of recourse strategy is given in Sect. 4.

Let $\xi \subseteq R$ be the set of requests that reveal to appear by the end of the horizon H. The set ξ is also called a *scenario*. We note $\xi^t \subseteq \xi$ the set of requests appearing at time $t \in H$, i.e., $\xi^t = \{r \in \xi : \Gamma_r = t\}$. We note $\xi^{1..t} = \xi^1 \cup ... \cup \xi^t$ the set of requests appeared up to time t.

A second stage solution is incrementally constructed at each time unit by following the skeleton provided by the first stage solution (x, τ). At a given time t of the horizon, we note (x^t, A^t) the current state of the second stage solution:

- x^t defines a set of vertex sequences describing the route operations performed up to time t. Unlike x, we define x^t on a graph that also includes the customer regions. Operations described in x^t must satisfy the time window and vehicle capacity constraints imposed by the VRPTW.
- $A^t \subseteq \xi^{1..t}$ is the set of *accepted* requests up to time t. Requests of $\xi^{1..t}$ that do not belong to A^t are said to be *rejected*.

We distinguish between requests that are accepted and those that are both accepted and satisfied. Up to a time t, an accepted request is said to be *satisfied* if it is visited in x^t by a vehicle. Accepted requests that are no yet satisfied must be *guaranteed to be eventually satisfied* according to their time window.

Figure 1 (right) illustrates an example of second stage solution being partially constructed at some moment of the time horizon.

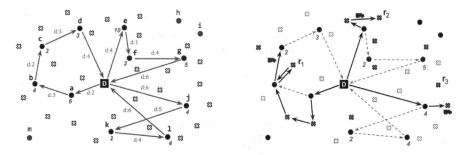

Fig. 1. On the left: first stage solution with $K = 3$ vehicles. The depot, waiting vertices and customer regions are represented by a square, circles and crosses respectively. Arrows represent vehicle routes and integers indicate waiting times at waiting locations. Values preceded by 'd' indicate travel times. Waiting vertices h, i and m are not part of the first stage solution. Here $\overline{on}(D) = 1$, $\underline{on}(a) = 3$, $\overline{on}(a) = 9$, $\underline{on}(b) = 12$, $\overline{on}(b) = 16$, etc. On the right: partial second stage solution (plain arrows). Filled crosses are accepted requests. Some accepted requests, such as r_1, have been satisfied (or the vehicle is currently traveling towards the location, $e.g.$, r_2), while some others are not yet satisfied ($e.g.$, r_3).

Before starting the operations (time 0), x^0 is a set of K sequences that only contain vertex 0, and $A^0 = \emptyset$. At each time unit $t \in H$, given a first stage solution (x, τ), a previous state (x^{t-1}, A^{t-1}) of the second stage solution and a set ξ^t of requests appearing at time t, the new state (x^t, A^t) is obtained by applying a specific recourse strategy $\mathcal{R}$:

$$(x^t, A^t) = \mathcal{R}\big((x, \tau), (x^{t-1}, A^{t-1}), \xi^t\big). \tag{1}$$

A necessary property of a recourse strategy is to avoid reoptimization. We consider that $\mathcal{R}$ avoids reoptimization if the computation of (x^t, A^t) is achieved in polynomial time.

We note $\mathrm{cost}(\mathcal{R}, x, \tau, \xi) = |\xi \backslash A^h|$ the final cost of a second stage solution with respect to a scenario ξ, given a first stage solution (x, τ) and under a recourse strategy $\mathcal{R}$. This cost is the number of requests that are rejected at the end h of the time horizon.

Optimal First Stage Solution. An optimal first stage solution (x, τ) to the SS-VRPTW-CR minimizes the expected cost of the second stage solution under a given strategy $\mathcal{R}$, satisfying statements (2) and (3):

$$\text{(SS-VRPTW-CR)} \quad \underset{x, \tau}{\text{Minimize}} \quad \mathcal{Q}^{\mathcal{R}}(x, \tau) \tag{2}$$

$$\text{s.t.} \quad (x, \tau) \text{ is a first stage solution.} \tag{3}$$

The objective function $\mathcal{Q}^{\mathcal{R}}(x, \tau)$, which is nonlinear in general, determines the *expected number of rejected requests*, i.e. requests that fail to be visited under recourse strategy $\mathcal{R}$ and first stage solution (x, τ):

$$\mathcal{Q}^{\mathcal{R}}(x, \tau) = \sum_{\xi \subseteq R} \Pr(\xi) \, \text{cost}(\mathcal{R}, x, \tau, \xi) \tag{4}$$

where $\Pr(\xi)$ defines the probability of scenario ξ. Since we assume independence between requests, we have $\Pr(\xi) = \prod_{r \in \xi} p_r \cdot \prod_{r \in R \setminus \xi} (1 - p_r)$.

4 Description of a Recourse Strategy

In order to avoid reoptimization, the set R of potential requests is ordered. Furthermore, given a first stage solution (x, τ) that visits the set W^x of waiting locations, each potential request $r = (c, \Gamma) \in R$ is assigned to exactly one waiting vertex (and hence, a vehicle) in W^x.

Informally, the recourse strategy accepts a new request if it is possible for the vehicle associated to its corresponding waiting vertex location to adapt its first stage tour to visit the customer. The vehicle will then travel from the waiting location to the customer and return to the waiting location. Time window constraints should be respected, and the already accepted requests should not be perturbed. In the recourse strategy we propose here, we assume the vehicles not to be constrained by a maximal capacity.

Request Ordering. Before computing first-stage solutions, we order R by increasing reveal time Γ_r first, end of time window l_r second and request number r to break ties. Let $<_R$ denote this total strict order on R. Whereas the remaining of the paper is based on the assumption of total order on Γ_r, the ordering criteria may be modified without loss of generality (*e.g.*, replacing l_r by e_r), as long as the total order remains strict and primarily based on Γ_r, i.e. $\forall r_1, r_2 \in R, \Gamma_{r_1} < \Gamma_{r_2} \Rightarrow r_1 <_R r_2$.

Request Assignment According to a First Stage Solution. Given a first-stage solution (x, τ), we assign each request of R to a waiting vertex visited in (x, τ). This assignment is computed for each first stage solution (x, τ) before the application of the recourse strategy. As an optimally fair distribution of the potential requests might be excessively expensive to compute, we propose the following heuristic.

Let $t_{r,w}^{\min} = \max\{\underline{on}(w), \Gamma_r, e_r - d_{w,r}\}$ be the minimum time for leaving waiting location w to satisfy request r. Indeed, a vehicle cannot handle r before (1) the vehicle is on w, (2) r is revealed, and (3) the beginning e_r of the time window minus the time $d_{w,r}$ needed to go from w to r.

Let $t_{r,w}^{\max} = \min\{l_r - d_{w,r}, \overline{on}(w) - d_{w,r} - s_r - d_{r,w}\}$ be the latest time at which a vehicle can handle r (which also involves a service time s_r) from waiting location w and still leave it in time $t \leq \overline{on}(w)$.

Given a first stage solution (x, τ), we assign each request $r \in R$ either to a waiting vertex of W^x or to $\bot$ (to denote that r is not assigned). We note $w(r)$ this assignment which is computed as follows:

- Let $W^x_r = \{w \in W^x : t^{\min}_{r,w} \leq t^{\max}_{r,w}\}$ be the set of feasible waiting locations for r
- If $W^x_r = \emptyset$ then set $w(r)$ to $\bot$ (r is always rejected)
- Else set $w(r)$ to the feasible vertex of W^x_r that has the least number of requests already assigned to it (break further ties w.r.t. vertex number)

Once finished, the request assignment ends up with a partition $\{\pi_\bot, \pi_1, ..., \pi_K\}$ of R, where π_k is the set of requests assigned to the waiting vertices visited by vehicle k and $\pi_\bot$ is the set of unassigned requests (such that $w(r) = \bot$). We note $\pi^w_k \subseteq \pi_k$ the set of requests assigned to $w \in W^x$ in route k. We note $\mathrm{fst}(\pi^w_k)$ the first request of π^w_k according to order $<_R$, and for each request $r \in \pi^w_k$ such that $r \neq \mathrm{fst}(\pi^w_k)$ we note $\mathrm{prv}(r)$ the request of π^w_k that immediately precedes r according to order $<_R$.

Using the Recourse Strategy to Adapt a First Stage Solution at a Current Time t. At each time step t, the recourse strategy is applied to compute the second stage solution (x^t, A^t), given the first stage solution (x, τ), the second stage solution (x^{t-1}, A^{t-1}) at the end of time $t - 1$, and the incoming requests ξ^t.

A^t is the set of accepted requests. It is initialized with A^{t-1}. Then, each incoming request of ξ^t is considered (taken by increasing order of $<_R$) and either accepted (added to A^t) or rejected (not added to A^t) by applying the following decision rule:

- Let k be the vehicle associated with r (i.e., $r \in \pi^k$)
- Let $y : R \to H$ be the function returning the time at which k finishes to satisfy all accepted requests that precede r (according to $<_R$) and reaches waiting vertex $w(r)$. Namely, $y(r)$ is the time at which k is available for r and is defined by:

  - If $r = \mathrm{fst}(\pi^w_k)$, then $y(r) = \underline{on}(w)$
  - else if $\mathrm{prv}(r) \notin A^t$ then $y(r) = y(\mathrm{prv}(r))$
  - else $y(r) = \max(y(\mathrm{prv}(r)) + d_{w,\mathrm{prv}(r)}, e_{\mathrm{prv}(r)}) + s_{\mathrm{prv}(r)} + d_{\mathrm{prv}(r),w}$
    If $y(r)$ allows k to reach r during its time window and to arrive in time to its next waiting location (*i.e.*, $y(r) \leq t^{\max}_{r,w(r)}$) then r is accepted and added to A^t; otherwise it is rejected.

Once A^t has been computed, vehicle operations for time unit t must be decided. Vehicles operate independently of each other. If vehicle k is traveling between a waiting location and a customer region, or if it is serving a request, then its operation remains unchanged; Otherwise, let w be the current waiting location (or the depot) of vehicle k:

- If $t = \overline{on}(w)$, the operation for k is "travel from w to the next waiting vertex (or the depot), as defined in the first stage solution"

- Otherwise, let $P = \{r \in \pi_k^w \,|\, c_r \notin x^t \wedge (r \in A^t \vee t < \Gamma_r)\}$ be the set of requests of π_k^w that are not yet satisfied and that are either accepted or with unknown revelation

  - If $P = \emptyset$, then the operation for k is "travel back to the depot"
  - Otherwise, let r^{next} be the smallest element of P according to $<_R$

    If $t < t_{r^{\text{next}},w}^{\min}$, then the operation for k is "wait until $t+1$"
    Otherwise, the operation is "travel to r^{next}, serve it and come back to w"

Figure 2 shows an example of second stage solution at a current time $t = 17$, from an operational point of view.

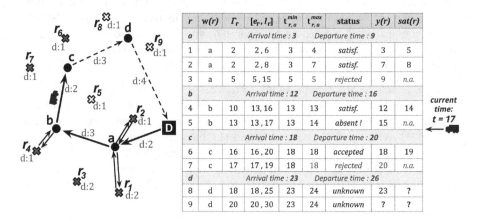

r	$w(r)$	Γ_r	$[e_r, l_r]$	$t_{r,a}^{min}$	$t_{r,a}^{max}$	status	$y(r)$	$sat(r)$
a			Arrival time : 3		Departure time : 9			
1	a	2	2 , 6	3	4	satisf.	3	5
2	a	2	2 , 8	3	7	satisf.	7	8
3	a	5	5 , 15	5	5	rejected	9	n.a.
b			Arrival time : 12		Departure time : 16			
4	b	10	13 , 16	13	13	satisf.	12	14
5	b	13	13 , 17	13	14	absent !	15	n.a.
c			Arrival time : 18		Departure time : 20			
6	c	16	16 , 20	18	18	accepted	18	19
7	c	17	17 , 19	18	18	rejected	20	n.a.
d			Arrival time : 23		Departure time : 26			
8	d	18	18 , 25	23	24	unknown	23	?
9	d	20	20 , 30	23	24	unknown	?	?

current
time:
$t = 17$

Fig. 2. Example of second stage solution at time $t = 17$, under strategy $\mathcal{R}1$. A filled cross represents a request that appeared, an empty one a request that is either still unknown (*e.g.*, r_8) or revealed as being absent (that is didn't appear, *e.g.*, r_5). Here $\pi_k = \langle r_a, r_1, \ldots, r_9 \rangle$ is the sequence of requests assigned to the vehicle, according to (x, τ). We assume $q_r = s_r = 0, \forall r \in R$. $sat(r)$ represents, for a request r, the time at which r gets satisfied.

5   Expected Cost of Second Stage Solutions

Provided a recourse strategy $\mathcal{R}$ and a first stage solution (x, τ) to the SS-VRPTW-CR, a naive approach for computing $\mathcal{Q}^{\mathcal{R}}(x, \tau)$ would be to literally follow Eq. (4), therefore using the strategy described by $\mathcal{R}$ in order to confront (x, τ) to each and every possible scenario $\xi \subseteq R$. Because there is an exponential number of scenarios with respect to $|R|$, this naive approach is not affordable in practice. In this section, we show how the expected number of rejected requests $\mathcal{Q}^{\mathcal{R}}(x, \tau)$ under the recourse strategy described in Sect. 4 may be computed in $\mathcal{O}(nh^2)$ using closed form expressions, in the special case where vehicles are of infinite capacity.

We assume that the potential request probabilities are independent from each other such that, for any couple of requests $r, r' \in R$, the probability $p_{r \cap r'}$ that both requests appear is given by $p_{r \cap r'} = p_r \cdot p_{r'}$.

Expected Cost. $Q^{\mathcal{R}}(x, \tau)$ is equal to the expected number of rejected requests, which in turn is equal to the expected number of requests that reveal to appear minus the expected number of accepted requests. The expected number of revealed requests is given by the sum of all request probabilities, whereas the expected number of accepted requests is equal to the sum, for every request r, of the probability that it belongs to A^h:

$$Q^{\mathcal{R}}(x, \tau) = \sum_{r \in R} p_r - \sum_{r \in R} \Pr\{r \in A^h\} = \sum_{r \in R} (p_r - \Pr\{r \in A^h\}) \qquad (5)$$

where the right-hand side of the equation comes from the independence hypothesis.

If we consider a request $r \in \pi_k$, the probability $\Pr\{r \in A^h\}$ only depends on the time at which vehicle k is available for r, which itself depends on previous operations. Recall the $y : R \to H$ function described in Sect. 4: $y(r)$ is that time. Whereas $y(r)$ is deterministic for a specific scenario, it is not anymore in the context of the computation of $\Pr\{r \in A^h\}$ and we are thus interested in its probability distribution. More specifically, we compute the probability that, at a time $t \in H$, a request r already appeared and the vehicle leaves $w(r)$ to satisfy it. Let's call this probability $g_1(r, t)$:

$$g_1(r, t) \equiv \Pr\{\text{request } r \text{ appeared at time } t' \leq t \text{ and departureTime}(r) = t\}$$

where departureTime(r) is the time at which the vehicle leaves vertex $w(r)$ in order to serve r, if r has been accepted. According to the recourse strategy, for a specific scenario we see that departureTime$(r) = \max(y(r), t^{\min}_{r,w(r)})$.

The probability $\Pr\{r \in A^h\}$ that a request r gets satisfied is the probability that both r appears and that departureTime$(r) \leq t^{\max}_{r,w}$, that is:

$$\Pr\{r \in A^h\} = \sum_{t=1}^{t^{\max}_{r,w}} g_1(r, t) = \sum_{t=t^{\min}_{r,w}}^{t^{\max}_{r,w}} g_1(r, t). \qquad (6)$$

The calculus of $g_1(r, t)$ is less obvious. Since departureTime(r) depends on previous operations on the same waiting location $w = w(r)$, we calculate $g_1(r, t)$ recursively starting from the first request $r_1 = \text{fst}(\pi^w_k)$ assigned to the waiting location, up to the current request r. The second stage solution strictly respects the first stage schedule when visiting the waiting vertices, that is, these are guaranteed to be visited according to their arrival $(\underline{on})$ and departure $(\overline{on})$ times. The base case is then:

$$g_1(r_1, t) = \begin{cases} p_{r_1}, & \text{if } t = \max(\underline{on}(w), t^{\min}_{r_1,w}) \\ 0 & \text{otherwise.} \end{cases} \qquad (7)$$

Indeed, if r_1 appeared then the vehicle leaves w at time $t^{\min}_{r_1,w}$, unless it has not yet reached w at that time. The general case of a request $r >_R r_1$, $r \in \pi^w_k$, depends on the time at which the vehicle gets rid of the preceding request prv(r).

Let $f(r,t)$ be the probability that, at time t, the vehicle either reaches back w after having served r, or discard r because it is not satisfiable or because it has revealed not to appear. It represents the time at which the vehicle becomes available for the next request after r in π_k^w, if any (computation of f is detailed below). We define $g_1(r,t)$ based on f-probabilities of the previous request $\text{prv}(r)$:

$$g_1(r,t) = \begin{cases} p_r \cdot f(\text{prv}(r),t) & \text{if} \quad t > t_{r,w}^{\min} \\ p_r \cdot \sum_{t'=\underline{on}(w)}^{t_{r,w}^{\min}} f(\text{prv}(r),t') & \text{if} \quad t = t_{r,w}^{\min} \\ 0 & \text{otherwise.} \end{cases} \tag{8}$$

Indeed, if $t > t_{r,w}^{\min}$ the vehicle leaves w to serve r as soon as it gets rid of the previous one $\text{prv}(r)$. In such case, $g_1(r,t)$ is the probability that both r has already appeared and the vehicle is available for it at time t, that is, finished with request $\text{prv}(r)$ at time t. At any time below $t_{r,w}^{\min}$, the probability that the vehicle leaves w must obviously be zero, since $t_{r,w}^{\min}$ is the minimum time for serving r from location $w = w(r)$. At time $t = t_{r,w}^{\min}$, we must consider the possibility that the vehicle was waiting for being able to serve r, but from an earlier time $t' < t_r^{\min}$. The overall probability that the vehicle leaves w for request r at time $t = t_{r,w}^{\min}$ is then p_r times all the f-probabilities that the vehicle was actually available from a time $\underline{on}(w) \leq t' \leq t_{r,w}^{\min}$.

The f-probabilities of a request r depend on what exactly happened to r. Namely, from a time t there are two cases: either r consumed operational time, or it didn't at all:

$$f(r,t) = g_1(r,t - S_r) \cdot \delta^w(r,t - S_r) + g_1(r,t) \cdot \left(1 - \delta^w(r,t)\right) + g_2(r,t). \tag{9}$$

where $S_r = d_{w,r} + s_r + d_{r,w}$ and the function $\delta^w(r,t)$ returns 1 iff request r is satisfiable from time t and vertex w, i.e., $\delta^w(r,t) = 1$ if $t \leq t_{r,w}^{\max}$, and $\delta^w(r,t) = 0$ otherwise.

The first term in the summation of the right hand side of Eq. 9 gives the probability that request r actually appeared and got satisfied. In such a case, $\text{departureTime}(r)$ must be the current time t, minus delay S_r needed for serving r.

The second and third terms of Eq. (9) add the probability that the vehicle was available time t, but that request r did not consume any operational time. There are only two possible reasons for that: either r actually appeared but was not satisfiable (second term), or r did not appear at all (third term), where $g_2(r,t)$ is the probability that r did not appear and is discarded at time t, and is computed as follows. For the base case of first potential request $r_1 = \text{fst}(\pi_k^w)$, we have:

$$g_2(r_1,t) = \begin{cases} 1 - p_{r_1} & \text{if} \quad t = \max(\underline{on}(w), \Gamma_{r_1}) \\ 0 & \text{otherwise} \end{cases} \tag{10}$$

The general case for $r \geq r_1$, $r \in \pi_k^w$, is quite similar to the one of function g_1. We just consider the probability $1 - p_r$ that r doesn't reveal and replace $t_{r,w}^{\min}$ by Γ_r:

$$g_2(r,t) = \begin{cases} (1 - p_r) \cdot f(\text{prv}(r), t) & \text{if } t > \max(\underline{on}(w), \Gamma_r) \\ (1 - p_r) \cdot \sum_{t'=\underline{on}(w)}^{\max(\underline{on}(w), \Gamma_r)} f(\text{prv}(r), t') & \text{if } t = \max(\underline{on}(w), \Gamma_r) \\ 0 & \text{otherwise.} \end{cases}$$

(11)

A Note on Implementation. Since we are interested in computing $\Pr\{r \in A^h\}$ for each request r separately, by following the definition of g_1, we only require the f-probability associated to $\text{prv}(r)$ to be already computed. This suggests a dynamic programming approach. Computing all the f-probabilities can then be incrementally achieved while filling up a 2-dimensional matrix containing all the f-probabilities.

Algorithm 1. Local search to compute a first stage solution of SS-VRPTW-CR

---

1 Let (x, τ) be an initial feasible first stage solution.
2 Initialize the neighborhood operator *op* to 1
3 **while** *some stopping criterion is not met* **do**
4 $\quad$ Select a solution (x', τ') at random in $\mathcal{N}_{op}(x, \tau)$
5 $\quad$ **if** *some acceptance criterion is met on* (x', τ') **then** set (x, τ) to (x', τ') and *op* to 1 ;
6 $\quad$ **else** change the neighborhood operator *op* to *op* % n_{op} +1 ;
7 **return** the best first stage solution computed during the search

---

Computational Complexity. Complexity of computing the expected cost is equivalent to the one of filling up a $|\pi_k^w| \times h$ matrix for each visited waiting location $w \in W^x$, in order to store all the $f(r,t)$ probabilities. By processing incrementally on each waiting location separately, each matrix cell can be computed in constant time using Eq. (9). In particular, once the probabilities in cells $(\text{prv}(r), 1 \cdots t)$ are known, the cell (r, t) such that $r \neq \text{fst}(\pi_k^w)$ can be computed in $\mathcal{O}(1)$ according to Eqs. (8)–(11). Given n customer regions and a time horizon of length h, we have at most $|R| = nh \geq \sum_{w \in W^x} |\pi_k^w|$ potential requests. It then requires at most $\mathcal{O}(|R|h) = \mathcal{O}(nh^2)$ constant time operations to compute $\mathcal{Q}^{\mathcal{R}}(x, \tau)$.

6   Local Search for the SS-VRPTW-CR

Algorithm 1 describes a Simulated Annealing [23] local search approach for approximating the optimal first stage solution (x, τ), minimizing $\mathcal{Q}^{\mathcal{R}}(x, \tau)$. The computation of $\mathcal{Q}^{\mathcal{R}}(x, \tau)$ is performed according to equations of Sect. 5 and is considered from now as a black box. Starting from an initial feasible first stage solution (x, τ), Algorithm 1 iteratively modifies it by using a set of $n_{op} = 9$ neighborhood operators. At each iteration, it randomly chooses a solution (x', τ') in the current neighborhood (line 4), and either accepts it and resets the neighborhood operator op to the first one (line 5), or rejects it and changes the neighborhood operator op to the next one (line 6). At the end, the algorithm simply returns the best solution (x^*, τ^*) encountered so far.

Initial Solution and Stopping Criterion. The initial first stage solution is constructed by randomly adding each waiting vertex in a route $k \in [1, K]$. All waiting vertices are thus initially part of the solution. The stopping criterion depends on the computational time dedicated to the algorithm.

Neighborhood Operators. We consider 4 wellknown operators for the VRP: relocate, swap, inverted 2-opt, and cross-exchange (see [24, 25] for detailed description). In addition, 5 new operators are dedicated to waiting vertices: 2 for either inserting or removing from W^x a waiting vertex w picked at random, 2 for increasing or decreasing the waiting time τ_w at random vertex $w \in W^x$, and 1 that transfers a random amount of waiting time units from one waiting vertex to another.

Acceptance Criterion. We use a Simulated Annealing acceptance criterion. Improving solutions are always accepted, while degrading solutions are accepted with a probability that depends on the degradation and on a temperature parameter, *i.e.*, the probability of accepting (x', τ') is $e^{-\frac{1 - Q^{\mathcal{R}}(x, \tau)/Q^{\mathcal{R}}(x', \tau')}{T}}$. The temperature T is updated by a *cooling factor* $0 < \alpha < 1$ at each iteration of Algorithm 1: $T \leftarrow \alpha \cdot T$. During the search process, T gradually evolves from an initial temperature T_{init} to nearly zero. A restart strategy is implemented by resetting the temperature to $T \leftarrow T_{\text{init}}$ each time T decreases below a fixed limit $T_{\min}$.

7   Experimentations

Test Instances. We have randomly generated instances for the SS-VRPTW-CR. Each test instance is drawn in a square of $[100, 100]$ distance units, and is characterized by:

- The number $|C| \in \{30, 50, 80\}$ of *customer regions*, randomly distributed in the square. Each customer $c \in C$ region hosts n_{TS} potential requests.
- The number $|W| \in \{20, 30, 50\}$ of *waiting vertices*, randomly distributed in the square.
- The size $h = 480$ of the *horizon* (corresponding to the number of minutes in an 8 h day).

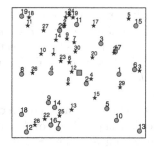

Fig. 3. Map representation of instance $a.1$. The depot (square) is located at the center. The instance counts 30 customer regions (stars) and 20 waiting vertices (circles). Although it is not visible here, the instance has a time horizon of 480 units and counts 24 time slots. If the operational day lasts 8 h, a time unit represents a 1 min in real time and each time slot lasts 20 min.

- The number $n_{TS} = 24$ of *time slots*. Time slots are introduced because it is not realistic to detail request probabilities for each time unit of the horizon (*i.e.*, every minute). We set n_{TS} to 24 so that the probability that a request appears at a customer region is specified for 20 min time slots.
- The number $K \in \{1, 3, 5, 10\}$ of available vehicles.

Travel times between vertices correspond to Euclidean distances, divided by a velocity parameter specified in the instance. Figure 3 shows an example of test instance. As a convention, the first time slot is associated to time unit 1 whereas time slot i is associated to time unit $1 + (i - 1) \cdot \lfloor h/n_{TS} \rfloor$. In our instance $a.1$, a potential request r associated to time slot 2 has a reveal time $\Gamma_r = 21$ and no potential request is associated to time units $[2, 20]$, $[22, 40]$, etc. All the test instances are available at http://becool.info.ucl.ac.be/resources/benchmarks-ss-vrptw-cr.

Potential Requests. Each potential request r, associated with a customer region and a time slot, comes with a deterministic service time $s_r = 10$. The time window $[e_r, l_r]$ is such that e_r is chosen uniformly in $[\Gamma_r, \min(\Gamma_r + \frac{h}{n_{TS}}], h)$, and l_r is chosen uniformly in $[\max(e_l, d_{0,r}), \max(e_l + 10, d_{0,r})]$.

Scale Parameter. A *scale* parameter is introduced in order to optimize expectations on coarser data, and therefore to speed-up computations. When equal to 1, expectations are computed while considering the original horizon. When $scale > 1$, expectations are computed from a coarse version of the initial horizon, scaled down by the factor $scale$. If $scale = 10$ for instance, then the horizon is scaled to $h' = 48$. All the time data, such as travel and service times, but also time windows and reveal times, are then scaled as well (rounding up to nearest integer). When working on a scaled horizon (i.e. scale ¿ 1), Algorithm 1 deals with an approximate but easier objective function $\mathcal{Q}^{\mathcal{R}}(x, \tau)$, in $\mathcal{O}(n(\frac{h}{scale})^2)$, and a reduced search space due to a coarse time horizon.

Algorithm 1 is then modified by simply adapting line 7 to return the best solution encountered so far, *according to the initial horizon*. Each time a new best solution is found during the search, its true expected cost is computed after scaling it up back to the original horizon, multiplying arrival, departure and waiting times by a factor *scale*.

Experimental Plan. All experiments are done under a cluster composed of 32 64-bits AMD Opteron 1.4 GHz cores. The code is developed in *C++11* and compiled with LLDB using -*O3* optimization flag. The Simulated Annealing parameters are set to $T_{init} = 5$, $T_{min} = 10^{-6}$ and $\alpha = 0.995$.

Table 1. Experimental results while varying horizon scale and computational time.

Scale	30 s				3 min				30 min			
	1	2	5	10	1	2	5	10	1	2	5	10
a.1	19.7	18.2	**15.0**	16.2	16.7	16.4	**14.9**	16.2	16.1	15.3	**14.9**	16.5
a.2	22.2	20.1	**16.4**	17.5	17.7	16.8	**16.2**	17.4	16.7	16.3	**16.2**	17.5
a.3	20.3	20.0	**14.4**	16.1	16.1	15.9	**14.0**	16.0	15.6	15.2	**14.0**	16.2
b.1	21.1	16.9	11.1	**11.0**	8.2	**6.3**	7.1	9.9	**5.6**	5.7	6.9	9.6
b.2	22.1	17.5	**9.6**	11.4	5.6	7.7	**6.8**	9.9	**5.1**	7.4	6.4	9.3
b.3	22.2	17.0	**10.8**	11.9	8.7	**7.2**	7.8	11.1	**6.2**	8.3	7.2	10.8
c.1	42.1	38.7	**23.6**	25.9	15.3	13.9	**12.2**	19.3	**8.3**	9.3	11.0	16.7
c.2	43.9	37.2	**25.8**	27.8	14.0	14.9	**13.5**	19.8	**9.9**	10.4	11.6	17.9
c.3	42.4	39.2	**24.3**	24.8	17.5	14.9	**11.7**	17.5	15.2	**8.8**	10.3	15.8
d.1	71.6	67.9	54.8	**54.3**	46.5	30.4	**26.1**	39.6	**11.8**	13.0	19.2	32.7
d.2	72.2	67.9	**52.8**	56.2	40.9	34.7	**25.7**	40.1	**12.6**	19.0	20.3	31.4
d.3	73.0	67.4	53.8	**51.5**	40.8	37.2	**23.0**	35.9	17.4	**11.9**	18.4	28.4

Results. Table 1 shows average experimental results over 10 runs on 12 instances: Instances *a.x* (resp. *b.x*, *c.x* and *d.x*) are such that $|C| = 30$ (resp. 30, 50 and 80), $|W| = 5$ (resp. 20, 30 and 50), and $K = 1$ (resp. 3, 5 and 10). Results are reported with *scale* $\in \{1, 2, 5, 10\}$ and with a CPU time limit $\in \{30, 180, 1800\}$ seconds.

Provided a limited computational time of 30 s, using a scaled horizon leads to better results. This is easily explained by the limited number of local search iterations performed when *scale* = 1. As the computational time increases to 3 min, working on the original horizon size tends to provide better results. This trend is confirmed by moving to 30 min. As the available computational time increases, the accuracy in the objective function eventually overtakes the computational efficiency provided by scaled horizons, especially for large instances such as *c.x* and *d.x*.

With their unique vehicle and because requests are uniformly distributed, instances *a.x* may suffer from an evaluation function being roughly uniform.

Sending the vehicle at some location to wait there is, most of the time, more or less equivalent to another location. Consequently, local optima are numerous and little diversified, the more promising ones being hard to detect when using scale 1 for only 30 min. In the contrary, using more vehicles (e.g. instances $b.x$) leads to a less uniform evaluation function. For example, concentrating all the vehicles in the same region would surely leads to poor results. On instances $a.x$, the diversification brought by scaled horizons then still prevails after 30 min. Given larger computation times (5 h), results on scales 5 and 10 do not show a significant improvement:

	a.1				a.2				a.3		
scale $\in \{1, 2, 5, 10\}$:	15.3	15.1	**14.9**	16.5	16.2	**15.8**	16.1	17.3	14.8	14.6	**14.0**	16.1

Scales 1 and 2 in contrary tend to take promising benefits of a larger computation time.

Figure 4 shows how, for instance $c.1$, the real objective function (i.e. according to the original horizon) evolves in average (over 10 runs) during an execution of Algorithm 1. By reducing both the granularity of the search space and the complexity of the objective function, the parameter *scale* can therefore be used as a tradeoff between responsiveness and good quality solutions on the long term. Figure 4 also shows that the parameter *scale* can dynamically be reduced during the search.

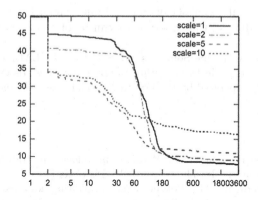

Fig. 4. Average evolution of the best real objective value in Algorithm 1, during 3600 s on instance $c.1$. During the first second, objective values rapidly decrease when optimizing on scaled horizon. Thereafter, depending on the available computation time, some scale factors reveal to be more efficient than others. For less than 1 min, *scale* = 5 leads to better results. With at least 10 min, using the original horizon is definitely better.

8   Conclusions and Research Directions

We introduced a new stochastic VRP, the SS-VRPTW-CR. Unlike existing SS-VRPs with random customers, we don't make any assumption on the moment at which a customer reveals its presence or absence. Instead, this is treated as a random variable as well. We proposed a recourse strategy for a special case of the SS-VRPTW-CR, when there is no maximal vehicle capacities. We showed how the exact expected cost can be computed in pseudo-polynomial time under this recourse strategy, and how to integrate in an efficient meta-heuristic method. Experiments are driven on generated test instances of various sizes. The average results show how a scale parameter, controlling the granularity of the time horizon, can be used to tune the optimization process in the case of limited computational times.

Maximal Vehicle Capacity Constraints. The recourse strategy and equations we give can be extended to take care of vehicle capacities. We are currently working on a generalized version of these equations.

Contribution to Online Optimization. Another potential application of the SS-VRPTW-CR goes to online optimization problems such as the DS-VRPTW. Because of the huge complexity of reoptimization, heuristic methods are often preferred, including the so called Sample Average Approximation (SAA, see [26]). SAA relies on Monte Carlo sampling, making decisions based on a subset of the scenarios. Thanks to recourse strategies, the SS-VRPTW-CR provides an upper bound on the expected cost of a first stage solution under optimal reoptimization. The SS-VRPTW-CR could therefore be used as a subroutine in order to heuristically solve the DS-VRTPW, whilst considering the whole set of scenarios instead of only a subset of sampled ones. In such a context, the scale parameter we introduce in the experiments can be of great contribution.

Acknowledgments. Christine Solnon is supported by the LABEX IMU (ANR-10-LABX-0088) of Université de Lyon, within the program "Investissements d' Avenir" (ANR-11-IDEX-0007) operated by the French National Research Agency (ANR).

References

1. Bent, R.W., Van Hentenryck, P.: Waiting and relocation strategies in online stochastic vehicle routing. In: IJCAI, pp. 1816–1821 (2007)
2. Ichoua, S., Gendreau, M., Potvin, J.Y.: Exploiting knowledge about future demands for real-time vehicle dispatching. Transp. Sci. **40**(2), 211–225 (2006)
3. Saint-Guillain, M., Deville, Y., Solnon, C.: A multistage stochastic programming approach to the dynamic and stochastic VRPTW. In: CPAIOR, pp. 357–374 (2015)
4. Branke, J., Middendorf, M., Noeth, G., Dessouky, M.: Waiting strategies for dynamic vehicle routing. Transp. Sci. **39**(3), 298–312 (2005)
5. Bertsimas, D.J.: A vehicle routing problem with stochastic demand. Oper. Res. **40**(3), 574–585 (1992)
6. Jaillet, P.: Probabilistic traveling salesman problems. Ph.D. thesis, Massachusetts Institute of Technology (1985)
7. Laporte, G., Louveaux, F.V., Mercure, H.: A priori optimization of the probabilistic traveling salesman problem. Oper. Res. **42**(3), 543–549 (1994)
8. Laporte, G., Louveaux, F.V.: The integer L-shaped method for stochastic integer programs with complete recourse. Oper. Res. Lett. **13**(3), 133–142 (1993)

9. Jezequel, A.: Probabilistic vehicle routing problems. Ph.D. thesis, Massachusetts Institute of Technology (1985)
10. Bertsimas, D.J., Chervi, P., Peterson, M.: Computational approaches to stochastic vehicle routing problems. Transp. Sci. **29**(4), 342–352 (1995)
11. Bianchi, L., Campbell, A.M.: Extension of the 2-p-opt and 1-shift algorithms to the heterogeneous probabilistic traveling salesman problem. Eur. J. Oper. Res. **176**(1), 131–144 (2007)
12. Bowler, N.E., Fink, T.M., Ball, R.C.: Characterisation of the probabilistic travelling salesman problem. Phys. Rev. E **68**(3), 036703 (2003)
13. Bianchi, L., Gambardella, L.M., Dorigo, M.: An ant colony optimization approach to the probabilistic traveling salesman problem. In: Guervós, J.J.M., Adamidis, P., Beyer, H.-G., Schwefel, H.-P., Fernández-Villacañas, J.-L. (eds.) International Conference on Parallel Problem Solving from Nature. LNCS, vol. 2439, pp. 883–892. Springer, Heidelberg (2002). doi:10.1007/3-540-45712-7_85
14. Waters, C.D.J.: Vehicle-scheduling problems with uncertainty and omitted customers. J. Oper. Res. Soc. **40**, 1099–1108 (1989)
15. Gendreau, M., Laporte, G., Séguin, R.: An exact algorithm for the vehicle routing problem with stochastic demands and customers. Transp. Sci. **29**(2), 143–155 (1995)
16. Séguin, R.: Problèmes stochastiques de tournées de vehicules, Université de Montréal (1994)
17. Gendreau, M., Laporte, G., Séguin, R.: A tabu search heuristic for the vehicle routing problem with stochastic demands and customers. Oper. Res. **44**(3), 469–477 (1996)
18. Gounaris, C.E., Repoussis, P.P., Tarantilis, C.D., Wiesemann, W., Floudas, C.A.: An adaptive memory programming framework for the robust capacitated vehicle routing problem. Trans. Sci. **50**(4), 1239–1260 (2014)
19. Campbell, A.M., Thomas, B.W.: Probabilistic traveling salesman problem with deadlines. Transp. Sci. **42**(1), 1–27 (2008)
20. Henchiri, A., Bellalouna, M., Khaznaji, W.: A probabilistic traveling salesman problem: a survey. In: FedCSIS Position Papers, vol. 3, pp. 55–60, September 2014
21. Sungur, I., Ren, Y.: A model and algorithm for the courier delivery problem with uncertainty. Transp. Sci. **44**(2), 193–205 (2010)
22. Chao, I.M., Golden, B.L., Wasil, E.A.: The team orienteering problem. Eur. J. Oper. Res. **88**(3), 464–474 (1996)
23. Kirkpatrick, S., Gelatt, C.D., Vecchi, M.P.: Optimization by simulated annealing. Science **220**(4598), 671–680 (1983)
24. Kindervater, G.A.P., Savelsbergh, M.W.P.: Vehicle routing: handling edge exchanges. In: Local search in combinatorial optimization, pp. 337–360 (1997)
25. Taillard, É., Badeau, P., Gendreau, M., Guertin, F., Potvin, J.Y.: A tabu search heuristic for the vehicle routing problem with soft time windows. Transp. Sci. **31**(2), 170–186 (1997)
26. Ahmed, S., Shapiro, A.: The sample average approximation method for stochastic programs with integer recourse (2002). Submitted for publication

Pre-scheduled Colony Size Variation
in Dynamic Environments

Michalis Mavrovouniotis[1(✉)], Anastasia Ioannou[2], and Shengxiang Yang[3]

[1] School of Science and Technology, Nottingham Trent University,
Clifton Lane, Nottingham NG11 8NS, UK
michalis.mavrovouniotis@ntu.ac.uk
[2] Department of Informatics, University of Leicester,
University Road, Leicester LE1 7RH, UK
ai63@le.ac.uk
[3] Centre for Computational Intelligence (CCI),
School of Computer Science and Informatics,
De Montfort University, The Gateway, Leicester LE1 9BH, UK
syang@dmu.ac.uk

Abstract. The performance of the $\mathcal{MAX}$-$\mathcal{MIN}$ ant system ($\mathcal{MMAS}$) in dynamic optimization problems (DOPs) is sensitive to the colony size. In particular, a large colony size may waste computational resources whereas a small colony size may restrict the searching capabilities of the algorithm. There is a trade off in the behaviour of the algorithm between the early and later stages of the optimization process. A smaller colony size leads to better performance on shorter runs whereas a larger colony size leads to better performance on longer runs. In this paper, pre-scheduling of varying the colony size of $\mathcal{MMAS}$ is investigated in dynamic environments.

1 Introduction

Ant colony optimization (ACO) is a metaheuristic inspired by the foraging behaviour of real ant colonies [2,3]. ACO algorithms have been successfully applied to many $\mathcal{NP}$-hard combinatorial problems such as the travelling salesman problem (TSP) [4] and vehicle routing problem (VRP) [7]. In this paper, we focus on a particular ACO variation, i.e., $\mathcal{MAX}$-$\mathcal{MIN}$ Ant System ($\mathcal{MMAS}$) [22], which is one of the best performing variations.

The construction of solutions from ants is biased by existing pheromone trails and heuristic information. Pheromone trails are updated according to the search experience and towards solution with good quality. This is similar to a learning reinforcement scheme. The behaviour and performance of $\mathcal{MMAS}$ algorithm depends strongly on the number of ants used [5,24]. When a given computational budget is available, e.g., the maximum number of function evaluations, a smaller number of ants will produce more algorithmic iterations whereas a larger number of ants less. Hence, the colony size affects the duration of the learning reinforcement [18].

© Springer International Publishing AG 2017
G. Squillero and K. Sim (Eds.): EvoApplications 2017, Part II, LNCS 10200, pp. 128–139, 2017.
DOI: 10.1007/978-3-319-55792-2_9

In [24], it was investigated that when fewer ants are used, the algorithm may converge quickly at early stages of the optimization process, but get stuck in the stagnation behaviour later on. In contrast, when more ants are used, the algorithm converges slower but to better solutions at later stages of the optimization process. Considering this $\mathcal{MMAS}$'s behaviour, it can be observed that the optimal number of ants depends on the stage of the optimization process. Therefore, $\mathcal{MMAS}$ can benefit from varying the number of ants. For example, a pre-schedule of varying the colony size may improve the performance of $\mathcal{MMAS}$ in dynamic environments. The key idea is to start a few ants when a change occurs and gradually increase the number of ants. In this way, $\mathcal{MMAS}$ will benefit from both merits of a small (fast convergence) and large (improve solution quality) colony size at different stages of the optimization process.

Several dynamic test cases of the dynamic TSP (DTSP) are generated for our study. The rest of the paper is organized as follows. Sections 2 and 3 describe the DOPs generated and the ACO algorithm used for this study, respectively. Section 4 discusses the importance of the colony size parameter. Section 5 presents the experimental study with discussions. Finally, Sect. 6 concludes this paper.

2 Dynamic Environment

2.1 Dynamic Travelling Salesman Problem (DTSP)

The DTSP is modelled by a fully connected weighted graph $G = (N, A)$, where $N = \{v_1, \ldots, v_n\}$ is a set of n nodes (e.g., cities) and $A = \{(v_i, v_j) \mid v_i, v_j \in N, i \neq j\}$ is a set of arcs (i.e., links), where n represents the size of a problem instance. Each arc $(v_i, v_j) \in A$ is associated with a non-negative value $d_{ij} \in \mathbb{R}^+$, which represents the distance between cities v_i and v_j. The objective of the problem is to find the shortest Hamiltonian cycle that starts from one node and visits each of the other cities once before returning to the starting city.

The distance matrix of the DTSP is subject to changes, which is defined as follows: $\mathbf{D}(t) = \{d_{ij}(t)\}_{n \times n}$, where t is the period of a dynamic change. A particular TSP solution $s = [s_1, \ldots, s_n]$ in the search space is specified by a permutation of the nodes (cities) and it is evaluated as follows:

$$f(s, t) = d_{s_n s_1}(t) + \sum_{i=1}^{n-1} d_{s_i s_{i+1}}(t). \tag{1}$$

2.2 DTSP Benchmark Generators

The concept of DTSPs was initially introduced by Psaraftis [20]. Since then, several variations of DTSPs were introduced, where the set of nodes N [1,9,10,12,13,25] and/or the cost from the set of arcs A [6,17,19,21,25] cause the weight matrix $\mathbf{W}(t)$ to change during the optimization process. However, there is still no any unified benchmark problem for DTSPs, which makes the comparison with algorithms from the literature a very challenging task. One popular benchmark is the DTSP where cities are exchanged: half of the cities from the problem instance are removed to create a spare pool [9,10,14], and the cities from the spare pool are then used to replace cities from the problem instance. Another popular benchmark is the DTSP where the weights of arcs change probabilistically [17,25] (the complete benchmark generator description is given in Sect. 2.3 since it is the benchmark generator we consider in the experiments). In [6,21], only the weights of arcs that belong to the best tour increase or decrease accordingly.

Younes *et al.* [26] introduced a benchmark generator for the DTSP with different modes: (1) topology changes as in [10], (2) weight changes in [6], and (3) swap cities. Based on the last mode (i.e., swap cities) of the aforementioned benchmark generator, a general dynamic benchmark generator for permutation-encoded problems (DBGP) was proposed that can generate test cases with known optima [15]. DBGP can convert any stationary TSP instance into a DTSP with specific properties (i.e., frequency and magnitude of changes). Although with DBGP one can observe how close to the optimum an algorithm converges, it sacrifices real-world models for the sake of benchmarking.

2.3 Generating Dynamic Test Cases

Considering the problem formulation above, a dynamic test case of a TSP can be generated by modifying the value of the arc between nodes v_i and v_j as follows:

$$w_{ij}(T+1) = \begin{cases} w_{ij}(0) + \mathcal{N}(\mu, \sigma), & \text{if } (i,j) \in A_S(T); \\ w_{ij}(T), & \text{otherwise;} \end{cases} \tag{2}$$

where $T = \lceil t/f \rceil$ is the environmental period index, f is the frequency of change, t is the evaluation count of the algorithm, $\mathcal{N}(\mu, \sigma)$ is a random number generated from a normal distribution with $\mu = 0$ and $\sigma = 0.2 \times w_{ij}(0)$, $w_{ij}(0)$ is the weight between nodes v_i and v_j for the initial instance and $A_S(T) \subset A$ contains exactly $\lceil m(n(n-1)) \rceil$ arcs in which their weights will be subject to changes (either increase or decrease) [25].

Since many real-world problems can be formulated as DTSPs and methods for solving static TSPs can be applied to solve them [8]; the dynamic changes generated in this paper can be generalized and may represent different factors depending on the application. For example, in logistics, the weight changes may represent traffic on the road system or in telecommunications the weight changes may represent delays on the network.

3 $\mathcal{MAX}$-$\mathcal{MIN}$ Ant System

3.1   Construct Solutions

One of the state-of-the-art ACO variations is the $\mathcal{MMAS}$ [22]. A colony of ω ants read pheromones in order to construct their solutions and write pheromones to store their solutions. Each ant k uses a probabilistic rule to choose the next node to visit. The decision rule of the kth ant to move from node v_i to node v_j is defined as follows:

$$p_{ij}^k = \frac{[\tau_{ij}]^\alpha [\eta_{ij}]^\beta}{\sum_{l \in \mathcal{N}_i^k} [\tau_{il}]^\alpha [\eta_{il}]^\beta}, \text{if } j \in \mathcal{N}_i^k, \tag{3}$$

where τ_{ij} and η_{ij} are the existing pheromone trail and heuristic information available a priori between nodes v_i and v_j, respectively. The heuristic information is defined as $\eta_{ij} = 1/d_{ij}(t)$, where $d_{ij}(t)$ is defined as in Eq. (1). $\mathcal{N}_i^k$ is the neighbourhood of unvisited nodes incident to node i available for ant k to select. α and β are the two parameters which determine the relative influence of τ_{ij} and η_{ij}, respectively.

3.2 Pheromone Update

The pheromone trails in $\mathcal{MMAS}$ are updated by applying evaporation as follows:

$$\tau_{ij} \leftarrow (1 - \rho) \tau_{ij}, \forall(v_i, v_j), \tag{4}$$

where ρ is the evaporation rate which satisfies $0 < \rho \leq 1$, and τ_{ij} is the existing pheromone value. After evaporation, the best ant deposits pheromone as follows:

$$\tau_{ij} \leftarrow \tau_{ij} + \Delta\tau_{ij}^{best}, \forall(v_i, v_j) \in T^{best}, \tag{5}$$

where $\Delta\tau_{ij}^{best} = 1/C^{best}$ is the amount of pheromone that the best ant deposits and C^{best} defines the solution quality of tour T^{best}. The best ant that is allowed to deposit pheromone may be either the best-so-far, in which case $C^{best} = C^{bs}$, or the iteration-best, in which case $C^{best} = C^{ib}$, where C^{bs} and C^{ib} are the solution quality of the best-so-far and the iteration best ant, respectively. The best-so-far ant is a special ant that may not necessarily belong in the current colony of ants as the iteration best ant. Both update rules are used in an alternate way in the implementation [23].

The lower and upper limits τ_{min} and τ_{max} of the pheromone trail values are imposed. The τ_{max} value is bounded by $1/(\rho C^{bs})$, where C^{bs} is initially the solution quality of an estimated optimal tour and later on is updated whenever a new best-so-far ant solution quality is found. The τ_{min} value is set to $\tau_{min} = \tau_{max}/2n$.

Since only the best ant is allowed to deposit pheromone, the colony may quickly converge towards the best solution found in the first iteration. Therefore, the pheromone trails are occasionally reinitialized to the τ_{max} value to increase exploration. For example, whenever the stagnation behaviour occurs or when no improved solution is found for a given number of iterations, the pheromone trails are reinitialized.

3.3   Adapting to Dynamic Changes

$\mathcal{MMAS}$ is able to use knowledge from previous environments via pheromone trails and can be applied directly to DOPs without any modifications [1, 16]. For example, when the changing environments are similar, the pheromone trails of the previous environment may provide knowledge to speed up the optimization process to the new environment. However, the algorithm needs to be flexible enough to accept the knowledge transferred from the pheromone trails, or eliminate the pheromone trails, in order to adapt well to the new environment. In particular, pheromone evaporation enables the algorithm to forget bad decisions made in previous iterations. When a dynamic change occurs, evaporation eliminates the pheromone trails of the previous environment from areas that are generated on the old optimum and helps ants to explore for the new optimum.

In case the changing environments are different, then pheromone reinitialization may be a better choice rather than transferring the knowledge from previous pheromone trails [1, 9, 10, 16]. For instance, when a change occurs, the pheromone trails are initialized with an equal amount.

4   Varying the Colony Size

4.1   Effect of the Colony Size in Dynamic Environments

A previous empirical study showed that the colony size of the $\mathcal{MMAS}$ algorithm, one of the best performing ACO algorithms, is sensitive to the properties of DOPs [18]. In particular, if for a given DOP only a certain computation budget, e.g., the maximum number of function evaluations, is available, then the colony size, i.e., the number of ants, is a very critical parameter. Since each ant in a colony corresponds to a single function evaluation, an unnecessarily large colony size may waste computations whereas an extremely small colony size may restrict the searching capabilities of ACO.

Furthermore, the colony size has a direct relation with the reinforcement learning period of ACO because it determines its duration: less ants corresponds to larger duration whereas more ants corresponds to smaller duration. Also the colony size determines how broad the search is at each iteration (e.g., more ants means broader search). Hence, the number of ants needs to be tuned accordingly in order not to waste computation resources and degrade the solution quality.

In this paper, we study the impact of the colony size on the performance of the $\mathcal{MMAS}$ algorithm for DOPs. This kind of problems in a nutshell are a series of stationary optimization problems that all need to be optimized. Therefore, it is straightforward that more challenges exist and the colony size will have impact on the performance of the algorithm. This is because it determines the number of iterations and the broadness of the search as in stationary optimization problems. For example, for a given DOP a predefined computation budged is available between each environmental change that is typically synchronized with the algorithm, i.e., every f evaluations a change occurs [15]. Therefore, an algorithm with a larger colony size means that it will perform a broader search (i.e.,

more evaluations per iteration) but it will have limited reinforcement learning
(i.e., less number of iteration) for each environmental change.

4.2 Pre-scheduling the Colony Size

The colony size of $\mathcal{MMAS}$ was investigated on the stationary TSP [24]. In
particular, the number of ants used shows a trade-off between the early and
later optimization process of the algorithm regarding the solution quality. At
early stages of the optimization process fewer ants result to better performance,
whereas at later stages more ants result to better performance. With fewer
ants the algorithm seems to initially progress faster but leads to the stagnation behaviour at later stages. More ants give better results only on later stages
of the optimization process. This behaviour of $\mathcal{MMAS}$ can be observed in Fig. 1.
Similar behaviour was observed for other problem instances (kroA150.tsp and
kroA200.tsp).

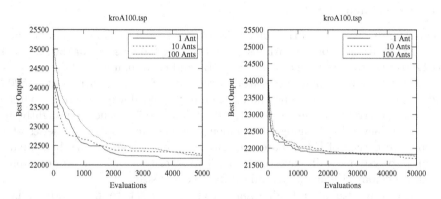

Fig. 1. Performance of $\mathcal{MMAS}$ with different fixed number of ants for a short run of
5000 evaluations (left) and a long run of 50,000 evaluations (right), respectively.

Clearly, at different stages of the optimization process the optimal colony size
of $\mathcal{MMAS}$ varies. Therefore, adjusting the colony size during the optimization
process seems a better choice rather than keeping a fixed colony size. In fact,
pre-scheduling the colony size in stationary environments has proved that it can
combine the merits of few ants on shorter runs and the merits of more ants on
longer runs [24]. However, in this paper, we are concerned with pre-schedules for
dynamic environments. Considering the observations in Fig. 1, a potential good
pre-schedule in a dynamic environment could be starting with a small colony
size when a change occurs to quickly converge and then gradually increase the
colony size to further improve the solution quality.

In particular, four pre-schedules are investigated which are defined as follows:

1. Pre-schedule 1: every 15 iterations add a single ant
2. Pre-schedule 2: every 10 iterations add a single ant
3. Pre-schedule 3: every 5 iterations add a single ant
4. Pre-schedule 4: every 2 iterations add a single ant

All schedules start with an initial colony size of 1 ant and increase by 1 ant at a time. When a change occurs the colony size is reset back to 1 and starts to grow until the next dynamic change occurs. An arbitrary number of different pre-schedules can exist but in this paper we consider these four to determine under which frequency of increasing the number of ants $\mathcal{MMAS}$ performs better. The size of the colony increases faster from pre-schedule 1 to pre-schedule 2, pre-schedule 3 and to pre-schedule 4.

5   Experimental Study

5.1   Experimental Setup

To investigate the effect of the colony size of $\mathcal{MMAS}$ in dynamic environments, three TSP stationary benchmark instances (i.e., kroA100.tsp, kroA150.tsp and kroA200.tsp) were obtained from TSPLIB[1] and corresponding DOPs are generated using the benchmark generator (described in Sect. 2.3) with f set to 5000 and 50000 function evaluations, indicating quickly and slowly changing environments, respectively, and m set to 0.1, 0.25, 0.5 and 0.75, indicating slightly, to medium, to severely changing environments, respectively. Totally, a series of 8 dynamic test cases of DTSPs are constructed from each stationary benchmark instance to systematically investigate $\mathcal{MMAS}$ algorithm with the proposed pre-scheduled colony size against standard fixed colony size.

The colony size of a traditional $\mathcal{MMAS}$ was set to fixed values, i.e., $\omega \in \{1, 2, 5, 10, 25, 50, 100\}$, and the results are compared with the pre-scheduled variation of $\mathcal{MMAS}$. The remaining parameters were set to typical values for DOPs as follows: $\alpha = 1$, $\beta = 5$ and $\rho = 0.8$ from our preliminary experiments.

5.2   Performance Measurement

For each DTSP, 30 independent runs of the $\mathcal{MMAS}$ were executed. For each run, 25 environments changes were allowed and the best so far ant after a dynamic change was recorded. The overall *offline performance* [11] is defined as follows:

$$\bar{P}_{offline} = \frac{1}{E} \sum_{i=1}^{E} \left(\frac{1}{R} \sum_{j=1}^{R} P_{ij}^* \right), \tag{6}$$

where E is the total number of function evaluations, R is the number of runs, P_{ij}^* is the best-so-far after a dynamic change of iteration i of run j.

---

[1] http://comopt.ifi.uni-heidelberg.de/software/TSPLIB95/.

5.3   Results and Discussion

The offline performance results of the $\mathcal{MMAS}$ algorithm on DTSPs with fixed and pre-scheduled colony sizes are presented in Table 1. Pairwise comparisons between the best fixed colony variation (1, 2, 5, 10, 25, 50 and 100 ants) against the best pre-scheduled colony variation (1, 2, 3 and 4 pre-schedules) using Mann–Whitney statistical tests are performed. The best variation of one type with a bold value indicates that is significantly better than the best variation of the other type. In case both variations types are in bold it indicates insignificantly difference between them. In Figs. 2 and 3, the dynamic offline performance for quickly and slowly changing environments against the algorithmic evaluations are plotted for the first 10 environments to better understand the behaviour of $\mathcal{MMAS}$. From the experimental results, the following observations can be drawn.

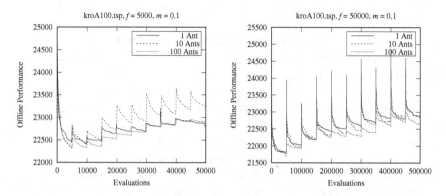

Fig. 2. Dynamic offline performance of $\mathcal{MMAS}$ with different fixed number of ants for quickly changing (left) and slowly changing (right) DTSPs, respectively.

First, the offline performance of fixed colony variations of $\mathcal{MMAS}$ with a larger size is better in most test cases. Only on few cases, i.e., when $m = 0.75$, a smaller colony size has better performance. These results were expected for slowly changing DTSPs, i.e., $f = 50000$, because more ants perform better in long runs. However, a large colony also performs better for quickly changing DTSPs, i.e., $f = 5000$. This is contradictory with the observations in Fig. 1, where a small colony size performed better in a shorter run (corresponds to a quickly changing environment). From Fig. 2, it can be observed that the performance up to the first environment (before any change occurs) the results match the one in Fig. 1. When a dynamic change occurs $\mathcal{MMAS}$ with fewer ants perform worst. This is possibly because the pheromone trails generated by fewer ants of the previous environment may not promote exploration when they are used in the new environment.

Second, the offline performance of pre-scheduled colony variations of $\mathcal{MMAS}$ that increase the colony size faster, e.g., Pre-schedule 3 and Pre-schedule 4,

Table 1. Comparison of $\mathcal{MMAS}$ variations regarding the results of the offline performance

$m \Rightarrow$	$f = 5000$				$f = 50000$			
	0.1	0.25	0.5	0.75	0.1	0.25	0.5	0.75
# ants	kroA100.tsp							
(1 ant)	23452	23565	23417	23584	22993	23125	22986	23159
(2 ants)	23378	23523	23381	23538	22967	23119	23004	23157
(5 ants)	23395	23575	23458	23648	23014	23152	23034	23188
(10 ant)	23390	23565	23410	23558	22984	23151	23007	23184
(25 ants)	22831	23030	23037	23085	22937	23135	23002	23134
(50 ants)	22892	23072	22933	23150	22880	23098	22975	23109
(100 ants)	22845	23016	22964	23128	22790	23092	23006	23112
Pre-schedule 1	23199	23385	23226	23284	22826	23055	22929	23055
Pre-schedule 2	23294	23318	23126	23193	22781	23038	22952	23081
Pre-schedule 3	22804	23050	**22740**	**22830**	**22609**	**22913**	**22803**	**22916**
Pre-schedule 4	**22707**	**22887**	23071	23144	22814	23066	22963	23090
# ants	kroA150.tsp							
(1 ant)	28892	29276	29473	29538	**28404**	**28797**	**28975**	**29004**
(2 ants)	28874	29260	29492	29588	28436	28842	29029	29060
(5 ants)	29020	29338	29610	29727	28558	28907	29082	29146
(10 ant)	28993	29308	29466	29568	28596	28922	29088	29188
(25 ants)	28600	28885	29229	29419	28578	28902	29057	29158
(50 ants)	28575	28897	29236	29300	28542	28861	29056	29156
(100 ants)	28596	28810	29237	29302	28508	28883	28966	29195
Pre-schedule 1	28832	29065	29163	29313	28474	28870	**28960**	29161
Pre-schedule 2	28856	29040	**29019**	29309	28491	28845	28995	29116
Pre-schedule 3	28566	28930	29189	29286	**28414**	28824	28994	29176
Pre-schedule 4	**28405**	**28701**	29334	**29143**	28500	28843	29004	29146
# ants	kroA200.tsp							
(1 ant)	31799	32405	32722	32829	31240	31712	32044	32103
(2 ants)	31635	32178	32588	32620	31219	31684	32029	32061
(5 ants)	31602	32148	32561	32592	31165	31656	32011	32017
(10 ant)	31543	31958	32409	32327	31131	31641	31992	31980
(25 ants)	31156	31529	32171	32105	31077	31583	31969	31987
(50 ants)	31191	31505	32138	32129	31055	31552	31973	31914
(100 ants)	31158	**31493**	32032	32113	**30982**	31468	31915	31802
Pre-schedule 1	31326	31692	32134	32086	31005	31503	31860	31895
Pre-schedule 2	31243	31534	31991	**31850**	**30978**	31463	31841	31825
Pre-schedule 3	31084	**31466**	**31882**	32101	31002	**31345**	**31806**	**31718**
Pre-schedule 4	**30935**	31643	31155	32248	31017	31549	31861	31858

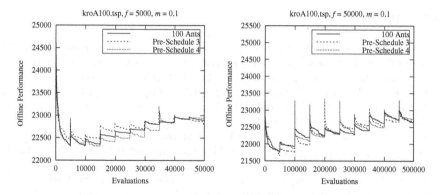

Fig. 3. Dynamic offline performance of the best fixed and pre-schedule $\mathcal{MMAS}$ variations for quickly changing (left) and slowly changing (right) DTSPs, respectively.

perform better in most test cases. Only in kroA150.tsp problem instance when $f = 50000$ none of the pre-scheduled variations perform better. This is because the results of fixed variation in Table 1 show that 1 ant outperforms other fixed variations. Therefore, a pre-schedule that increases the colony size will not be helpful. For the remaining cases, either Pre-schedule 3 or Pre-schedule 4 performs better. This shows that the speed of increasing the colony size is problem dependent.

Finally, the comparisons between the fixed and pre-scheduled variation show that with the exception of kroA150.tsp when $f = 50000$, the best performing pre-schedule variation outperforms the best performing fixed variation in many DTSPs. From Fig. 3, it can be observed that a pre-scheduled colony size is able to maintain a better offline performance than a fixed colony size.

6 Conclusions

The optimal colony size of $\mathcal{MMAS}$ algorithms varies at different stages of the optimization process. More precisely, a small colony size works better for short runs and a large colony size works better for long runs in stationary environments. This paper, investigates different pre-schedules for DTSPs, where $\mathcal{MMAS}$ begins with a single ant and gradually increase its colony size in dynamic environments. When a dynamic change occurs, the colony is reset back to a single ant. The key idea of the pre-schedule is to combine the benefits of small and large colonies. The experiments for different DTSP test cases showed that a varying colony size has a promising performance when compared with a fixed colony size. However, the performance of the pre-schedule of the varying colony strongly depends on the properties of the DTSP. Hence, a direct future work would be to self-adapt the colony size of $\mathcal{MMAS}$. In this way, a possibly automatic pre-schedule will be generated for different DTSPs.

Acknowledgement. This work was supported by the Engineering and Physical Sciences Research Council (EPSRC) of U.K. under Grant EP/K001310/1.

References

1. Angus, D., Hendtlass, T.: Ant colony optimisation applied to a dynamically changing problem. In: Hendtlass, T., Ali, M. (eds.) IEA/AIE 2002. LNCS (LNAI), vol. 2358, pp. 618–627. Springer, Heidelberg (2002). doi:10.1007/3-540-48035-8_60
2. Colorni, A., Dorigo, M., Maniezzo, V.: Distributed optimization by ant colonies. In: Vaerla, F., Bourgine, P. (eds.) Proceedings of the European Conference on Artificial Life, pp. 134–142. Elsevier Publishing (1991)
3. Dorigo, M., Maniezzo, V., Colorni, A.: Ant system: optimization by a colony of cooperating agents. IEEE Trans. Syst. Man Cybern. Part B Cybern. **26**(1), 29–41 (1996)
4. Dorigo, M., Gambardella, L.M.: Ant colony system: a cooperative learning approach to the traveling salesman problem. IEEE Trans. Evol. Comput. **1**(1), 53–66 (1997)
5. Dorigo, M., Stützle, T.: Ant colony optimization. MIT Press, Cambridge (2004)
6. Eyckelhof, C.J., Snoek, M.: Ant systems for a dynamic TSP. In: Dorigo, M., Caro, G., Sampels, M. (eds.) ANTS 2002. LNCS, vol. 2463, pp. 88–99. Springer, Heidelberg (2002). doi:10.1007/3-540-45724-0_8
7. Gambardella, L.M., Taillard, E.D., Agazzi, C.: MACS-VRPTW: a multicolony ant colony system for vehicle routing problems with time windows. In: New Ideas in Optimization, pp. 63–76 (1999)
8. Gueta, L., Chiba, R., Ota, J., Arai, T., Ueyama, T.: A practical and integrated method to optimize a manipulator-based inspection system. In: IEEE International Conference on Robotics and Biomimetics, ROBIO 2007, pp. 1911–1918, December 2007
9. Guntsch, M., Middendorf, M.: Pheromone modification strategies for ant algorithms applied to dynamic TSP. In: Boers, E.J.W. (ed.) EvoWorkshops 2001. LNCS, vol. 2037, pp. 213–222. Springer, Heidelberg (2001). doi:10.1007/3-540-45365-2_22
10. Guntsch, M., Middendorf, M.: Applying population based ACO to dynamic optimization problems. In: Dorigo, M., Caro, G., Sampels, M. (eds.) ANTS 2002. LNCS, vol. 2463, pp. 111–122. Springer, Heidelberg (2002). doi:10.1007/3-540-45724-0_10
11. Jin, Y., Branke, J.: Evolutionary optimization in uncertain environments-a survey. IEEE Trans. Evol. Comput. **9**(3), 303–317 (2005)
12. Kang, L., Zhou, A., McKay, B., Li, Y., Kang, Z.: Benchmarking algorithms for dynamic travelling salesman problems. In: Congress on Evolutionary Computation, CEC2004, vol. 2, pp. 1286–1292, June 2004
13. Li, C., Yang, M., Kang, L.: A new approach to solving dynamic traveling salesman problems. In: Wang, T.-D., Li, X., Chen, S.-H., Wang, X., Abbass, H., Iba, H., Chen, G.-L., Yao, X. (eds.) SEAL 2006. LNCS, vol. 4247, pp. 236–243. Springer, Heidelberg (2006). doi:10.1007/11903697_31
14. Mavrovouniotis, M., Yang, S.: A memetic ant colony optimization algorithm for the dynamic travelling salesman problem. Soft Comput. **15**(7), 1405–1425 (2011)
15. Mavrovouniotis, M., Yang, S., Yao, X.: A benchmark generator for dynamic permutation-encoded problems. In: Coello, C.A.C., Cutello, V., Deb, K., Forrest, S., Nicosia, G., Pavone, M. (eds.) PPSN 2012. LNCS, vol. 7492, pp. 508–517. Springer, Heidelberg (2012). doi:10.1007/978-3-642-32964-7_51

16. Mavrovouniotis, M., Yang, S.: Adapting the pheromone evaporation rate in dynamic routing problems. In: Esparcia-Alcázar, A.I. (ed.) EvoApplications 2013. LNCS, vol. 7835, pp. 606–615. Springer, Heidelberg (2013). doi:10.1007/978-3-642-37192-9_61
17. Mavrovouniotis, M., Yang, S.: Ant colony optimization with immigrants schemes for the dynamic travelling salesman problem with traffic factors. Appl. Soft Comput. **13**(10), 4023–4037 (2013)
18. Mavrovouniotis, M., Yang, S.: Empirical study on the effect of population size on max-min ant system in dynamic environments. In: Proceedings of the 2016 IEEE Congress on Evolutionary Computation (CEC 2016), pp. 853–860 (2016)
19. Melo, L., Pereira, F., Costa, E.: Multi-caste ant colony algorithm for the dynamic traveling salesperson problem. In: Tomassini, M., Antonioni, A., Daolio, F., Buesser, P. (eds.) ICANNGA 2013. LNCS, vol. 7824, pp. 179–188. Springer, Heidelberg (2013). doi:10.1007/978-3-642-37213-1_19
20. Psaraftis, H.: Dynamic Vehicle Routing Problems, pp. 223–248. Elsevier (1988)
21. Simões, A., Costa, E.: CHC-based algorithms for the dynamic traveling salesman problem. In: Chio, C., et al. (eds.) EvoApplications 2011. LNCS, vol. 6624, pp. 354–363. Springer, Heidelberg (2011). doi:10.1007/978-3-642-20525-5_36
22. Stützle, T., Hoos, H.: $\mathcal{MAX}$-$\mathcal{MIN}$ ant system and local search for the traveling salesman problem. In: IEEE International Conference on Evolutionary Computation, pp. 309–314 (1997)
23. Stützle, T., Hoos, H.H.: $\mathcal{MAX}$-$\mathcal{MIN}$ ant system. Future Gener. Comput. Syst. **16**(8), 889–914 (2000)
24. Stützle, T., López-Ibáñez, M., Pellegrini, P., Maur, M., de Oca, M.M., Birattari, M., Dorigo, M.: Parameter adaptation in ant colony optimization. In: Hamadi, Y., Monfroy, E., Saubion, F. (eds.) Autonomous Search, pp. 191–215. Springer, Heidelberg (2012)
25. Tinós, R., Whitley, D., Howe, A.: Use of explicit memory in the dynamic traveling salesman problem. In: Proceedings of the 2014 Conference on Genetic and Evolutionary Computation, pp. 999–1006. ACM, New York (2014)
26. Younes, A., Calamai, P., Basir, O.: Generalized benchmark generation for dynamic combinatorial problems. In: Proceedings of the 2005 Genetic and Evolutionary Computation Conference, pp. 25–31. ACM Press (2005)

An Online Packing Heuristic
for the Three-Dimensional Container Loading
Problem in Dynamic Environments
and the Physical Internet

Chi Trung Ha[1(✉)], Trung Thanh Nguyen[2(✉)], Lam Thu Bui[1(✉)],
and Ran Wang[2(✉)]

[1] Le Quy Don Technical University, Hanoi, Vietnam
eldic2009@gmail.com, lambt@lqdtu.edu.vn
[2] Liverpool John Moores University, Liverpool, UK
T.T.Nguyen@ljmu.ac.uk, r.wang@2015.ljmu.ac.uk

Abstract. In this paper, we consider the online three-dimensional container loading problem. We develop a novel online packing algorithm to solve the three-dimensional bin packing problem in the online case where items are not known well in advance and they have to be packed in real-time when they arrive. This is relevant in many real-world scenarios such as automated cargo loading in warehouses. This is also relevant in the new logistics model of Physical Internet. The effectiveness of the online packing heuristic is evaluated on a set of generated data. The experimental results show that the algorithm could solve the 3D container loading problems in online fashion and is competitive against other algorithms both in the terms of running time, space utilization and the number of bins.

Keywords: Dynamic optimization · Online optimization · Dynamic environments · 3D bin packing problem · 3D container loading problem · Online packing heuristic · Physical internet · Benchmark problems

1 Introduction

The three-dimensional bin packing problem (3D-BPP), a special class of bin packing problems [1, 2], is a NP-hard combinatorial optimization problem [3, 4], where the primary aim is to load a finite number of items of different sizes using the smallest possible number of bins. In logistics and supply chains, the 3D-BPP is also called the three-dimensional container loading problem (3D-CLP). It has many industrial and commercial applications, such as loading goods to containers and pallets, cargo and ship stowage loading, etc. 3D-CLP has been studied extensively by a lot of researchers with different objective functions and constraints by using diverse methods as surveyed and discussed in [5, 6].

Although many studies have addressed the 3D-CLP, most have focused exclusively on volume utilization and ignored other practical requirements. In real world problems, a number of practical constraints and requirements need to be satisfied, such as loading

© Springer International Publishing AG 2017
G. Squillero and K. Sim (Eds.): EvoApplications 2017, Part II, LNCS 10200, pp. 140–155, 2017.
DOI: 10.1007/978-3-319-55792-2_10

feasibility, stability, weight balance, operational safety product handling, and the prevention of cargo damage during container shipping. But only a few works have addressed those mentioned requirements [7–9].

Furthermore, most existing works focused on the static (offline) multidimensional CLP. Only few works have addressed the online or dynamic 3D-CLP where knowledge about items' arrival is not known in advance and items have to be packed right after they arrive. The online 3D-CLP has many applications in automatic or robotic cargo loading in warehouse storages. It will also become very common in a new logistics model, the Physical Internet [10], which is considered the future of smarter logistics [11]. This logistics model proposes to move, pack and unpack goods in the same way as information are being transported, pack and unpack in the digital internet. In the Physical Internet logistics model, items will arrive in real-time with not much notification, and they will need to be packed immediately to avoid any delay.

To solve the online/dynamic 3D-CLP, one needs to follow a dynamic optimization approach, in which the problem is solved online when time goes by [12], i.e. packing solutions need to be provided immediately in real-time whenever one or a set of items arrive.

The classical online one-dimensional CLP problem was introduced in [13–15], where items are coming one by one and each must be packed immediately and irrevocably into a bin without any knowledge of future items and the goal is to minimize the maximal number of bins ever used over all times.

The issue we are addressing in this work is to develop an online packing heuristic for 3D-CLP with online arrival of items, and test its performance against other online and static algorithms. The algorithm must make decisions immediately and irrevocably based only on a part of the input without any knowledge of the future part. This is different to the static (offline) case where an algorithm knows the whole information about items and containers before making any decision. The algorithm should guarantee that all items are loaded more realistically in the containers, with one door from the one side, and avoid the problem of blocked items (see Fig. 3).

The remainder of this paper is organized as follows. In Sect. 2 basic concepts of online 3D-BPP are introduced. In Sect. 3 we discuss about building a packing heuristic for the online case. Section 4 discusses generating problem data and testing the performance of algorithms. Finally, conclusions are given in Sect. 5.

2 Problem Definition

Since the online 3D-CLP in this work is formed from the classical 3D-CLP, it is defined as follows: suppose that *IPS* is an item packing sequence where items are coming in an online fashion, *CLS* is a container loading sequence and there are enough containers for the whole *IPS*.

Let N is the total number of items, and let M is the total number of user containers over all the time of loading process. We assumed that all item and container have the shape of a cube, where the length, width, and height of the container are oriented with the x-axis, y-axis and z-axis respectively in the Cartesian coordinate system. So the point $(0, 0, 0)$ is the deepest-bottom-left corner of a container. Let L_j, W_j, H_j and c_i be the container length, width, height and the cost of the j-th container, respectively. Let the lowercase letters l_i, w_i, h_i be the length, width, and height of i-th item.

2.1 Objective and Constraints

The objective is to minimize the total cost of all used containers:

$$\sum_{i=1}^{M} c_i \rightarrow min \tag{1}$$

If the containers are homogeneous, then the cost of all containers are the same, in this case the objective is to minimize the number M. This objective function is similar to maximize the utilization or minimize the wasted space:

$$\sum_{i=1}^{M} (L_j * W_j * H_j) - \sum_{i=1}^{M} (l_j * w_j * h_j) \rightarrow min \tag{2}$$

For the constraints of the online problem, this work takes into account the basic geometric constraints, according to [5]: (1) the items are assumed to be placed orthogonally, that is, the edges of the boxes have to be either parallel or perpendicular to those of the containers and within the container's dimension; (2) all items are packed and (3) items do not overlap with each other. More detailed explanation of the similar model can be found in [8, 16, 17]. We also consider a specific constraint that the items can be rotated because it is an important operational factor in both the research and the real world. There are, at most, six different rotation types (0 to 5) for each packed item in a container. They are: l-w-h, w-l-h, l-h-w, w-h-l, h-l-w, and h-w-l (see Fig. 1).

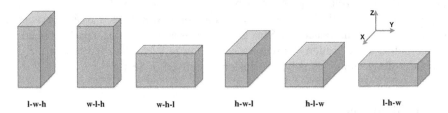

l-w-h   w-l-h   w-h-l   h-w-l   h-l-w   l-h-w

Fig. 1. Six types of item orientation

2.2 Empty Maximal Spaces

To indicate the exact position where an item can be loaded into a particular container, many concept of coordinates of objects have been used, for example the concept of corner points [2, 18, 19], and the concept of extreme points [20, 21]. In this work, we use the concept of empty maximal spaces (EMSs) to represent the free spaces in bins. In this concept, for each container to be used, we list the largest empty orthogonal

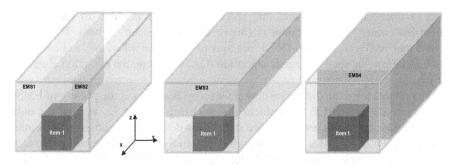

Fig. 2. Empty maximal spaces

spaces (that are not inscribed by any other space) available for packing. This concept is used in many recent studies [22–24]. Each empty maximal space is represented by a pair of their vertices with minimum and maximum coordinates: deepest bottom left vertex and highest top right vertex. Figure 2 shows four empty maximal spaces in a container where item1 is placed in the middle front of the container. The difference process introduced by [25] is also used in this work to calculate and update the list of EMSs.

3 Online Packing Heuristic

For the static 3D-CLP, usually, a packing algorithm follows a certain type of heuristic packing strategy. The input of a packing algorithm includes a sequence of packing items (IPS), which can be static or online, and a sequence of loading containers (CLS). The packing algorithm will then convert these sequences into a solution, where each item is assigned an exact position and an exact orientation inside a container. Depending on the type of 3D-CLP and the priority of selection of items and positions, one of many available packing heuristics can be used, such as First Fit Decreasing Algorithm (FFDA), Best-Fit Decreasing Algorithm (BFDA) [26], Bottom-Left-Fill, Bottom-Left-Back-Fill [27], etc.

[28] introduced a packing strategy called Deepest-Bottom-Left with Fill heuristic (DBLF). This heuristic has gained its popularity in various works e.g. [8, 28, 29]. This heuristic always searches for a space with the minimal x (deepest) coordinate to place the current item. And it uses z (bottom) and y (left) coordinates as tie breakers. This heuristic is also used and modified in [30]. [17] showed two drawbacks of DBLF: First, only one coordinate (x) plays the dominant role in choosing the candidate space; second, only one of the two factors: the item or the space, is determined. The other factor is then selected based on certain priority rules. This results in a potential loss of good combinations that may lead to better solutions (i.e. a solution with a smaller wasted space); In [17], authors proposed a new packing heuristic called Best Match First Packing Heuristic (BMF). In this heuristic, EMSs are sorted in order of smallest coordinate values of the vertices to the deepest-bottom-left point of the container (with coordinates $(x, y, z) = (0, 0, 0)$). Then BMF searches for the best combination

(space-box-orientation), in which the space as close as possible to the deepest-bottom-left corner of the container is chosen to place the current item. The authors showed that BMF outperforms DBLF in terms of utilization when they are combined with a metaheuristic such as genetic algorithm (GA) or differential evolution algorithm (DE).

We find that the main difference between the two heuristics is the priority of EMSs, but in both BMF and DBLF, the problem of items being blocked, i.e. an item cannot be loaded through the container's entrance door to its designated locations due to other existing items blocking its way, is not considered. In Subsect. 3.1 we will propose an online packing heuristic (OnlineBPH) for the online 3D-BPP. The OnlineBPH is inspired from the Deepest-Bottom-Left order in DBLF and the idea of choosing the best combination (space-item-orientation) in BMF. In this new algorithm also we implemented an improvement in space selection to avoid the problem of item being blocked, so that the loading solution provide by packing heuristics can be more realistic and implementable in the real-world.

3.1   Empty Maximal Space Selection

For two EMSs in the same container, we first compare their deepest (the x-value) coordinate values of the two vertices, while the EMS with the smaller value is given higher priority. If they are at the same deep level, we compare the bottom (the z-value) coordinate values and assign the higher priority to the EMS with the smaller one. If the two values are still the same, we compare the y-values. Furthermore, the heuristic always check if the item can be loaded from the door of the container or not by checking the x-value of the selected EMS. The reason behind this is to avoid the blocking problem, where an item can be fit in the space, but the loading process is unfeasible. When the deepest-bottom-left space is selected for an item, but the length dimension of this EMS does not extend to the entrance of the container, then other loaded items can block its loading ways. For example, in Fig. 3 if the items are loaded in order item1, item2, item3 then item4, then after item2 is loaded, item 3 cannot be placed in the assigned space, because item 2 has blocked its way.

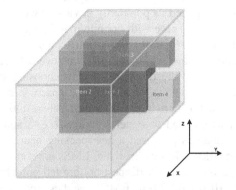

Fig. 3. Blocking problem in loading process

3.2   Placement Selection

OnlineBPH also inherits two parameters Kb and Ke from [17] but in different manner: to determine the placement assignment, for Kb items (if items are arriving one by one then $Kb = 1$) and the first Ke EMSs in the each opened container, the heuristic finds all the feasible placement assignments with allowed rotations of the items. When one item has several feasible placements in a free EMS, the one that has the smallest margin (from the faces of item to the faces of EMS) is selected. The triad (item, rotation, ems) pair with the largest fill ratio is chosen.

The three main differences between our online packing heuristic (OnlineBPH) and BMF are: (1) BMF has information about all items while OnlineBPH only has information about the limited number of items that have arrived. (2) BMF will place an item in the *first opened container (bin)* that it has found a suitable space; while OnlineBPH considers all combinations of (bin, item, ems, and rotation) in *all opened containers* first before deciding which one is the best. (3) the OnlineBPH always check either the item can be loaded from the door of the container or not by checking the x-value of the selected EMS.

3.3   Pseudo-code of OnlineBPH

Pseudo-code of OnlineBPH is described in Fig. 4. At each step OnlineBPH decides packing information of one item in sequence (item will be packed in which container, at which position and in which orientation). For this, there are two phases to determine a placement of one item. First, the algorithm considers all opened containers and the information about the first Ke empty maximal spaces in *EMSs* list of each opened container, and look ahead Kb item in online *IPS* Then it selects the best tetrad of (*container, item, orientation, ems*) to pack an item. If there are no feasible tetrad, the second phase is triggered to open a new suitable container for the item. *FindNewSuitableContainer* returns the container that can fit the item with the largest fill ratio. In the case of identical containers, the next empty container in *CLS* is chosen. Note that the initial EMS of a container cover its whole space, so containers with different dimensions will have initial EMSs with different sizes.

4   Experiments

4.1   Benchmark Problems

Due to the lack of proper data for online 3D-CLP, we follow the approach described in [31] to generate test problems for the case of identical container packing problems. We generated 4 classes (I, II, III and IV) of instances. For classes I, II and III, specific distributions are chosen (Table 2), where l_j, w_j and h_j are length, with and height of j-th generated item, whereas L, W, H are respectively length, with and height of the identical containers.

Input: An online item packing sequence *IPS* and a container loading sequence *CLS*;

Output: *Packing solution PS for IPS* or **null** if not found;

1.	Let *OC* be the *list of opened containers*;
2.	$OC \leftarrow \emptyset$; $PS \leftarrow \emptyset$;
3.	**while** *items are arriving* or *IPS* $\neq$ *null* **do**
4.	Let *P* be a queue of candidate placements;
5.	$Kb \leftarrow$ *numbers of arrived items*;
6.	Update *IPS*;
7.	*itemplaced* $\leftarrow$ 0;
	// *Phase 1: try to put an item to an opened container at the DBL ems;*
8.	**for each** $c \in OC$ **do**
9.	Let *EMSc* be *the sorted list of the ems of container c* in the
10.	*deepest-bottom-left-first* order
11.	$j \leftarrow 0$;
12.	**while** $j < Ke$ **and** $j < EMSc.size$ **do**
13.	**for** $i \leftarrow$ 0 **to** Kb **do**
14.	**for each** *allowed rotation io of item i* **do**
15.	**if** *IPS[i] can be placed* in *EMSc[j]* with *io* and is *not blocked by others* **then**
16.	add this placement combination to *P*;
17.	$j = j + 1$;
18.	**if** $P \neq \emptyset$ **then**
19.	add the placement indicted by *P*[0] to *PS*;
20.	update *IPS* and *EMS* lists;
21.	*itemplaced* $\leftarrow$ 1;
	// *Phase 2: Open a new container to load current item to its DBL corner;*
22.	**if** *itemplaced* = 0 **then**
23.	$c = FindNewSuitableContainer(CLS, i)$;
24.	**if** $c \neq null$ **then**
25.	*EMSc* be the initial *empty maximal spaces* in *c*;
26.	**for each** *allowed rotation io* **do**
27.	**if** *IPS[i] can be placed in EMSc* with orientation *io* **then**
28.	add this placement combination to *P*;
29.	**if** $P \neq \emptyset$ **then**
30.	move *c* from *CLS* to *OC*;
31.	add the placement indicted by *P*[0] to *PS*;
32.	update *IPS* and *EMS* lists;
33.	*itemplaced* $\leftarrow$ 1;
34.	**if** *itemplaced* = 0 **then**
35.	**return** *null*;
36.	**return** *Packing solution PS*;

Fig. 4. Pseudo-code of packing heuristic for Online 3D-CLP

For class IV, the following four types (types 1, 2, 3, and type 4) of uniformly distribution are defined in the terms of the length L, width W and height H of the containers (Table 1). To generate class IV, instances of type 1 are selected with probability 70%, instances of types 2, 3, 4 are selected with probability 10% each.

To evaluate the performance of algorithms, we classified instances into groups in terms of the problems sizes (number of items): small (less than 50 items), medium (from 50 up to 200 items), or large (more than 200 items). For classes I, II, and III, we generated for each class 5 datasets of instances in sizes of 20, 40 (small), 60, 80 (medium) and 1000 items (large). For class IV, we generated 2 datasets of small size (40 items) and large size (1000 items). In each dataset, there are 100 instances generated. Table 2 shows the classes of test problems.

Table 1. Type of random items in instances

Type of uniformly distribution in dimensions of items	l_j	w_j	h_j
Type 1	$\left[1, \frac{1}{3}L\right]$;	$\left[\frac{2}{3}W, W\right]$;	$\left[1, \frac{1}{2}H\right]$;
Type 2	$\left[\frac{1}{2}L, L\right]$;	$\left[1, \frac{1}{2}W\right]$;	$\left[\frac{2}{3}H, H\right]$;
Type 3	$\left[1, \frac{1}{2}L\right]$;	$\left[\frac{1}{2}W, W\right]$;	$\left[\frac{1}{2}H, H\right]$;
Type 4	$\left[\frac{2}{3}L, L\right]$;	$\left[1, \frac{1}{2}W\right]$;	$\left[1, \frac{1}{2}H\right]$;

Table 2. Classes of test problems

Data set No.	Category	Sizes of containers (L*W*H)	No. of items	No. of instances	Item sizes (l*w*h)
I_20	Small	30*30*30	20	100	Uniformly random in [1, 10]
I_40	Small	30*30*30	40	100	Uniformly random in [1, 10]
I_60	Medium	30*30*30	60	100	Uniformly random in [1,10]
I_80	Medium	30*30*30	80	100	Uniformly random in [1,10]
I_1000	Large	30*30*30	1000	100	Uniformly random in [1,10]
II_20	Small	100*100*100	20	100	Uniformly random in [1,35]
II_40	Small	100*100*100	40	100	Uniformly random in [1,35]
II_60	Medium	100*100*100	60	100	Uniformly random in [1,35]
II_80	Medium	100*100*100	80	100	Uniformly random in [1,35]

(continued)

Table 2. (*continued*)

Data set No.	Category	Sizes of containers (L*W*H)	No. of items	No. of instances	Item sizes (l*w*h)
II_1000	Large	100*100*100	1000	100	Uniformly random in [1,35]
III_20	Small	100*100*100	20	100	Uniformly random in [1,100]
III_40	Small	100*100*100	40	100	Uniformly random in [1,100]
III_60	Medium	100*100*100	60	100	Uniformly random in [1,100]
III_80	Medium	100*100*100	80	100	Uniformly random in [1,100]
III_1000	Large	100*100*100	1000	100	Uniformly random in [1,100]
IV_40	Small	100*100*100	40	100	Probability 70% of type 1, probability 10% of each types 2, 3, 4
IV_1000	Large	100*100*100	1000	100	Probability 70% of type 1, probability 10% of each types 2, 3, 4

4.2 Computational Results

All the proposed approach and algorithms have been coded in C and executed on a system with the following configuration: Intel® Core™ i5-4590 CPU @(3.30 Ghz, 3.30 Ghz) with 8.00 GB RAM, Windows 7 Enterprise 64-bit.

Tables 3 and 4 show the average results of OnlineBPH on 100 generated instances for each dataset. We tested the proposed algorithm for both cases of fixed orientation and free (6-ways) orientation of items. To evaluate efficiency of the approach, we selected different combination of parameters Kb and Ke.

Let S be the number of tetrads (*container, item, orientation, ems*), obviously, S is proportional to $Kb * Ke * OC$ *size* $*$ *number of allowed orientations of item*. For $Kb = 3$, $Ke = 3$ or $Ke = 5$, the value of S is larger than in the case where $Kb = 1$ or $Ke = 1$. As shown in Tables 3 and 4, in the case of fixed orientation when $Kb = 3$ and $Ke = 3$ the algorithm gives better results, but in the case of six way orientations, with $Kb = 1$ and $Ke = 1$, the algorithm is more efficient both in utilization and computational time.

To compare the performance of OnlineBPH, we implemented three other algorithms from the literature:

- The online packing algorithm in [31] (Algorithm 1), this online heuristic is based on a layer-building approach;
- Algorithm864, proposed in [19] - a static approximation packing heuristic - where items are sorted by non-increasing volume. In this work the concept of corner points

Table 3. OnlineBPH performance in case of fixed orientation of items

Data set No.	Total No. of items	Sizes of containers (L*W*H)	(Kb = 1; Ke = 1)			(Kb = 1; Ke = 3)			(Kb = 3; Ke = 3)			(Kb = 3; Ke = 5)		
			Avg. No of bins	Avg. Util.	Running times	Avg. No of bins	Avg. Util.	Running times (s)	Avg. No of bins	Avg. Util.	Running times	Avg. No of bins	Avg. Util.	Running times (s)
I_20	20	30*30*30	1	12.69%	0.002	1	12.69%	0.0017	1	12.69%	0.0015	1	12.69%	0.0014
I_40	40	30*30*30	1	24.49%	0.011	1	24.49%	0.0103	1	24.49%	0.0097	1	24.49%	0.0095
I_60	60	30*30*30	1	37.14%	0.02	1	37.14%	0.0191	1	37.14%	0.0209	1	37.14%	0.0202
I_80	80	30*30*30	1.03	48.61%	0.03	1.03	48.61%	0.0295	1.02	48.96%	0.0308	1.01	49.24%	0.031
I_1000	1000	30*30*30	8.09	76.53%	0.28	8.12	76.26%	0.2785	8.05	76.89%	0.3059	8.13	76.17%	0.2988
II_20	20	100*100*100	1	11.72%	0.003	1	11.72%	0.0033	1	11.72%	0.003	1	11.72%	0.0026
II_40	40	100*100*100	1	23.51%	0.022	1	23.51%	0.0231	1	23.51%	0.024	1	23.51%	0.0233
II_60	60	100*100*100	1.01	34.34%	0.05	1	34.55%	0.0508	1	34.55%	0.0571	1.01	34.34%	0.058
II_80	80	100*100*100	1.03	45.73%	0.079	1	46.65%	0.1049	1.04	45.55%	0.0848	1.1	43.94%	0.0862
II_1000	1000	100*100*100	9.51	61.91%	1.051	9.65	61.12%	1.0277	8.88	66.22%	1.107	9.14	64.30%	1.1053
III_20	20	100*100*100	5.32	47.36%	0.001	5.48	45.95%	0.0002	5.28	47.83%	0.0003	5.27	47.92%	0.0003
III_40	40	100*100*100	9.54	53.26%	0.001	9.59	52.87%	0.001	9.51	53.44%	0.0011	9.53	53.27%	0.0011
III_60	60	100*100*100	13.56	57.17%	0.002	13.68	56.65%	0.002	13.52	57.30%	0.0021	13.59	57.00%	0.002
III_80	80	100*100*100	17.23	59.15%	0.003	17.39	58.57%	0.0023	17.25	59.07%	0.0029	17.29	58.97%	0.0028
III_1000	1000	100*100*100	173.6	74.40%	0.072	173.8	74.32%	0.0717	174.1	74.16%	0.1404	175	73.81%	0.1481
IV_40	40	100*100*100	2.61	54.34%	0.009	2.6	54.51%	0.0091	2.46	57.73%	0.0087	2.49	57.03%	0.0088
IV_1000	1000	100*100*100	44.74	76.17%	0.345	44.61	76.39%	0.3214	44.55	76.50%	0.4287	44.44	76.69%	0.414

Table 4. OnlineBPH performance in case of free (six ways) orientations of items

Data set No.	Total No. of items	Sizes of containers (L*W*H)	(Kb = 1; Ke = 1)			(Kb = 1; Ke = 3)			(Kb = 3; Ke = 3)			(Kb = 3; Ke = 5)		
			Avg. No of bins	Avg. Utl.	Running times (s)	Avg. No of bins	Avg. Utl.	Running times (s)	Avg. No of bins	Avg. Utl.	Running times (s)	Avg. No of bins	Avg. Utl.	Running times (s)
I_20	20	30*30*30	1	12.69%	0.001	1	12.69%	0.002	1	12.69%	0.001	1	12.69%	0.001
I_40	40	30*30*30	1	24.49%	0.009	1	24.49%	0.009	1	24.49%	0.009	1	24.49%	0.008
I_60	60	30*30*30	1	37.14%	0.021	1	37.14%	0.02	1	37.14%	0.02	1	37.14%	0.02
I_80	80	30*30*30	1	49.55%	0.033	1	49.55%	0.032	1	49.55%	0.036	1	49.55%	0.034
I_1000	1000	30*30*30	7.26	85.42%	0.328	7.33	84.63%	0.335	7.25	85.53%	0.382	7.41	83.75%	0.378
II_20	20	100*100*100	1	11.72%	0.003	1	11.72%	0.003	1	11.72%	0.003	1	11.72%	0.003
II_40	40	100*100*100	1	23.51%	0.023	1	23.51%	0.026	1	23.51%	0.023	1	23.51%	0.023
II_60	60	100*100*100	1	34.55%	0.061	1	34.55%	0.063	1	34.55%	0.066	1	34.55%	0.063
II_80	80	100*100*100	1.01	46.38%	0.103	1	46.65%	0.105	1.04	45.64%	0.115	1.03	45.91%	0.113
II_1000	1000	100*100*100	10.23	57.91%	1.334	10	58.99%	1.372	10.01	59.08%	1.693	9.87	59.88%	1.636
III_20	20	100*100*100	4.5	56.59%	0.001	4.64	54.64%	4E-04	4.56	55.50%	0.001	4.61	54.96%	6E-04
III_40	40	100*100*100	8.09	63.02%	0.002	8.26	61.68%	0.002	8.26	61.68%	0.002	8.3	61.39%	0.002
III_60	60	100*100*100	11.8	65.77%	0.003	11.9	65.31%	0.003	11.91	65.14%	0.005	12.05	64.46%	0.004
III_80	80	100*100*100	15.06	67.79%	0.005	15.2	67.21%	0.005	15.35	66.54%	0.007	15.37	66.40%	0.007
III_1000	1000	100*100*100	159.9	80.75%	0.227	161	80.39%	0.241	161.66	79.89%	0.604	162.6	79.40%	0.64
IV_40	40	100*100*100	2.54	55.89%	0.009	2.7	52.68%	0.008	2.71	52.43%	0.007	2.99	47.06%	0.006
IV_1000	1000	100*100*100	42.55	80.10%	0.341	44.2	77.06%	0.333	46.23	73.73%	0.679	52	65.57%	0.645

and a branch & bound procedure are employed to verify whether a set of boxes can be placed into a container. The algorithm also assumes that unlimited identical bins are given.

- A static metaheuristic approach (DE+BMF), introduced in [17] - a differential evolution algorithm (DE) with the Best-Match-First Packing heuristic (BMF). As shown by the authors, this is one of the best combinations of a metaheuristic and a packing heuristic for static 3D container loading problem so far.

Firstly, we tested OnlineBPH and Algorithm1 for all instances in an online manner. Then when all information about instances is gathered, the Algorithm864 and DE+BMF is applied to the test cases in an offline (static) manner. The parameters of DE are set as follows: G = 200; Np = 80; F = 0.85; Cr = 0.5; the parameters of BMF Kb = 3; Ke = 3 (as recommended by the authors). The results for 17 classes of instances are showed in Table 5. For each dataset (each has 100 instances), if an algorithm cannot solve more than 20 out of 100 instances then the algorithm is given N/A, i.e. no score. If an algorithm takes more than averagely 3600 s (1 h) per instance, it is also given N/A. If an algorithm can solve more than 20 instances but not all 100 instances, the average value of utilization, number of used bins and average time is calculated for the solved cases only, and the scores are given in italic font.

From Table 5 we observe that in terms of computational time the Algorithm1 is the fastest, closely followed by OnlineBPH and the static Algorithm864. The static DE+BMF is significantly slower than the other three in magnitudes of thousands to hundreds of thousands. The static DE+BMF also takes more than 3600 s to solve the large instances with 1000 items (hence the N/A).

In the terms of solution quality (utilization or number of used bins), OnlineBPH and static DE+BMF achieved the best scores for problems of classes I and II (although DE+BMF failed to solve the largest cases with 1000 items). In problems of classes III and IV, DE+BMF is slightly better than OnlineBPH but again it failed in the largest cases while OnlineBPH still succeeded. Online Algorithm 1 performed the worst in terms of solution quality. Static Algorithm864 is bettern than online Algorithm 1, but it struggled to solve all the 100 instances in most datasets, failed to find solutions in some datasets, and its scores are generally worse than that of OnlineBPH and static DE+BMF.

Overall OnlineBPH seems to be the most well-rounded taking into account both computational time and solution quality. It is generally the second-best in both categories and its scores are not far off the best scores and in many cases match the best scores. It is interesting to see that although it is expected that an optimal online solution cannot be as good as an optimal static/offline solution, OnlineBPH is actually just slightly worse than the best available static solutions (provided by DE+BMF). OnlineBPH's solutions are even better than the static solutions found by Algorithm864.

Here we will try to analyse the reason for the good/bad performance of the algorithms. OnlineBPH is fast because it is an online algorithm, being able to consider just one item at a time. OnlineBPH can produce solutions with good quality because (1) it considers all available containers and choose the most suitable for the current item; and (2) it utilize the EMS concept effectively by taking into account all feasible placements with all possible rotations.

Table 5. A comparison of dynamic Algorithm1, dynamic OnlineBPH, static Algorithm864 and static DE+BMF (N/A means no score due to less than 20 over 100 instances solved, or due to solving time greater than 3600 s)

Data set No.	Total No. of items	Sizes of containers (L*W*H)	Online Algorithm 1 [31]			OnlineBPH (free rotation)			Static Algorithm864 [19]			Static DE+BMF [17]		
			Avg. No of bins	Avg. Util.	times (s)	Avg. No of bins	Avg. Util.	times (s)	Avg. No of bins	Avg. Util.	times (s)	Avg. No of bins	Avg. Util.	times (s)
I_20	20	30*30*30	1	12.69%	0.001	1	12.69%	0.0014	1	12.69%	0.001	1	12.69%	8.3
I_40	40	30*30*30	1.04	23.93%	0.001	1	24.49%	0.0091	1	24.49%	0.001	1	24.49%	45.73
I_60	60	30*30*30	1.99	18.72%	0.001	1	37.14%	0.021	1	N/A	0.001	1	37.14%	106.7
I_80	80	30*30*30	2	24.77%	0.001	1	49.55%	0.033	N/A	N/A	N/A	1	49.55%	238.7
I_1000	1000	30*30*30	21.77	28.43%	0.001	7.26	85.42%	0.328	N/A	N/A	N/A	N/A	N/A	N/A
II_20	20	100*100*100	1	11.72%	0.001	1	11.72%	0.003	1	11.72%	0.001	1	11.72%	13.66
II_40	40	100*100*100	1.37	18.90%	0.001	1	23.51%	0.023	1	N/A	0.001	1	23.51%	100.6
II_60	60	100*100*100	2.02	17.13%	0.001	1	34.55%	0.061	1	N/A	0.002	1	34.55%	303.7
II_80	80	100*100*100	2.38	20.21%	0.001	1	46.65%	0.105	N/A	N/A	N/A	1	46.65%	478.7
II_1000	1000	100*100*100	25.23	23.18%	0.001	9.87	59.88%	1.636	N/A	N/A	N/A	N/A	N/A	N/A
III_20	20	100*100*100	8	31.40%	0.001	4.5	56.59%	0.001	5.354	47.00%	0.005	3.94	64.81%	5.69
III_40	40	100*100*100	15.87	31.90%	0.001	8.09	63.02%	0.002	9.522	54.71%	0.005	7.2	71.09%	16.45
III_60	60	100*100*100	23.83	32.45%	0.001	11.8	65.77%	0.003	13.28	58.94%	0.005	10.45	73.94%	30.05
III_80	80	100*100*100	31.24	32.53%	0.001	15.06	67.79%	0.005	16.57	61.50%	0.006	13.53	75.39%	44.26
III_1000	1000	100*100*100	395.08	32.67%	0.001	159.9	80.75%	0.227	162.5	79.48%	1.076	N/A	N/A	N/A
IV_40	40	100*100*100	3.76	37.28%	0.001	2.54	55.89%	0.009	3.103	47.53%	0.006	2.14	65.55%	70.06
IV_1000	1000	100*100*100	81.68	41.72%	0.001	42.55	80.10%	0.341	44.32	76.89%	0.485	N/A	N/A	N/A

Algorithm1 is fast because like OnlineBPH it is an online algorithm. Algorithm1 provides solutions with the worst quality because it is over simplified. Its layer-building approach is efficient only in the case of weakly heterogeneous items [6]. This is much less effective than the mechanisms in OnlineBPH, Algorithm864 and DE+BMF. These three compute and consider a much larger number of placement combinations.

In most data sets, Algorithm864 cannot find the solutions for all instances because it does not allow the rotation of items. Due to that, if one of the items' original dimension exceeds the corresponding dimension of the container then algorithm will stop. Algorithm864 also trades the computational quality for computational time to make it fast. That is why a static algorithm like Algorithm864 can still be nearly as fast as online algorithms like Algorithm 1 and OnlineBPH. As a trade-off, the quality of Algorithm864 is worse than OnlineBPH, even that Algorithm864 is a static algorithm.

DE+BMF can provide the best results for the static case because it relies on one of the best packing heuristics, BMF, to pack items into a container, and it relies on an efficient meta-heuristics, DE, to find the optimal sequence of containers. The downside of DE+BMF is that it is very slow. Being a static algorithm it needs to consider all items before making a decision. In addition, the use of a population-based algorithm like DE also slow down the decision making process. The large amount of time needed for DE+BMF to find a solution in the large-scale cases (like the data sets with 1000 items) is simply not realistic in real-world scenarios.

There is also another issue with Algorithm864 and DE+BMF: these algorithm do not check the problem of items being blocked, so their output may not be used directly for real loading process. Our experiments show that the solutions provided by these algorithms can have a large number of blocked items, meaning that not all items can be loaded into the containers in the sequence provided by the algorithms. This situation is mitigated by OnlineBPH because it always check either the item can be loaded from the door of the container first before selecting an EMS. Due to a lack of space we are not able to provide detailed experimental results on this issue, but this will be further investigated and published in a future publication.

In summary, OnlineBPH seems to be able to provide a good balance of time and utilization. Being an online algorithm it is obviously the only choice if items need to be handled/loaded in real-time or if there is no storage areas and/or buffers for incoming items. However, even in situations where items can be handled offline and there are ample storage areas for incoming items, OnlineBPH can still provide a good alternative to current state-of-the-arts static algorithms like DE+BMF. OnlineBPH is significantly faster; its solutions are just slightly less good in the tested cases; and it eliminates the need of having storage areas.

5   Conclusion

This work presented an online packing heuristic to solve the three-dimensional bin packing problem in dynamic environments and in the Physical Internet context. The effectiveness of the online packing heuristic is evaluated on a set of generated data. The experimental results show that the algorithm could solve the 3D container loading problems in an online fashion and is competitive against one of best static algorithms both in the terms of running time, space utilization and number of bins. The algorithm also avoids the problem of blocked item and allows the loading process in the containers to be more realistic.

Acknowledgement. This work is supported by a Newton Institutional Links grant funded by the UK BEIS via the British Council, a Newton Research Collaborations Programme (3) grant funded by the UK BEIS via the Royal Academy of Engineering, and a Seed-corn project funded by the Chartered Institute of Logistics and Transport.

The authors thank anonymous reviews for their suggestions and contributions and corresponding editor for his/her valuable efforts.

References

1. Bui, L.T., Baker, S., Bender, A., Abbass, H.A., Barlow, M., Saker, R.: A grid-based heuristic for two-dimensional packing problems. In: 2011 IEEE Congress on Evolutionary Computation (CEC), pp. 2329–2336 (2011)
2. Martello, S., Pisinger, D., Vigo, D.: The three-dimensional bin packing problem. Oper. Res. **48**, 256–267 (2000)
3. Anily, S., Bramel, J., Simchi-Levi, D.: Worst-case analysis of heuristics for the bin packing problem with general cost structures. Oper. Res. **42**, 287–298 (1994)
4. Scheithauer, G.: Algorithms for the container loading problem. In: Gaul, W., et al. (eds.) Operations Research Proceedings 1991, pp. 445–452. Springer, Heidelberg (1992)
5. Bortfeldt, A., Wäscher, G.: Constraints in container loading–a state-of-the-art review. Eur. J. Oper. Res. **229**, 1–20 (2013)
6. Zhao, X., Bennell, J.A., Bektaş, T., Dowsland, K.: A comparative review of 3D container loading algorithms. Int. Trans. Oper. Res. **23**, 287–320 (2016)
7. Junqueira, L., Morabito, R., Yamashita, D.S.: Three-dimensional container loading models with cargo stability and load bearing constraints. Comput. Oper. Res. **39**, 74–85 (2012)
8. Moon, I., Nguyen, T.V.L.: Container packing problem with balance constraints. OR Spectr. **36**, 837–878 (2014)
9. Liu, D.S., Tan, K.C., Huang, S.Y., Goh, C.K., Ho, W.K.: On solving multiobjective bin packing problems using evolutionary particle swarm optimization. Eur. J. Oper. Res. **190**, 357–382 (2008)
10. Montreuil, B.: Toward a Physical Internet: meeting the global logistics sustainability grand challenge. Logistics Res. **3**, 71–87 (2011)
11. ALICE, Global Supply Network Coordination and Collaboration research & innovation roadmap. ALICE - Alliance for Logistics Innovation through Collaboration in Europe (2014)
12. Nguyen, T.T., Yang, S., Branke, J.: Evolutionary dynamic optimization: a survey of the state of the art. Swarm Evol. Comput. **6**, 1–24 (2012)
13. Berndt, S., Jansen, K., Klein, K.-M.: Fully dynamic bin packing revisited, arXiv preprint arXiv:1411.0960 (2014)
14. Coffman, J., Edward, G., Garey, M.R., Johnson, D.S.: Dynamic bin packing. SIAM J. Comput. **12**, 227–258 (1983)
15. Epstein, L., Levy, M.: Dynamic multi-dimensional bin packing. J. Discrete Algorithms **8**, 356–372 (2010)
16. Feng, X., Moon, I., Shin, J.: Hybrid genetic algorithms for the three-dimensional multiple container packing problem. Flex. Serv. Manuf. J. **27**, 451–477 (2015)

17. Li, X., Zhang, K.: A hybrid differential evolution algorithm for multiple container loading problem with heterogeneous containers. Comput. Ind. Eng. **90**, 305–313 (2015)
18. Lodi, A., Martello, S., Vigo, D.: Heuristic algorithms for the three-dimensional bin packing problem. Eur. J. Oper. Res. **141**, 410–420 (2002)
19. Martello, S., Pisinger, D., Vigo, D., Boef, E.D., Korst, J.: Algorithm 864: general and robot-packable variants of the three-dimensional bin packing problem. ACM Trans. Math. Softw. (TOMS) **33**, 7 (2007)
20. Baldi, M.M., Crainic, T.G., Perboli, G., Tadei, R.: The generalized bin packing problem. Transp. Res. Part E Logistics Transp. Rev. **48**, 1205–1220 (2012)
21. Crainic, T.G., Perboli, G., Tadei, R.: Extreme point-based heuristics for three-dimensional bin packing. Informs J. Comput. **20**, 368–384 (2008)
22. Parreño, F., Alvarez-Valdés, R., Oliveira, J., Tamarit, J.M.: A hybrid GRASP/VND algorithm for two-and three-dimensional bin packing. Ann. Oper. Res. **179**, 203–220 (2010)
23. Gonçalves, J.F., Resende, M.G.: A biased random key genetic algorithm for 2D and 3D bin packing problems. Int. J. Prod. Econ. **145**, 500–510 (2013)
24. Gonçalves, J.F., Resende, M.G.C.: A parallel multi-population biased random-key genetic algorithm for a container loading problem. Comput. Oper. Res. **39**, 179–190 (2012)
25. Lai, K., Chan, J.W.: Developing a simulated annealing algorithm for the cutting stock problem. Comput. Ind. Eng. **32**, 115–127 (1997)
26. Christensen, S.G., Rousøe, D.M.: Container loading with multi-drop constraints. Int. Trans. Oper. Res. **16**, 727–743 (2009)
27. Tiwari, S., Fadel, G., Fenyes, P.: A fast and efficient compact packing algorithm for free-form objects. In: ASME 2008 International Design Engineering Technical Conferences and Computers and Information in Engineering Conference, pp. 543–552 (2008)
28. Karabulut, K., İnceoğlu, M.M.: A hybrid genetic algorithm for packing in 3d with deepest bottom left with fill method. In: International Conference on Advances in Information Systems, pp. 441–450 (2004)
29. Kang, K., Moon, I., Wang, H.: A hybrid genetic algorithm with a new packing strategy for the three-dimensional bin packing problem. Appl. Math. Comput. **219**, 1287–1299 (2012)
30. Wang, H., Chen, Y.: A hybrid genetic algorithm for 3d bin packing problems. In: 2010 IEEE Fifth International Conference on Bio-Inspired Computing: Theories and Applications (BIC-TA), pp. 703–707 (2010)
31. Wang, R., Nguyen, T.T., Kavakeb, S., Yang, Z., Li, C.: Benchmarking Dynamic Three-Dimensional Bin Packing Problems Using Discrete-Event Simulation. In: Squillero, G., Burelli, P. (eds.) EvoApplications 2016. LNCS, vol. 9598, pp. 266–279. Springer, Heidelberg (2016). doi:10.1007/978-3-319-31153-1_18

Advancing Dynamic Evolutionary Optimization Using In-Memory Database Technology

Julia Jordan[1,2], Wei Cheng[3], and Bernd Scheuermann[1(✉)]

[1] Hochschule Karlsruhe, University of Applied Sciences, Karlsruhe, Germany
`bernd.scheuermann@hs-karlsruhe.de`
[2] CAS Software AG, Karlsruhe, Germany
[3] SAP Innovation Center Network, Potsdam, Germany

Abstract. This paper reports on IMDEA (In-Memory database Dynamic Evolutionary Algorithm), an approach to dynamic evolutionary optimization exploiting in-memory database (IMDB) technology to expedite the search process subject to change events arising at runtime. The implemented system benefits from optimization knowledge persisted on an IMDB serving as associative memory to better guide the optimizer through changing environments. For this, specific strategies for knowledge processing, extraction and injection are developed and evaluated. Moreover, prediction methods are embedded and empirical studies outline to which extent these methods are able to anticipate forthcoming dynamic change events by evaluating historical records of previous changes and other optimization knowledge managed by the IMDB.

Keywords: Dynamic evolutionary algorithm · Associative memory · Prediction · In-memory databases

1 Introduction

For decades *Evolutionary Algorithms (EA)* [1] have been established heuristics to tackle NP-hard optimization problems which are inherent to countless industrial applications. Typically, the search for good solutions to such problems can consume up to several hours or even days. The hitherto best solution found, e.g. a production schedule, would then be used for planning and executing operations. In practice, however, several aspects like the objective function, the size of the problem instance or constraints may be subject to changes. In such *dynamic optimization* scenarios, it is essential that every relevant change of the optimization problem is taken into account. However, calculation time is commonly restricted and usually one cannot afford to restart optimization from scratch. Instead it is often advisable to exploit existing optimization knowledge from the running optimization to quickly react to and to recover from dynamic changes arriving.

This paper reports on the implementation and on the empirical evaluation of *IMDEA (In-Memory database Dynamic Evolutionary Algorithm)*, a dynamic

© Springer International Publishing AG 2017
G. Squillero and K. Sim (Eds.): EvoApplications 2017, Part II, LNCS 10200, pp. 156–172, 2017.
DOI: 10.1007/978-3-319-55792-2_11

EA which interfaces with an in-memory database (IMDB) [2] and exploits its strengths to expedite the search process in dynamically changing environments. It is shown, how in-memory databases can be used as a large capacity knowledge store that embodies a persistent associative memory to the optimization algorithm. Such knowledge includes, e.g. historical logs of visited search areas, environmental data, and recorded change events. In contrast to previous work, where a memory is usually implemented by storing knowledge in data objects inside the EA, it is examined to which extent in-memory database technology can help increase and manage the amount of stored knowledge in order to better guide the optimization process. Furthermore, the database is employed as a storage for predictive knowledge that is accessed and analyzed to make the optimizer better prepared for prospected changes, to quickly respond to such changes and to easier recover from their impact.

The remainder of the paper is structured as follows: Sect. 2 introduces to dynamic evolutionary computing. Section 3 briefly reviews related work and outlines how IMDEA contributes to progress beyond. Section 4 describes the architecture and the methods of the system implemented. Subsequently, a sample of results from extensive experiments are presented in Sect. 5. Concluding remarks are provided in Sect. 6.

2   Dynamic Evolutionary Optimization

Prior to introducing the EA, the static Knapsack Problem shall be defined and henceforth be used to exemplify the strategies proposed in this paper. In its static variant, the 0/1 Knapsack Problem [3] is described by a set of n items of weight w_j and value v_j where $j \in \{1, \ldots, n\}$. A candidate solution $X = (x_1, \ldots, x_n)$ represents a subset of all items, with $x_j \in \{0, 1\}$ indicating if item j is included in the knapsack which has a capacity of C. The goal is to maximize the total value of items included in the knapsack such that the sum of their weights is less or equal to the knapsack capacity: Maximize

$$f(X) = \sum_{j=1}^{n} v_j x_j \text{ subject to } \sum_{j=1}^{n} w_j x_j \leq C, x_j \in \{0, 1\}. \qquad (1)$$

As the Knapsack Problem is known to be $NP - hard$, EA [1] are one possible heuristic to search for near optimal solutions. Inspired by the principles of natural evolution, the main idea behind evolutionary optimization is to represent solutions of an optimization problem as a set of individuals called population. The size of the population shall be denoted as p. An individual $i \in \{1, \ldots, p\}$ is encoded in a chromosome X_i representing the individual's genotype. In the case of the Knapsack Problem, individual i is encoded as n-bit chromosome $X_i = (x_{i,1}, \ldots x_{i,n})$ with $x_{i,j} \in \{0, 1\}$, where $x_{i,j} = 1$ means that item number j is contained in the knapsack of individual i, and $x_{i,j} = 0$ otherwise. The *dynamic* Knapsack Problem introduces time-dependent variance: capacity $C(t)$, weights $w_j(t)$ and values $v_j(t)$ are considered dynamic over time t.

The goal of an EA is to incrementally improve the *fitness* of the best individual, which represents its solution quality, by mimicking the principles of natural selection, recombination, mutation and survival of the fittest (cf. [1] for more details). Overweight individuals are invalid but in dynamic problems it is more advisable to reduce their fitness by a penalty cost term than considering them as completely unsuitable, since a change event could lead an invalid solution to become valid or even the best. Hence, IMDEA calculates the fitness of individual i with genotype $X_i(t)$ as

$$fit\left(X_i(t)\right) = \sum_{j=1}^{n} \left(v_j(t)x_{ji}(t)\right) \cdot \left(1 - \max\left\{0; \frac{\sum_{j=1}^{n}\left(w_j(t)x_{ji}(t)\right)}{C(t)} - 1\right\}^{\lambda}\right) \quad (2)$$

with external parameter λ representing the penalty weight.

For dynamic optimization the goal is not to localize a global stationary optimum but to track moving optima [4]. It is assumed that the problem instances before and after a change are related to each other, thus reusing prior optimization knowledge is more beneficial than a restart [5]. If prior solutions are intended to be reused, good individuals will have to be stored in a so-called *direct* memory. A memory that additionally stores information on the corresponding problem instance is called *associative* memory [6,7]. It allows to reuse individuals that had been successful under similar circumstances. Predictive analysis can be used for tracking optima by calculating the prospected path of an optimum through the solution space or by anticipating the nature of the next change [8,9]. A successful dynamic EA should include a *memory* and a *predictive* component and it should maintain *diversity* throughout the run because a diverse population can better react to a change than a converged one [4].

3   Related Work and Progress Beyond

Related work started with early contributions by Fogel et al. [10] and Goldberg [1]. A recent state of the art survey by Nguyen et al. [4] summarizes papers on evolutionary dynamic optimization of the past 20 years, benchmark generators and performance measures. Cruz et al. [11] provide a list of about 40 artificial and real world problems as well as papers addressing them.

Hatzakis et al. [12] integrate auto-regression and moving average analysis into a multiobjective EA to forecast optimal regions. Rossi et al. [8] use an EA that learns the movement of the optimum and adjusts the fitness function accordingly to force the population into promising areas of the solution space. Simões and Costa [9,13–15] published several papers on linear and nonlinear regression to predict the generation of the next change. They use *Marcov Chains* to anticipate the nature of the next change and they include a direct memory.

Fitness Sharing [16] is a widely used diversity management technique. Fitness sharing calculates the so-called *shared fitness* for each individual i depending on its distance $d(i, k)$ (e.g. hamming distance) to all other individuals k:

$$fit^*(X_i(t)) = \frac{fit(X_i(t))}{\sum_{k=1}^{p}\left(1 - \min\left\{1; \frac{d(i, k)}{\sigma_s}\right\}^{\alpha}\right)}. \tag{3}$$

Parameter α is a constant which defines the shape of the sharing function and is commonly set to 1 [17]. Further strategies to maintain diversity are, e.g., *Deterministic Crowding Selection* [18] and *Mating Restricted Tournament (MRT)* [19].

Grefenstette et al. [7] published one of the early papers on an associative memory. Branke [5] worked on direct memory and suggests to compute an *importance value* for each individual to decide which individuals to store in the memory. Yang introduced EA with direct [20] and with associative [21,22] memory.

Previous approaches to memory-extended EAs appear to be implemented as data objects within the algorithm. Online analytical processing using IMDB was explored by Plattner [23], however an extensive review of prior work yields that no previous publication on evolutionary computation has ever used database technology as knowledge store. Hence, this paper introduces IMDEA, an approach to dynamic evolutionary optimization exploiting IMDB technology as storage for associative memory and for prediction knowledge.

4 The Dynamic In-Memory Database Evolutionary Algorithm (IMDEA)

4.1 In-Memory Databases

Plattner [2] introduces the characteristics and advantages of IMDB: The rapid decline of prices for RAM storage during the last decade comes along with an increase in chip capacities and expedited access times. IMDBs provide a vast amount of storage capacity to the database residing entirely in main memory. And compared to disc-resident databases, data access times are reduced dramatically. This can also be attributed to flexible table encoding (row-store or column-store), as well as improved data compression and partitioning techniques. Therefore IMDBs suggest themselves as a technology to support dynamic evolutionary computing. This paper proposes to use the IMDB to store and efficiently maintain optimization knowledge in terms of an associative memory and prediction data. The storage volume required depends on (1) the optimization problem instance, (2) the extraction and replacement strategy, and (3) the number of generations executed. A set of preliminary experiments indicates that such storage requirements can easily exceed 1 GB of data, effectively managed by an IMDB. The product chosen for this paper is SAP HANA (High Performance Analytics Appliance) [24], which is the market-leading IMDB [25], and it has shown to excel in many application scenarios [25] with practical relevance. The IMDEA system is implemented in *SAP HANA Extended Application Services* [26], which is the common approach for native HANA applications.

4.2   Architectural Overview

Figure 1 visualizes the architecture of the IMDEA. The core algorithm, based on the dynamic EA approach introduced in Sect. 2, is started reading a set of parameters and the problem definition. Since the problem is considered dynamic, a simulator continuously adapts this problem definition, whereupon the changes are propagated to the core algorithm. A set of individuals is perpetually extracted from the current population and persisted into an associative memory held in an IMDB. Whenever necessary this memory is queried for suitable individuals which are injected into the core algorithm. A predictive analytics component processes the knowledge stored in the IMDB to better prepare the algorithm for forthcoming dynamic changes.

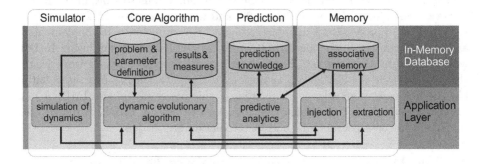

Fig. 1. Architectural overview

4.3   Simulator

For simulating a dynamically changing environment, several approaches are proposed in literature. Simulators like the *Moving Peaks Benchmark* by Branke [5] are not suitable for binary encoded problems like the Knapsack Problem as they assume real-valued search spaces. The *XOR Generator* by Yang et al. [22] is designed for binary encoded problems but creates dynamics by manipulating genotypes. A better approach would be to adjust the problem definition itself. The framework proposed by Li and Yang [27] appears to be an adequate approach and therefore inspired the implementation of the IMDEA simulator. This approach is closer to real world dynamics, avoids manipulating the population and leads to measurable dynamic environments which are crucial for an associative memory that stores environmental information.

The simulator creates environments $e(t)$, which are considered to represent the definition of the optimization problem at time t, where the time is supposed to be the generation number. The environment is constituted by a tuple of problem parameters that are subject to change. In the case of the knapsack problem, the environment $e(t) = (C(t), v(t), w(t))$ shall be signified by the knapsack capacity $C(t)$, its item weights $w(t) = (w_1(t), \ldots, w_n(t))$ and item values

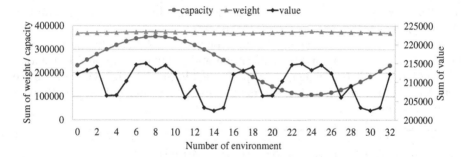

Fig. 2. Sample scenario simulating a dynamic knapsack problem, cycle length $L = 32$.

$v(t) = (v_1(t), \ldots, v_n(t))$. The simulator is implemented to change the environment at a constant frequency of T generations. Furthermore, it is assumed that the environment changes in a cyclic manner at a cycle length of L. Hence any environment will recur every $L \cdot T$ generations. The specific environment sequence used in this paper is visualized in Fig. 2.

4.4 Pseudocode for IMDEA

Listing 1.1 illustrates the IMDEA as pseudocode. The functions concerning memory and prediction are described in Sects. 4.5 and 4.6. After preparing the IMDB for the upcoming optimization and loading the problem definition and several parameters (line 1) the IMDEA initializes all necessary variables (line 2–6). There are population-objects for temporary saving parents, children, individuals from the memory and individuals provided by the predictive component (line 3–4).

The population is initialized (line 7), whereupon the population size is defined by one of the loaded parameters and the IMDEA enters its main while-loop. If a change is predicted for the current generation t, IMDEA will update the population with the individuals provided by the predictive component (line 9). In the first generation this condition is false. Changes are simulated every T generations (line 10) and the fitness of all individuals is evaluated (line 13).

Lines 12–22 are entered every time a change occured: If the accuracy of the predictive component for the current change lies below a threshold, that means that the change was anticipated badly and there is a high possibility that the individuals, which had been provided by the predictive component to prepare the EA for this change, are not suitable for the new environment. Thus the memory will be searched for individuals from a similar environment to update the population (line 13–17). Otherwise no measures will be taken.

Lines 18–21 illustrate the prediction cycle that is run after every change: The new change is saved in the IMDB (line 18). Using this prediction knowledge the IMDEA anticipates the generation of the next change and the expected environment (line 19–20). Afterwards IMDEA searches the associative memory for individuals that had been successful in an environment similar to the expected one (line 21, cf. Sect. 4.6 for more detail). These individuals will be used to update the population before the next change (line 9).

Lines 23–26 execute the standard functions of an EA, namely selection of at least two parents, recombination, mutation and population update. Extraction of good individuals to the memory is performed in line 27 (cf. Sect. 4.5 for more details). Finally the algorithm enters the next generation unless the stopping condition is met.

```
1   initializeIMDB(); env = loadProblem(); par = loadParameters();
2   pop = newPopulation(); fitness = newFitnessArray();
3   parents = newPopulation(); children = newPopulation();
4   memoryPop = newPopulation(); predictionPop = newPopulation();
5   acc = 0.0; predictedGen = −1; predictedEnv = newEnvironment();
6   t = 0;
7   pop = initializePopulation(par.populationSize);
8   while (stopping condition not met)
9       if (t == predictedGen) pop = updatePopulation(predictionPop); endif
10      if ((t mod par.T) == 0) env = simulateChanges(env); endif
11      fitness = evaluateFitness(pop);
12      if (change occured in current generation t)
13          acc = computePredictionAccuracy(env, predictedEnv);
14          if (acc < par.accuracyThreshold)
15              memoryPop = getIndividualsFromMemory(env);
16              pop = updatePopulation(memoryPop);
17          endif
18          saveChangesInPredictionKnowledge(env);
19          predictedGen = predictGenerationOfNextChange();
20          predictedEnv = predictNewEnvironment();
21          predictionPop = getIndividualsFromMemory(predictedEnv);
22      endif
23      parents = selectForReproduction(pop, fitness, par.numberOfParents);
24      children = recombineParents(parents);
25      children = mutateIndividuals(children);
26      pop = updatePopulation(pop, children);
27      if ((t mod par.extractionPeriod) == 0) extraction(pop, fitness); endif
28      t = t + 1;
29  endwhile
```

Listing 1.1. Pseudocode for IMDEA

4.5 Associative Memory

An *associative* memory has the advantage that after a change the EA can reuse individuals that had been successful in a similar environment before. It needs to address four main issues [4]: (1) how to organize the memory, (2) when to *extract* which individuals from the EA to the memory (3) how to *update* the memory and (4) when to *inject* individuals from the memory to the EA (cf. Fig. 1).

WEIGHT				VALUE			
ENVID	WEIGHT001	...	WEIGHT500	ENVID	VALUE001	...	VALUE500
Integer	Double	...	Double	Integer	Double	...	Double
0	533,000	...	852,000	0	276,000	...	103,000
1	599,625	...	852,000	1	299,544	...	103,000
...		...	...	...		...	...

CAPACITY		GENOTYPES				
ENVID	CAPACITY	ENVID	INDIVIDUAL	GENE001	...	GENE500
Integer	Double	Integer	Integer	Integer		Integer
0	231001,0000	0	8	1	...	0
1	255267,3097	0	3	1	...	1
...	...	...	...		...	...

Fig. 3. Database schema of associative memory for knapsack instance with 500 items

The associative memory of IMDEA is organized in column tables on the IMDB. Figure 3 illustrates database schema of the memory for a knapsack instance with $j = 500$ items. The tables are organized according to the problem definition. Table *GENOTYPES* stores good individuals of earlier generations. Each column *GENE-j* ($j = \{001..500\}$) stores one gene x_j, which is 1 if item j is chosen, and 0 otherwise (cf. Eq. 1). The other three tables contain environmental information. Every environment is referenced by an *ENV-ID* in the first column of all tables. Column *WEIGHT-j/VALUE-j* in table *WEIGHT/VALUE* stores weight w_j, or value v_j of item j, respectively. When a change is detected, the IMDEA compares the current environment to the environmental information from the memory. If a suitable environment is found in the memory, good solutions from table *GENOTYPES* are injected into the IMDEA. These solutions had previously been successful in a similar environment. The *similarity* of two environments $e_1 = e(t_1)$ and $e_2 = e(t_2)$ at times t_1 and t_2 is computed as a weighted sum as follows:

$$sim(e_1, e_2) = \eta_c \cdot sim_C(e_1, e_2) + \eta_w \cdot sim_W(e_1, e_2) + \eta_v \cdot sim_V(e_1, e_2) \quad (4)$$

with $\eta_c, \eta_w, \eta_v \in [0,1]$ and $\eta_c + \eta_w + \eta_v = 1$. Similarities sim_C, sim_W and sim_V signify the proportion of capacities ($C(t_1)$ and $C(t_2)$), weights ($w(t_1)$ and $w(t_2)$), and values ($v(t_1)$ and $v(t_2)$), respectively:

$$sim_C(e_1, e_2) = \min\left\{\frac{C(t_1)}{C(t_2)}, \frac{C(t_2)}{C(t_1)}\right\}, \quad (5)$$

$$sim_W(e_1, e_2) = \frac{1}{n} \cdot \sum_{j=1}^{n} \min\left\{\frac{w_j(t_1)}{w_j(t_2)}, \frac{w_j(t_2)}{w_j(t_1)}\right\}, \quad (6)$$

$$sim_V(e_1, e_2) = \frac{1}{n} \cdot \sum_{j=1}^{n} \min\left\{\frac{v_j(t_1)}{v_j(t_2)}, \frac{v_j(t_2)}{v_j(t_1)}\right\}. \quad (7)$$

The min-function normalizes the outcome between 0 and 1. An alternative way to calculate sim_W and sim_V is

$$sim_W\left(e_1, e_2\right) = \frac{1}{n} \cdot \sum_{j=1}^{n} st_W\left(e_1, e_2, j\right) \text{ with} \tag{8}$$

$$st_W\left(e_1, e_2, j\right) = \begin{cases} 1, & \text{if } \min\left\{\dfrac{w_j(t_1)}{w_j(t_2)}, \dfrac{w_j(t_2)}{w_j(t_1)}\right\} \geq \tau_W \\ 0 & \text{otherwise} \end{cases}. \tag{9}$$

The first calculation (6, 7) is more flexible because it does not declare items as dissimilar based on a threshold. The second calculation (8, 9) on the other hand allows for a strict control of the similarity threshold τ_W if required and prevents the commingling of similarities of different items. This paper uses the second calculation because it focuses on the performance of the IMDEA for environments that reappear in exactly the same way.

The *extraction* of good individuals from the population is performed at equally spaced intervals. Copies of the individuals are stored in the IMDB. Yang [20] uses dynamic time patterns for extraction to reduce the risk that extraction and change coincide. As this paper combines an associative memory with predictive analytics, the prediction on change periods can be used to adapt the extraction period accordingly. As recommended by Grefenstette and Ramsey [7] we extract 50% of the population after a change. To decide which individuals to extract the IMDEA calculates an *importance value* based on [5] for each individual i as

$$imp\left(i\right) = \gamma_f \cdot imp_{fit}\left(i\right) + \gamma_d \cdot imp_{div}\left(i\right) + \gamma_a \cdot imp_{age}\left(i\right) \tag{10}$$

with $\gamma \in [0, 1]$ and $\gamma_f + \gamma_d + \gamma_a = 1$. The terms $imp_{fit}\left(i\right)$, $imp_{div}\left(i\right)$ and $imp_{age}\left(i\right)$ express the relative importance of individual i with respect to the fitness, diversity and age of the population. At generation t these importance terms are computed as follows:

$$imp_{fit}\left(i\right) = \frac{fitness\left(i\right)}{\sum_{k=1}^{p} fitness\left(k\right)}, \tag{11}$$

$$imp_{div}\left(i\right) = \frac{\sum_{k=1}^{p} d\left(i, k\right)}{\sum_{h=1}^{p} \sum_{k=1}^{p} d\left(h, k\right)}, \tag{12}$$

$$imp_{age}\left(i\right) = \frac{age\left(i, t\right)}{\sum_{k=1}^{p} age\left(k, t\right)}, \tag{13}$$

where $d\left(h, k\right)$ is the Hamming distance between individuals h and k. The age of an individual i in generation t is $age\left(i, t\right) = 0$ if the individual was created in generation t, and $age\left(i, t - 1\right) + 1$ otherwise. The population is sorted descending by importance and the 50% with the highest importance value are extracted.

If the current environment does not exist in the memory so far, the new environmental information is stored in the in-memory database and the extracted individuals are *inserted* to the memory. The IMDEA checks whether the current environment already exists in the memory by applying Eq. 4. If a similar environment exists in the memory, the extracted individuals will be used to *update* table $GENOTYPES$ (see Fig. 3). In this case the extracted individuals and the memory individuals are merged and Eq. 10 is used to decide which individuals become the new memory individuals.

When the associative memory is called by the IMDEA (i.e. due to a new prediction output or during *injection* after an unpredicted change, cf. Sect. 4.4), the environmental tables in the memory are searched for an environment similar to the new environment based on Eq. 4. If the search is successful, the stored individuals from the memory will replace similar individuals in the population of the EA. Otherwise only immigrants will be generated to increase diversity.

4.6   Change Prediction

The associative memory component interacts with the predictive analytics component. Prediction is triggerd after each change and aims to anticipate the generation and nature of the next change. Therefor *prediction knowledge* on previous changes is stored in the in-memory database (cf. Fig. 1). This paper uses the *Predictive Analysis Library (PAL)* [28]. HANA is organized in two layers [26]. Applications, like the implemented EA, run as part of the *control flow logic*. Interaction with the data is controlled by the *calculation logic*. PAL is part of the calculation logic and is thus very suitable for the IMDEA because the predictive algorithms run close to the data they analyze. Furthermore PAL is well compatible with the HANA IMDB. Its functionality is based on stored procedures. The input data has to be stored in database tables and must be organized in the specific way required by the respective procedure.

PAL comprises functions for statistics, time series analysis, regression, clustering, classification and preprocessing of data [28]. Simões et al. [9] showed the effectiveness of regression for prediction. Therefore this paper uses polynomial regression to predict upcoming changes. Other methods like *forecast smoothing* or *neural networks* are potential candidates for predictive analytics as well but polynomial regression has a slight advantage regarding computation time. Based on the previous changes that are stored in the *prediction knowledge*, the IMDEA calls the stored procedure from PAL for polynomial regression to calculate

- the anticipated generation of the next change,
- which of the parameters C, w_j and v_j are going to change and
- how they will change (cf. Listing 1.1).

PAL stores its output in dedicated database tables from where the results are selected. Based on the output of the predictive analytics component the expected environment can be simulated and the IMDEA searches the associative memory for individuals, which had been successful in an environment similar to the simulated one. If such individuals are found, they remain in a temporary buffer

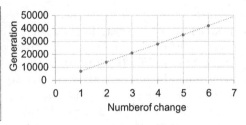

PREDICT-NEXT-GENERATION-INPUT		
ID	Y	X1
Integer	Integer	Integer
...	...	...
4	28000	4
5	35000	5
6	42000	6

Fig. 4. Prediction of the generation of the next change using regression

in order to be injected right before the anticipated change occurs. If no suitable individuals are found in the memory, immigrants will be inserted to the population when the next change occurs to increase diversity.

Figure 4 illustrates an example for the calculation of the generation of the next change in a scenario where change occurs every 7000 generations ($T = 7000$). The input table for the stored procedure is organized in the way required by PAL [28, p. 273]. The dotted line in the diagram illustrates the corresponding regression function, which is used to calculate the generation of the 7th change. The next step of the prediction is to analyze which of the parameters C, w_j and v_j are going to change. Therefor information on how often the parameters changed before is used: the more often they changed, the higher the likelihood that they are going to change next time. Afterwards their new numerical value is anticipated with the same PAL procedure as described above.

In order to measure the efficiency of the implemented predictive analysis, every time a change occurs the *prediction accuracy* is calculated as $acc = 1 - err$. The prediction error err is One if the actual change occurs too early or if no prediction was made at all. Otherwise err is calculated as the arithmetic mean of the relative error of each parameter.

5 Evaluation Results

Extensive tests were conducted to evaluate the performance the associative memory and the predictive component of IMDEA. This paper uses a knapsack instance with 500 items [29], a constant population size p of 40 individuals, *mating restriction* [19] and *Fitness Sharing* to maintain diversity with $\alpha = 1$ and $\sigma_s = 257.6$ based on [16] and a quadratic penalty in the fitness function ($\lambda = 0.5$, Eq. 2).

Based on *Design of Experiment (DoE)* principles a 2^3 full factorial design was prepared to evaluate the effect of the three factors *associative memory*, *polynomial regression prediction* and *diversity maintenance*. In the diagrams each factor combination is coded with three letters, the first one indicating whether predictive analysis was used (P) or not (O), the second one indicating the same for diversity maintenance (D or O) and the third one standing for associative memory (M or O). For each factor combination ten tests were run. Each test ran for eight hours simulating dynamic changes with $T = 7000$ and $L = 32$ (cf. Sect. 4.3, Fig. 2) resulting in more than 1000000 generations, 150 changes and five repetitions of each environment. The main performance measures for evaluation are *decrease* and *recovery* of the fitness after a change, mean *best fitness* per factor, *computation time* and *prediction accuracy*.

Figure 5 compares the best fitness per generation. The best fitness declines over the generations because the diagram shows a stage of decreasing capacity. Figure 6 shows the arithmetic mean of the percentaged decrease of the best fitness per factor combination averaged over all changes as well as the arithmetic mean of the best fitness over all generations (cf. [4], $\overline{F}_{BOG}$).

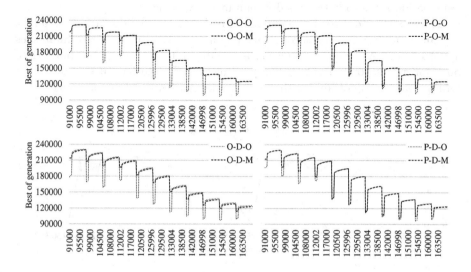

Fig. 5. Excerpt of the best-of-generation

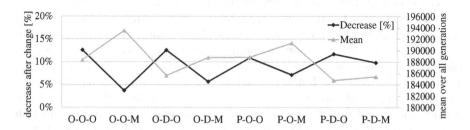

Fig. 6. Mean best fitness and percentaged decrease of best fitness

Both diagrams clearly show, that using the IMDB as associative memory for the IMDEA has a positive effect on the fitness for recurring environments. In the scenario with no dynamic adaptation (O-O-O) the average decrease of the best fitness after a change is 12.55%. However when using an IMDB memory (O-O-M) the decrease drops to only 3.70%. That is merely about a quarter of the decrease of the non-adapted EA. Correspondingly the implemented memory in average also realizes the highest outcome for the best fitness.

On the other hand, Figs. 5 and 6 show that combining the associative memory with *Fitness Sharing*, mating restriction and polynomial regression prediction does not further improve the algorithm but diminishes it. Using only diversity maintenance (O-D-O) or prediction (P-O-O) results in an improvement compared to the non-adapted EA, too (O-O-O). If prediction or diversity maintenance is used and the memory is added (O-D-M, P-O-M, P-D-M), the results will be better than without memory (O-D-O, P-O-O, P-D-O). But no factor combination leads to better results than memory alone.

The idea behind diversity maintenance is that a diverse population can adapt to changes more easily than a converged population. Yet for IMDEA it diminishes the algorithm. A logical explanation is the difficulty of finding an appropriate value for σ_s, as pointed out by Sareni et al. [17]. The test results suggest that *Fitness Sharing* is not always the best solution for diversity maintenance.

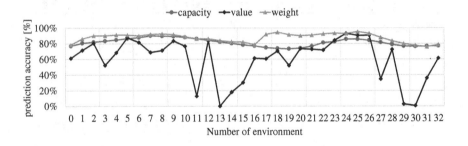

Fig. 7. Prediction accuracy per environment

The reason for the negative effect of the predictive component is not the prediction itself but the hardness of predictability. Figure 7 illustrates the prediction accuracy (cf. Sect. 4.6) for each environment. The simulator was programmed to simulate changes that are hard to predict on purpose, because easy changes such as linear increase are no challenge for predictive analysis. Therefore the simulator includes a sine function (capacity, cf. Fig. 2) which is relatively easy to predict and small jumps (value, cf. Fig. 2) based on [27] which are hard to predict. Figure 7 shows that polynomial regression can estimate a sine function with an accuracy of about 82%. However the jumps are so hard to predict, that the polynomial regression varies significantly from the actual jumps. As a result there are some cases where the memory is queried for individuals from the wrong environment which are then inserted to the EA before the next change. Due to these individuals originating from the wrong environment the prediction weakens the performance of the memory.

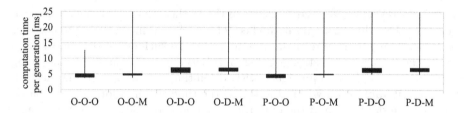

Fig. 8. Computation time per generation

Communication between IMDEA and the IMDB needs to be taken into account when evaluating its performance. IMDEA is implemented as an application within the IMDB thus reducing communication overhead to a minimum. It uses PAL for predictive analysis to ensure that the prediction is carried out as close as possible to the stored data. Figure 8 illustrates the computation time in milliseconds per generation for each factor combination as box plot diagram. The ordinate is limited to 25 $\frac{ms}{g}$. Diversity maintenance raises the average computation time from 5 $\frac{ms}{g}$ to 7 $\frac{ms}{g}$ because extra time to compute the shared fitness is required. Prediction and memory do not influence the average computation time but the maximum values every T generations: During each prediction cycle more than 30 s of computational cost are lost in the IMDB. This is due to the used library and can not be improved by IMDEA. *Extraction* and *injection* require 500 ms to read from the IMDB and to write into it.

Similar to results obtained by Yang [22] and Branke [5] these tests conducted with IMDEA prove the effectiveness of a memory, but in contrast to previous work IMDEA introduces the benefit of storing large amounts of data in an IMDB. IMDEA accomplishes a high prediction accuracy for linear changes but for noisy environments it is not able to outperform existing approaches like Simões [9].

After determining that memory alone has the best effect of the performance of the IMDEA, further test were conducted to evaluate interdependences between changes and the extraction periodicity. The results show, that there is no correlation between the extraction periodicity and the severity of jumps. However, there is a strong interdependence between the extraction periodicity and the frequency of change. If changes occur often, extraction will have to take place often as well. For a low frequency of change a less frequent extraction strategy is beneficial. This strong interdependence leads to the conclusion that in dynamic environments where the frequency of change itself is fluctuating, the EA performs best if the memory component constantly and automatically adapts its extraction points according to the frequency of change.

6   Conclusion

This paper reported on an implemented approach to dynamic evolutionary optimization exploring the possibilities of integrating in-memory computing into evolutionary algorithms. Empirical studies suggest that an in-memory database (e.g. SAP HANA) can enable the optimizer to learn from the decisions of the past and to make better informed decisions in the forthcoming iterations of the optimization algorithm. This positive effect of associative memory seems becomes particularly apparent in recurring environments. In such cases, the contribution of associative memory is strong. Using an IMDB allows storing and maintaining huge amounts of data on previously visited solutions. By implementing the optimizer as an application within the IMDB the time required for communication between the database and the optimizer is reduced to 500 ms. The test results also indicate, that there is a strong interdependence between the frequency of change and the extraction strategy, meaning that the interval for extraction needs to adapt to the frequency of change in order to ensure maximum efficiency of the associative memory.

Additionally, the results demonstrate that some changes (i.e. jumps) are hard to predict. To improve the accuracy of predictive analysis of stored knowledge, further evaluation of suitable analysis methods such as different regression models, forecast smoothing or neural networks may be explored. The optimizer could include a learning component to automatically improve the selection of the best prediction method. Alternate approaches of implementing the predictive component – besides PAL – should be tested to reduce the computation time of the prediction cycle. Future work targets the associative memory by testing alternate database schemes addressing typical access patterns. It is also envisaged to apply IMDEA to other usage scenarios including, e.g., constrained-based product configuration systems [30], a form of the SAT problem.

Acknowledgments. The work for this paper was generously supported by the HPI Future SOC Lab in the scope of the project "Big Data in Bio-inspired Optimization".

References

1. Goldberg, D.E.: Genetic Algorithms in Search, Optimization and Machine Learning. Addison-Wesley, Reading (1989)
2. Plattner, H.: A Course in in-Memory Data Management: The Inner Mechanics of in-Memory Databases. Springer, Heidelberg (2014)
3. Kellerer, H., Pferschy, U., Pisinger, D.: Knapsack Problems. Springer, Heidelberg (2004)
4. Nguyen, T.T., Yang, S., Branke, J.: Evolutionary dynamic optimization: a survey of the state of the art. Swarm Evol. Comput. **6**, 1–24 (2012)
5. Branke, J.: Memory enhanced evolutionary algorithms for changing optimization problems. In: Congress on Evolutionary Computation, CEC 1999, pp. 1875–1882 (1999)
6. Yang, S.: Explicit memory schemes for evolutionary algorithms in dynamic environments. In: Yang, S., Ong, Y.S., Jin, Y. (eds.) Evolutionary Computation in Dynamic and Uncertain Environments. SCI, vol. 51, pp. 3–28. Springer, Berlin London (2007)
7. Grefenstette, J.J., Ramsey, C.L.: Case-based initialization of genetic algorithms. In: Proceedings of the 5th ICGA, pp. 84–91 (1993)
8. Rossi, C., Abderrahim, M., Díaz, J.C.: Tracking moving optima using Kalman-based predictions. Evol. Comput. **16**, 1–30 (2008)

9. Simões, A., Costa, E.: Prediction in evolutionary algorithms for dynamic environments. Soft Comput. **18**, 1471–1497 (2014)
10. Fogel, L., Owens, A., Walsh, M.: Artificial Intelligence Through Simulated Evolution. Wiley, New York (1966)
11. Cruz, C., Gonzalez, J.R., Pelta, D.A.: Optimization in dynamic environments: a survey on problems, methods and measures. Soft Comput. **15**, 1427–1448 (2011)
12. Hatzakis, I., Wallace, D.: Dynamic multi-objective optimization with evolutionary algorithms. In: Cattolico, M. (ed.) Proceedings of the 8th Annual Conference on Genetic and Evolutionary Computation, GECCO 2006, pp. 1201–1208. ACM, New York (2006)
13. Simões, A., Costa, E.: Variable-size memory evolutionary algorithm to deal with dynamic environments. In: Giacobini, M. (ed.) EvoWorkshops 2007. LNCS, vol. 4448, pp. 617–626. Springer, Heidelberg (2007). doi:10.1007/978-3-540-71805-5_68
14. Simões, A., Costa, E.: Evolutionary algorithms for dynamic environments: prediction using linear regression and Markov chains. In: Rudolph, G., Jansen, T., Beume, N., Lucas, S., Poloni, C. (eds.) PPSN 2008. LNCS, vol. 5199, pp. 306–315. Springer, Heidelberg (2008). doi:10.1007/978-3-540-87700-4_31
15. Simões, A., Costa, E.: Prediction in evolutionary algorithms for dynamic environments using Markov chains and nonlinear regression. In: Rothlauf, F. (ed.) Proceedings of the 11th Annual Conference on Genetic and Evolutionary Computation, GECCO 2009, pp. 883–890. ACM, New York (2009)
16. Deb, K., Goldberg, D.E.: An investigation of niche and species formation in genetic function optimization. In: Proceedings of the 3rd ICGA, San Francisco, CA, USA. Morgan Kaufmann Publishers Inc., pp. 42–50 (1989)
17. Sareni, B., Krähenbühl, L.: Fitness sharing and niching methods revisited. IEEE Trans. Evol. Comput. **2**, 97–106 (1998)
18. Mahfoud, S.W.: Niching methods for genetic algorithms. Ph.D. thesis, University of Illinois UMI Order No. GAX95-43663 (1995)
19. Ishibuchi, H., Shibata, Y.: Mating scheme for controlling the diversity-convergence balance for multiobjective optimization. In: Deb, K. (ed.) GECCO 2004. LNCS, vol. 3102, pp. 1259–1271. Springer, Heidelberg (2004). doi:10.1007/978-3-540-24854-5_121
20. Yang, S.: Memory-based immigrants for genetic algorithms in dynamic environments. In: Proceedings of the 7th Annual Conference on Genetic and Evolutionary Computation, GECCO 2005, pp. 1115–1122. ACM, New York (2005)
21. Yang, S.: Associative memory scheme for genetic algorithms in dynamic environments. In: Rothlauf, F., Branke, J., Cagnoni, S., Costa, E., Cotta, C., Drechsler, R., Lutton, E., Machado, P., Moore, J.H., Romero, J., Smith, G.D., Squillero, G., Takagi, H. (eds.) EvoWorkshops 2006. LNCS, vol. 3907, pp. 788–799. Springer, Heidelberg (2006). doi:10.1007/11732242_76
22. Yang, S., Yao, X.: Population-based incremental learning with associative memory for dynamic environments. Evol. Comput. **12**, 542–561 (2008)
23. Plattner, H.: A common database approach for OLTP and OLAP using an in-memory column database. In: Proceedings of the 2009 ACM SIGMOD International Conference on Management of Data, pp. 1–2. ACM, New York (2009)
24. Silvia, P., Frye, R., Berg, B.: SAP HANA - An Introduction. Rheinwerk Verlag, Birmingham (2016)
25. Plattner, H., Leukert, B.: The In-Memory Revolution: How SAP HANA Enables Business of the Future. Springer, Heidelberg (2015)
26. SAP: SAP HANA XS JavaScript Reference: SAP HANA Platform SPS 12, Document Version: 1.0, 11 May 2016

27. Li, C., Yang, S.: A generalized approach to construct benchmark problems for dynamic optimization. In: Li, X., Kirley, M., Zhang, M., Green, D., Ciesielski, V., Abbass, H., Michalewicz, Z., Hendtlass, T., Deb, K., Tan, K.C., Branke, J., Shi, Y. (eds.) SEAL 2008. LNCS, vol. 5361, pp. 391–400. Springer, Heidelberg (2008). doi:10.1007/978-3-540-89694-4_40
28. SAP: SAP HANA Predictive Analysis Library (PAL): SAP HANA Platform SPS 11, Document Version: 1.0, 25 November 2015
29. Beasley, J.E.: mknapcb3 (2004). http://people.brunel.ac.uk/~mastjjb/jeb/orlib/files/mknapcb3.txt. Accessed 25 August 2016
30. Klein, M., Greiner, U., Genßler, T., Kuhn, J., Born, M.: Enabling interoperability in the area of multi-brand vehicle configuration. In: Gonçalves, R.J. (ed.) Enterprise Interoperability II, pp. 759–770. Springer, London (2007)

Road Traffic Rules Synthesis Using Grammatical Evolution

Eric Medvet[(✉)], Alberto Bartoli, and Jacopo Talamini

Department of Engineering and Architecture, University of Trieste, Trieste, Italy
emedvet@units.it

Abstract. We consider the problem of the automatic synthesis of road traffic rules, motivated by a future scenario in which human and machine-based drivers will coexist on the roads: in that scenario, current road rules may be either unsuitable or inefficient. We approach the problem using Grammatical Evolution (GE). To this end, we propose a road traffic model which includes concepts amenable to be regulated (e.g., lanes, intersections) and which allows drivers to temporarily evade traffic rules when there are no better alternatives. In our GE framework, each individual is a set of rules and its fitness is a weighted sum of traffic efficiency and safety, as resulting from a number of simulations where all drivers are subjected to the same rules. Experimental results show that our approach indeed generates rules leading to a safer and more efficient traffic than enforcing no rules or rules similar to those currently used.

Keywords: Simulation · Road traffic model · Stochastic evolution · Driverless cars

1 Introduction and Related Work

Car driving is one of the tasks that in a not far away future will be carried out by machines, rather than by humans. In a *driverless car* scenario a machine must be able to take a number of decisions in real time, with a limited and possibly noisy perception of the environment. Such decisions must take into account the need of abiding by the rules of the road and the presence of other moving, possibly hardly predictable, agents (pedestrian, bikers, other cars, either driverless or with a human driver).

Current traffic rules have been written for a scenario where humans drive cars and may hence be suboptimal in a driverless car scenario, or even in a scenario where both machines and humans drive cars. In this work, we take a fresh look at traffic rules and investigate the possibility of devising a novel set of rules that are amenable to automation and, at the same time, able to improve *global* indexes computed over the full population of vehicles. In particular, we focus on optimizing the global *traffic efficiency* and *safety*. We believe that, broadly speaking, an approach of this kind could lead to significant advantages to the society as a whole and that the driverless car revolution could offer a unique opportunity in this respect.

© Springer International Publishing AG 2017
G. Squillero and K. Sim (Eds.): EvoApplications 2017, Part II, LNCS 10200, pp. 173–188, 2017.
DOI: 10.1007/978-3-319-55792-2_12

We propose a framework based on Grammatical Evolution (GE) and our contribution is as follows. First, we propose and experimentally evaluate a model for road traffic including the road graph, the cars, and the rules-aware drivers who try to abide by, but can possibly evade, the rules; the model is detailed enough to include concepts such as lanes, collisions, and safety distance, which are significant to our study. Second, we propose a language to define rules which can be enforced in our model: rules are predicates and the language is given in the form of a context-free grammar. Third and finally, we propose and experimentally evaluate a method for the automatic synthesis of rules based on GE: individuals represent sets of rules (i.e., regulations) and their fitness capture the degree to which, according to the results of several simulations, traffic regulated by the set of rules is efficient and safe.

Our experimental evaluation shows that, using GE, it is possible to obtain sets of rules which result in safer (less collisions) and more efficient traffic, w.r.t. both unregulated traffic and a set of hand-written rules designed to resemble a (simplified) real world set of rules.

To the best of our knowledge, no other studies concerning the automatic synthesis of road traffic rules have been proposed before. Recent research has focused on how driverless cars should behave with respect to the existing rules: by proposing flexible control strategies which minimize the number of violated rules [14], by approaching the (highway) driverless algorithm design with rules complying as a first goal (legal safety) [15], or by formalizing rules for the sake of accountability after collisions involving driverless cars [10]. A much deeper problem in this area consists in determining which decision should be taken by a driverless car when facing a situation where only less-than-ideal outcomes are possible [4,5]. In such a case, the decision may result in some sacrifice involving car users (passengers) or other people (e.g., pedestrians). This fundamental problem is orthogonal to our work.

Traffic is regulated not only by rules but also by the infrastructure, e.g., road markings and signs. In this area, several proposals have been made to modify the working principle of traffic lights in order to avoid congestion (e.g., [16]), also resorting to evolutionary computation [12]. More recently, motivated by the emergence of more automated vehicles, Tachet et al. even proposed the replacement of traffic lights with a novel (for road traffic) flow regulation solution build upon slot-based systems [13].

From a more general point of view, automatic synthesis of rules is a task which fits particularly well GE, since the language of the rules can be described in terms of a grammar and candidate solutions may be evaluated by means of simulated application of the corresponding set of rules: for instance, in [2] GE has been used to generate trading rules for spot foreign-exchange markets. Moreover, recent works showed that GE is suitable for addressing real problems with complex grammars, such as learning of string similarity functions [1], or designing components of vehicle routing algorithms [3].

2 Road Traffic Model

We consider a scenario with continuous space and discrete time in which a number of cars move according to their driving algorithms.

2.1 Roads and Cars

A *road graph* is a directed graph $\mathcal{G} = (S, I)$ in which edges represent road sections, vertices represent road intersections, and where each vertex is connected to at least two edges. A *road section* $p \in S$ is characterized by a length $l(p) \in \mathbb{R}, l(p) > 0$ and a width $w(p) \in \mathbb{N}, w(p) > 0$: the former represents the length of the section between two intersections and the latter represents the number of lanes in the section. A *road intersection* $p \in I$ is characterized by a size $w(p) \in \mathbb{N}, w(p) > 0$: without loss of generality, we assume that the size of an intersection is equal to the largest width among the sections connecting the intersection.

A *car* is an agent which moves on the road graph. At a given time step, the car is positioned somewhere on the road graph, i.e., its position can be determined in terms of the section/intersection, lane and distance from the section/intersection origin. The car movement is determined in terms of two speeds, i.e., along the section and along the lanes—see Fig. 1.

In detail, a car is a tuple (p, x, y, v_x, v_y, s) where p, x, y constitute the *position*, $v_x \in \mathbb{R}$ is the *linear speed*, $v_y \in \{-1, 0, 1\}$ is the lane-changing speed, and $s \in \{\text{alive}, \text{dead}\}$ is the *status*. Within the position, $p \in S \cup I$ is the section or intersection where the car is. If $p \in S$, $x \in [0, l(p)]$ and $y \in \{1, \dots, w(p)\}$ are the linear and lane coordinates of the car within the road section p—we assume that $x = 0$ refers to the starting side of p. If $p \in I$, $x \in [0, w(p)]$ is the coordinate of the car within the intersection and y is not relevant.

At each time step, if the status of a car is $s = $ dead, the position is not updated. Otherwise, if the status is $s = $ alive, the position (p, x, y) of a car is updated as follows. If $p \in S$ and $0 \le x + v_x \le l(p)$, then its position at the next step is $(p, x + v_x, \min(\max(y + v_y, 0), w(p)))$. Otherwise, if $p \in S$ and $x + v_x < 0$ or $x + v_x > l(p)$, then its position at the next step is $(p', 0, 0)$, where $p' \in I$ is the appropriate intersection between the two connected by p. Otherwise, if $p \in I$ and $x + |v_x| \le w(p)$ then its position at the next step is $(p, x + |v_x|, 0)$. Otherwise and finally, if $p \in I$ and $x + |v_x| > w(p)$, then its position at the next step is (p', x_0, y_0), where $p' \in S$ is one of the sections connecting p and $x_0 = 0, y_0 = 0$ or $x_0 = l(p'), y_0 = w(p')$ depending on whether p' starts or ends in p, respectively—in the latter case, if $v_x > 0$, then at the next step it is set to $-v_x$. Concerning the choice of p', let $\{p'_1, \dots, p'_n\} \subseteq S$ be the set of sections connecting p, then p' is set to p'_j, where j is chosen randomly in $\{1, \dots, n\}$. In other words, a car moves on a section according to its speeds; whenever it reaches the end (or the beginning) of the section, it enters the connected intersection. While in an intersection, the car remains inside according to its linear speed and the intersection size. When exiting an intersection, it enters a connecting section.

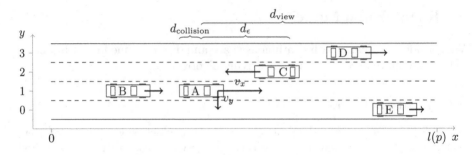

Fig. 1. A visualization of some of our model definitions. A car A is traveling with a positive linear speed v_x and a negative lane speed $v_y = -1$ on a road section on which there are other 4 cars. With respect to A, car C is the 1-lane closest car, because it is on $y_C = 2 = y_A + 1$ and its distance from A is $\Delta x \leq d_{\text{view}}$; moreover, $\delta v_1 = $ opposite, since C is traveling in the opposite direction w.r.t. A, and $\epsilon_1 = $ T, since C is closer than d_{epsilon} to A. There are no other j-lane closest cars for A: in facts B is behind (not ahead) A, D is two lanes away from A, and E distance to A is larger than d_{view}.

At each time step, a *collision* may occur between a pair of cars. A collision occurs if two cars meet on the same intersection or if two cars meet on the same lane of the same road section. If a collision occurs, the status of the two cars is set to dead. In detail, let $(p_1^{(k)}, x_1^{(k)}, y_1^{(k)})$ and $(p_2^{(k)}, x_2^{(k)}, y_2^{(k)})$ be the positions of the two cars at time step k, a collision occurs at k if at least one of the following conditions is met:

- $p_1^{(k)} = p_2^{(k)} \in I$ and $\left| x_1^{(k)} - x_2^{(k)} \right| < d_{\text{collision}}$;
- $p_1^{(k)} = p_2^{(k)} \in S$ and $y_1^{(k)} = y_2^{(k)}$ and $\left| x_1^{(k)} - x_2^{(k)} \right| < d_{\text{collision}}$;
- $p_1^{(k)} = p_1^{(k-1)} = p_2^{(k)} = p_2^{(k-1)} \in I$ and $\text{sign}(x_1^{(k)} - x_2^{(k)}) \neq \text{sign}(x_1^{(k-1)} - x_2^{(k-1)})$;
- $p_1^{(k)} = p_1^{(k-1)} = p_2^{(k)} = p_2^{(k-1)} \in S$ and $y_1^{(k)} = y_2^{(k)}$ and $\text{sign}(x_1^{(k)} - x_2^{(k)}) \neq \text{sign}(x_1^{(k-1)} - x_2^{(k-1)})$;
- $p_1^{(k-1)} = p_2^{(k-1)} \in I$ and $p_2^{(k)} = p_2^{(k-1)}$ and $p_1^{(k)} \neq p_1^{(k-1)}$ and $x_1^{(k-1)} \leq x_2^{(k-1)}$;
- $p_1^{(k-1)} = p_2^{(k-1)} \in S$ and $p_2^{(k)} = p_2^{(k-1)}$ and $p_1^{(k)} \neq p_1^{(k-1)}$ and $y_1^{(k-1)} = y_2^{(k-1)}$ and $v_{x,1}^{(k)} > 0$ and $x_1^{(k-1)} \leq x_2^{(k-1)}$;
- $p_1^{(k-1)} = p_2^{(k-1)} \in S$ and $p_2^{(k)} = p_2^{(k-1)}$ and $p_1^{(k)} \neq p_1^{(k-1)}$ and $y_1^{(k-1)} = y_2^{(k-1)}$ and $v_{x,1}^{(k)} < 0$ and $x_1^{(k-1)} \geq x_2^{(k-1)}$;

where $d_{\text{collision}}$ is a parameter which represents the minimal distance between two cars—note that with any $d_{\text{collision}} > 0$ the capacity of the road graph is limited.

2.2 Driver

A *driver* is an algorithm according to which the linear and lane-changing speeds of a car are updated. In particular, at each time step, the algorithm execution is based on the processing of (a) a set of input variables, (b) a set of state variables, (c) the driver's car tuple, (d) a set of unmodifiable parameters and results in (a) the output of a non-empty sequence of actions and (b) the modification of the state variables.

The input variables are based on the concept of *j-lane closest car*, with $j \in \{-1, 0, 1\}$. The j-lane closest car is the closest car ahead of the driver's car on the $y + j$ lane such that its linear distance is $\Delta x < d_{\text{view}}$, where y is the lane of the driver's car and d_{view} is a driver's parameter. For the sake of brevity, we omit a more formal definition, which covers also the case in which the driver's car is in (or close to) an intersection. Note that the j-lane closest car could not exist for some j, if no cars are closer than d_{view} or there is no $y + j$-th lane.

The *input variables* are the following—see Fig. 1 for a visual interpretation of the variables.

- Three *relative movement* variables δv_{-1}, δv_0, and δv_1. The value of δv_j is defined in $\{\varnothing, \text{opposite}, -1, 0, 1\}$ and is determined as follows. If there is no j-lane closest car, then $\delta v_j = \varnothing$. Otherwise, let $(p', x', y', v_x', v_y', s')$ the j-lane closest car: if $\text{sign}\, v_x \neq \text{sign}\, v_x'$, then $\delta v_j = \text{opposite}$, otherwise $\delta v_j = \text{sign}\,(|v_x'| - |v_x|)$. In other words, δv_j says if there is a j-lane closest car and, if any, if it moves in the opposite direction or, otherwise, is becoming closer ($\delta v_j = -1$), farther ($\delta v_j = 1$), or has the same linear speed, w.r.t. the driver's car.
- Three *closeness* variables $\epsilon_{-1}, \epsilon_0, \epsilon_1$. The value of ϵ_j is a boolean which is true if and only if there is a j-lane closest car and its distance Δx from the driver's car is $\Delta x \leq d_\epsilon$, where $d_\epsilon < d_{\text{view}}$ is a driver's parameter. In other words, ϵ_j is set if the j-lane closest car, if any, is closer than a threshold.

The *state variables* include a single variable $d \in \mathbb{R}, d \geq 0$, which represents the distance the driver still wants to go and which is updated at each time step as $d^{(k+1)} = d^{(k)} - |v_x^{(k)}|$. The *parameters* include $d_{\text{view}}, d_\epsilon$ (whose meaning was described above), a value $v_{\max} \in \mathbb{R}, v_{\max} \geq 0$, and a value $v_\Delta \in \mathbb{R}, 0 < v_\Delta < v_{\max}$: $v_{\max}$ is the maximum linear speed the driver's car can reach and v_Δ represents the acceleration/deceleration of the driver's car.

The output of the driver's algorithm is a non-empty sequence A of *actions*, i.e., an ordered subset of the set $\mathcal{A}$ of possible driver's action, with $\mathcal{A} = \{\uparrow, \nearrow, \rightarrow \searrow, \downarrow, \swarrow, \leftarrow, \nwarrow, \varnothing\}$. An action determines how v_x and v_y are updated, as shown in Table 1.

In other words, an up arrow corresponds to accelerating and a down arrow corresponds to braking; a right arrow corresponds to moving on the right lane and a left arrow corresponds to moving on the left lane, and so on. The driver executes only one of the actions in A. The action which is actually performed is chosen after processing A according to a procedure that is detailed in Sect. 2.4 which takes traffic rules into account.

The driver's algorithm is presented in the form of a multiway branch control in Table 2. The rationale for the proposed algorithm is to resemble the behavior of a "reasonable" driver who aims at traveling a distance d while avoiding trivial

Table 1. Driver's actions.

$a \in \mathcal{A}$	$v_x^{(k+1)}$	$v_y^{(k+1)}$
↑	$\text{sign}\,(v_x^{(k)}+v_\Delta)\min(|v_{\max}|,\,\left|v_x^{(k)}\right|+v_\Delta)$	0
↗	$\text{sign}\,(v_x^{(k)}+v_\Delta)\min(\left|v_x^{(k)}\right|,\,\left|v_x^{(k)}\right|+v_\Delta)$	$-\text{sign}\,v_x^{(k)}$
→	$v_x^{(k)}$	$-\text{sign}\,v_x^{(k)}$
↘	$\text{sign}\,(v_x^{(k)}+v_\Delta)\max(0,\,\left|v_x^{(k)}\right|-v_\Delta)$	$-\text{sign}\,v_x^{(k)}$
↓	$\text{sign}\,(v_x^{(k)}+v_\Delta)\max(0,\,\left|v_x^{(k)}\right|-v_\Delta)$	0
↙	$\text{sign}\,(v_x^{(k)}+v_\Delta)\max(0,\,\left|v_x^{(k)}\right|-v_\Delta)$	$\text{sign}\,v_x^{(k)}$
←	$v_x^{(k)}$	$\text{sign}\,v_x^{(k)}$
↖	$\text{sign}\,(v_x^{(k)}+v_\Delta)\min(\left|v_x^{(k)}\right|,\,\left|v_x^{(k)}\right|+v_\Delta)$	$\text{sign}\,v_x^{(k)}$
∅	$v_x^{(k)}$	0

Table 2. The driver's algorithm.

	δv_1	δv_0	δv_{-1}	ϵ_1	ϵ_0	ϵ_{-1}	$d \le x_{\text{stop}}$	A
1	∀	∀	∀	∀	∀	∀	{T}	{↓,↘,↙}
2	{∅,1}	{∅,1}	{∅,1}	∀	∀	∀	∀	{↑,↗,↖,∅,↓}
3	∀	{∅,1}	∀	∀	∀	∀	∀	{↑,∅,↓}
4	∀	{−1,0}	∀	∀	{F}	∀	∀	{↑,∅,↓}
5	{∅,1}	{−1,0}	∀	{F}	{T}	∀	∀	{↖,∅,↓}
6	∀	{−1,0}	{∅,1}	∀	{T}	{F}	∀	{↗,∅,↓}
7	∀	{0}	∀	∀	{T}	∀	∀	{∅,↓}
8	∀	{−1}	∀	∀	{T}	∀	∀	{↓}
9	∀	{opposite}	∀	∀	∀	{F}	∀	{→,↘,↓}
10	∀	{opposite}	∀	{F}	∀	∀	∀	{←,↙,↓}
11	∀	{opposite}	∀	∀	{T}	∀	∀	{↘,↙,↓}
12	∀	∀	∀	∀	∀	∀	∀	{↓,↘,↙}

collisions: that goal is pursued by—in essence—trying to travel at the max linear speed while avoiding hitting other cars on the same lane. In detail, each row of Table 2 represents a proposition and the corresponding output A. The proposition is composed of the conjunction of membership checks on input variables and on the result of the comparison of the state variable d against x_{stop}, which is defined as $x_{\text{stop}} = k_{\text{stop}}v_x + \frac{1}{2}\left(k_{\text{stop}}^2 - k_{\text{stop}}\right)v_\Delta$ where $k_{\text{stop}} = \left\lceil \frac{v_x}{v_\Delta} \right\rceil$; x_{stop} represents the distance the driver's car would run if it constantly decrease its speed until stopping. For instance, row 4 proposition is $\delta v_0 \in \{−1,0\} \wedge \epsilon_0 \in \{F\}$, row 5 proposition is $\delta v_1 \in \{∅,1\} \wedge \delta v_0 \in \{−1,0\} \wedge \epsilon_1 \in \{F\} \wedge \epsilon_0 \in \{T\}$. The output is determined as follows: if the row 1 proposition is true, then the output is the row 1 A; otherwise, if the row 2 proposition is true, then the output is the row 2 A, and so on—note that the last row proposition is always true, hence it is guaranteed that a non empty sequence is always output.

2.3 Rules

A *traffic rule* is a predicate defined on a set of variables concerning a car and its driver, its j-lane closest cars, and the road graph. A car *breaks* a rule at a given time step if the corresponding predicate is false.

The variables on which a traffic rule can be defined include: (a) variables concerning the car and the corresponding driver: $\hat{v}_x$, $v_{\max}$, v_Δ, d_{view}, d_ϵ, p, $\hat{x}$, and $\hat{y}$, where $\hat{v}_x = |v_x|$, $\hat{x} = l(p) - x$ and $\hat{y} = y$, if $v_x \geq 0$, and $\hat{x} = x$ and $\hat{y} = w(p) - y$, otherwise; (b) variables concerning the car j-lane closest cars: δv_{-1}, δv_0, δv_1, Δx_{-1}, Δx_0, and Δx_1, where Δx_j is defined as in Sect. 2.2 and is set to $+\infty$ if the corresponding $\delta v_j = \varnothing$; (c) variables concerning the road graph section or intersection in which the car is: $l(p)$ and $w(p)$.

The set of possible traffic rules is defined by a context-free grammar which we here present with the Backus-Naur Form (r is the rule) in Fig. 2.

$$r ::= \langle\text{conditions}\rangle$$
$$\langle\text{conditions}\rangle ::= \langle\text{condition}\rangle \mid \langle\text{conditions}\rangle \vee \langle\text{condition}\rangle$$
$$\langle\text{condition}\rangle ::= \langle\text{baseCondition}\rangle \mid \neg\langle\text{baseCondition}\rangle$$
$$\langle\text{baseCondition}\rangle ::= \langle\text{numericCondition}\rangle \mid \langle\text{deltaCondition}\rangle \mid \langle\text{graphCondition}\rangle$$
$$\langle\text{numericCondition}\rangle ::= \langle\text{numericVariable}\rangle \leq \langle\text{numericValue}\rangle$$
$$\langle\text{numericVariable}\rangle ::= \hat{v}_x \mid v_{\max} \mid v_\Delta \mid d_{\text{view}} \mid d_\epsilon \mid \hat{x} \mid \hat{y} \mid \Delta x_{-1} \mid \Delta x_0 \mid \Delta x_1 \mid l(p) \mid w(p)$$
$$\langle\text{numericValue}\rangle ::= \langle\text{digit}\rangle.\langle\text{digit}\rangle\text{E}\langle\text{exp}\rangle$$
$$\langle\text{digit}\rangle ::= 0 \mid 1 \mid 2 \mid 3 \mid 4 \mid 5 \mid 6 \mid 7 \mid 8 \mid 9$$
$$\langle\text{exp}\rangle ::= -1 \mid 0 \mid 1$$
$$\langle\text{deltaCondition}\rangle ::= \delta v_{-1} = \langle\text{deltaValue}\rangle \mid \delta v_0 = \langle\text{deltaValue}\rangle \mid \delta v_1 = \langle\text{deltaValue}\rangle$$
$$\langle\text{deltaValue}\rangle ::= \varnothing \mid \text{opposite} \mid -1 \mid 0 \mid 1$$
$$\langle\text{graphCondition}\rangle ::= p \in S$$

Fig. 2. Backus-Naur Form of the context-free grammar for the traffic rules.

For example, the rule stating that "the maximum speed of a car is 20" is written as $\hat{v}_x \leq 20$. The rule stating that "the car should stay on the rightmost free lane" is written as $\hat{y} \leq 0 \vee \Delta x_{-1} \leq 10$, where 10 represents a distance within which a lane is not considered free. The rule stating that "the car should proceed slowly when approaching an intersection" is written as $\neg\hat{x} \leq 20 \vee \hat{v}_x \leq 10$.

2.4 Rules-Aware Driver

A *rules-aware driver* is a driver that selects exactly one *winning action* out of a sequence $A = (a_1, a_2, \dots)$ of actions, given a set R of traffic rules. In brief, a rules-aware driver selects the action which, if repeated for the next steps, will cause the least number of broken rules.

More in detail, the selection is performed as follows. First, for each action a_i in A, the sequence A_i of future actions consisting of a_i repeated k_{advance} times is considered. Second, the number n_i of future broken rules caused by A_i is computed as the sum of the number of rules that would be broken at each future step $k+j$, with $0 \leq j \leq |A_i|$. Third and finally, the winning action is determined as the action a_{i^*} for which $\frac{n_{i^*}}{|A_{i^*}|}$ is the lowest—in case of tie, the action with the lowest index in A is selected. When computing n_i, the rules-aware driver predicts the future variable values assuming that: (i) the j-lane closest cars, if any, will maintain the same speeds of step k; (ii) no other j-lane closest cars will appear; (iii) the driver's car will update consistently with the sequence of actions A_i. If a sequence A_i is such that the future position p of the car changes, the sequence is truncated to the last element before that change.

3   Grammatical Evolution

Grammatical Evolution (GE) [11] is a form of grammar-based Genetic Programming (GP) [6] which can evolve strings belonging to a language $\mathcal{L}(\mathcal{G})$ defined by a context-free grammar $\mathcal{G}$. In brief, GE operates on *genotypes*, which are variable-length bit strings, maps them to *phenotypes*, which are strings of $\mathcal{L}(\mathcal{G})$, and finally associates them with fitness values in $\mathbb{R}$.

The genotype-phenotype mapping procedure is the distinguishing trait of GE. In this procedure, the genotype is viewed as a variable-length integer string where each i-th integer, called *codon* and denoted by g_i, is obtained by decoding bits from the $(8(i-1))$-th to the $(8i-1)$-th, included, in the genotype g. The procedure is iterative and starts by setting the phenotype to $p = s_0$, s_0 being the grammar starting symbol, a counter i to 0, and a counter w to 0. Then, the following steps are iterated.

1. The leftmost non-terminal s in p is expanded using the j-th option (zero-based indexing) in the production rule r_s for s in $\mathcal{G}$, with j being the remainder of the division between the value g_i of the i-th codon (zero-based indexing) and the number $|r_s|$ of options in r_s, i.e., $j = g_i \bmod |r_s|$.
2. The counter i is incremented by 1; if i exceeds the number of codons, i.e., if $i > \frac{|g|}{8}$, then i is set to 0 and w is incremented by 1—the latter operation is called wrapping and w represents the number of wraps performed during the mapping.
3. If w exceeds a predefined threshold n_w, the mapping is aborted, i.e., a null phenotype is returned which will be associated to the worst possible fitness.
4. If p contains at least one non-terminal to be expanded, return to step 3, otherwise end.

The search engine of GE, i.e., the way in which the population of individuals is updated across subsequent generations, is conventionally based on Genetic

Algorithms (GA). In Sect. 4.2 we provide the evolutionary parameters values which we used in our experimentation.

In order to adapt the general-purpose GE framework to a specific case, one has to provide a grammar, which implicitly define the phenotype space, and a *fitness function* f, which maps a phenotype to a number in $\mathbb{R}$. In our case, phenotypes are sets of rules and hence we modified the grammar of Fig. 2, which describes the language for defining a single rule r, by replacing the first rule in order to make it defining a rule set R, as follows:

$$R ::= \langle \text{conditions} \rangle \mid \langle \text{conditions} \rangle \wedge \langle \text{conditions} \rangle$$

Rules within a set or rules are separated by a conjunction $\wedge$.

Concerning the fitness function, we aimed at defining a function which captures two desired high-level objectives of a set R of road traffic rules: (i) traffic flow regulated by R should allow car drivers to reach their destination without taking too long time, i.e., with a large average speed, and (ii) traffic flow regulated by R should result in no or few collisions. It can be noted that, in principle, the two objectives are conflicting: for instance (and simplifying), a set R imposing a very low speed limit will likely prevent many collisions, but will cause long traveling times for all drivers; on the other hand, a set R not imposing any speed limit will allow drivers to quickly reach their destination, but will likely result in many collisions.

We implemented these high-level objectives by means of two indexes which can be measured for each single driver. The *average speed ratio* (ASR) is the ratio between the actual average speed $\frac{d_{tot}}{k_{tot}}$ a driver traveled at and the maximum theoretical average speed v_{max}. The *collision-per-time* (CpT) is the ratio between the number $n_{collision}$ of collisions a car had during its travel and k_{tot}, where $n_{collision} \in \{0, 1\}$. For the former index, the greater, the better; the opposite for the latter. Hence, instead of ASR, we considered $1 - \text{ASR}$, i.e., $\left(1 - \frac{d_{tot}}{k_{tot}} \frac{1}{v_{max}}\right)$. We associate a rule set R with a fitness value which is a linear combination of the two indexes averaged across all cars n_{car} during a number n_{sim} of simulations:

$$f(R) = \alpha_{time} \frac{1}{n_{sim}} \frac{1}{n_{car}} \sum_{cars} \left(1 - \frac{d_{tot}}{k_{tot}} \frac{1}{v_{max}}\right) + \alpha_{collision} \frac{1}{n_{sim}} \frac{1}{n_{car}} \sum_{cars} \frac{n_{collision}}{k_{tot}}$$

(1)

where α_{time} and $\alpha_{collision}$ are the weights.

4 Experiments

We performed two experimental campaigns. The first one aimed at validating our road traffic model. The second one aimed at verifying the effectiveness of our GE-based approach for the synthesis of road traffic rules.

4.1 Validation of the Road Traffic Model

We performed a number of simulations in order to validate our proposed model for the road traffic scenario. In particular, we were interested in: (i) finding

Table 3. Model and simulation parameters.

Param	Meaning	Value
$d_{\text{collision}}$	Minimum distance between cars without collision	1
k_{removal}	Time steps before collided cars remotion	100
d_{view}	Driver's view distance	30
d_ϵ	Driver's safety distance	10
v_{max}	Driver's maximum speed	$\sim U(1.5, 3.5)$
v_Δ	Driver's acceleration (deceleration)	0.1
k_{advance}	Driver's rules forethought time steps	10
$d^{(0)}$	Driver's distance to travel (i.e., initial d)	2000
$|S|$	Number of road sections	5
$|I|$	Number of road intersections	4
$w(p), p \in S$	Number of lanes	$\in \{2, 3, 4\}$
$l(p), p \in S$	Section length	$\in \{100, 100\sqrt{2}\}$
n_{car}	Cars in the simulation	$\in \{2, 5, 8, 11, 14, 17, 20\}$
k_{dead}	Dead car removal time steps	100
k_{max}	Simulation time steps	5000

appropriate values for the model ($d_{\text{collision}}$, d_{view}, d_ϵ, v_{max}, v_Δ, k_{advance}, and all the values concerning the road graph) and simulation ($d^{(0)}$, n_{car}, k_{dead}, and k_{max}) parameters; (ii) verifying if the model behaves consistently when varying the number of cars in the road graph; (iii) verifying if a set of manually crafted rules causes a sound modification of the model behavior w.r.t. the absence of rules. To this end, after an exploratory experimentation, we set the values of the parameters as shown in Table 3. In order to simulate different drivers, we set different values, chosen randomly according to a uniform distribution, for the driver-related parameter v_{max}.

We performed each simulation by maintaining constant the number n_{car} of cars in the graph during the whole simulation. To this end, during the simulation, we removed a car and added a new one in a random position whenever at least one of the two following conditions was met: (a) the driver's state variable d (i.e., the distance the driver still wants to travel) became lower or equal to zero, or (b) exactly k_{dead} time steps passed since the car state s switched from alive to dead, i.e., since the step when the car was involved in a collision. Concerning the former condition, we recall that drivers do not have a specific destination; instead, their goal is to travel for a predefined distance.

Table 4 shows the set of 8 rules that we manually crafted in order to resemble a (simplified) typical road traffic regulation. The set contains rules regulating the driver's behavior w.r.t. lane to stay on (i.e., "stay on the right", rules 1 and 2), rules stating how the driver's should approach intersection (3, 4, and 5), rules

Table 4. Hand-written rules.

	Rule	Explanation
1	$\hat{y} \leq 0.0\text{E}0 \vee \Delta x_{-1} \leq 2.0\text{E}1$	Stay on the rightmost free lane
2	$\hat{y} \leq 1.0\text{E}0$	Stay on the first or second rightmost lane
3	$\neg \hat{x} \leq 3.0\text{E}1 \vee \hat{v}_x \leq 1.5\text{E}0$	When close to end of (inter)section, proceed slowly
4	$\neg \hat{x} \leq 2.0\text{E}1 \vee \hat{v}_x \leq 0.5\text{E}0$	When closer to end of (inter)section, proceed more slowly
5	$\neg \hat{x} \leq 3.0\text{E}1 \vee \hat{y} \leq 0.0\text{E}0$	When close to end of (inter)section, stay on the rightmost lane
6	$\neg \Delta x_0 \leq 2.0\text{E}1$	Do not travel too close to the preceding car
7	$\neg \hat{v}_x \leq 0 \vee \Delta x_0 \leq 2.0\text{E}1$	When too close to the preceding car, stop
8	$\hat{v}_x \leq 2.4\text{E}0$	Do not exceed a maximum speed

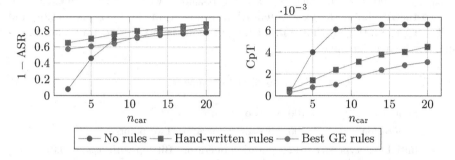

Fig. 3. Values of the two indexes vs. the number n_{car} of cars in the simulation, obtained by performing 10 simulation for each value of n_{car} and each of the three set of rules.

imposing a safety distance (6 and 7), and a rule prohibiting speeding (8). We adjusted the numeric values in the rules by exploratory experimentation, with the aim of reducing the number of collisions while not heavily affecting ASR.

Figure 3 shows the results of our first experimentation (along with the results of the rules inference experimentation, discussed in the next section). The figure shows the value of the two indexes ($1 - \text{ASR}$, left, and CpT, right) vs. the number n_{car} in the simulation, that is, vs. the injected traffic. There is one curve for each of the three following sets of rules: an empty set (no rules), the set of rules of Table 4 (hand-written rules), and a set of generated rules (best GE rules)—we here discuss the results corresponding to the first two curves. Each point of the curve is obtained by averaging the values of the index collected in 10 simulations.

Observing the plots of Fig. 3, it can be seen that the relation between the amount of traffic (n_{car}) and the two indexes looks sound, i.e., consistent with what happens in real world road traffic: the greater the number of traveling cars, the lower the average speed (i.e., the longer the time to destination) and the greater the overall number of collisions. From another point of view, there is a trade-off between efficiency and safety of the road traffic, like in the real world.

Moreover, by comparing the curves related to no rules and hand-written rules, it can be seen that enforcing a road traffic regulation results in a different point in the above-mentioned trade off: with the hand-written rules traffic is in general less efficient but safer. This findings suggest that our models for the road graph, the car, and the driver are sufficiently consistent with the real word and hence, in our opinion, adequate to investigate the feasibility of an automatic synthesis of road traffic rules.

4.2   Synthesis of Traffic Rules

In our second experimental campaign, we investigated the feasibility of the automatic synthesis of traffic rules using GE. To this end, we run 30 different evolutionary searches using the parameters shown in Table 5 and, concerning the fitness function (see Eq. 1), setting $n_{car} = 10$, $n_{sim} = 10$, $\alpha_{time} = 1$, and $\alpha_{collision} = 100$. For the weights α_{time} and $\alpha_{collision}$, we chose the values according to the results of the experimentation discussed in the previous section and reflecting the intuition that minimizing collisions is more important than maximizing the average speed.

Table 5. GE parameters.

Population	100	Crossover rate	0.9
Generations	100	Crossover operator	Two-points
Initial genotype size	512	Mutation operator	Bit flip with $p_{mut} = 0.01$
Max wraps	10	Selection	Tournament with size 5

We first analyze extensively the set of rules which obtained the best fitness among the final generations of the 30 runs, which is shown in Table 6 and discussed later. We experimentally verified how this set of best GE rules affected the traffic with different amounts of injected traffic by running 10 simulations for each value of $n_{car} \in \{2, 5, 8, 11, 14, 17, 20\}$. In other words, since GE rules were generated with $n_{car} = 10$, we evaluated the generalization ability of our rules synthesis approach. The results are shown in Figs. 3 and 4.

Figure 3 shows the values of the two indexes $(1 - ASR$ and CpT) vs. n_{car} for the three set of rules: no rules, hand-written rules, and best GE rules. It can be seen that the generated rules always obtain better index values w.r.t. hand-written rules, for both $1 - ASR$ and CpT—the difference being always statistically significant ($p < 0.001$ with the Mann–Whitney U test) with the sole exception of CpT for $n_{car} = 2$, for which $p < 0.05$. That is, GE rules allow to reduce the number of collisions and increase the average speed.

Figure 4 shows the same results of Fig. 3 from another point of view, by plotting the overall number of collisions in the simulation (i.e., $\sum n_{collision}$, on

Table 6. Best GE rules.

	Rule	Possible explanation
1	$\Delta x_{-1} \leq 4.8\mathrm{E}0$	Stay within some distance from the car on right lane
2	$\neg \hat{v}_x \leq 1.1\mathrm{E}1$	Maintain at least a minimum speed
3	$\neg \delta v_0 = \mathrm{opposite} \vee \delta v_0 = 1 \vee$ $\neg p \in S \vee \Delta x_0 \leq 0.3\mathrm{E}1$	When in an section, stay close to a car coming on the same lane
4	$\hat{v}_x \leq 1.2\mathrm{E}0$	Do not exceed a maximum speed

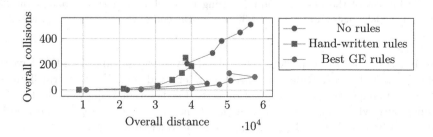

Fig. 4. Overall number of collisions in the simulation against the overall traveled distance in the simulation averaged across simulations with the same n_{car}.

y-axis) against the overall traveled distance in the simulation (i.e., $\sum d_{\mathrm{tot}}$, on x-axis), averaged across simulations with the same n_{car}, one curve for each set of rules. The figure allows to appreciate the trade-off between traffic efficiency and safety: the larger the overall distance, the larger the overall number of collisions. However, it can also be seen that the curve of GE rules strictly dominates both the other two curves (no rules and hand-written rules), hence suggesting that GE rules may be a better way of regulating road traffic regardless of the amount of cars in the graph—i.e., not only for the n_{car} for which the GE rules were generated. This latter finding seems to confirm the good generalization ability of our approach.

Figure 4 also shows another interesting property of our traffic model, namely it highlights the congestion condition. In facts, in both the cases where the traffic is regulated (hand-written and GE rules), there is a maximum number of cars in the graph ($n_{\mathrm{car}} = 17$) after which no further increasing in the overall distance can be obtained, while an increasing in overall number of collisions occurs. Interestingly, despite the fact that the maximum injected traffic before congestion in the two cases is the same, with GE rules the resulting overall distance is greater and the resulting overall number of collisions is smaller.

Table 6 shows in detail the best GE rules: it can be seen that the set consists of four rules, one of which (the 2nd) is clearly always broken in our simulations, since it tries to impose a minimum linear speed which cannot be reached with the parameters shown in Table 3. Rule 4 is easily understandable and its inclusion in

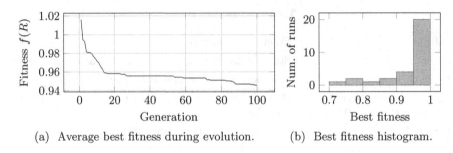

(a) Average best fitness during evolution.

(b) Best fitness histogram.

Fig. 5. Fitness of the best individual: during the evolution, averaged across the 30 runs, on the left; histogram w.r.t. the 30 runs at the end of the evolution, on the right.

best individual is not surprising. The role, if any, of rules 1 and 3 on the drivers' behavior is not clear. Rule 3 is hard to understand, i.e., hard to translate in natural language: the third disjunction says that the remaining part of the rule applies only when the car is in a section (since if $p \in I \equiv p \notin S$, the rule is true); the first and second disjunctions can be rewritten as $\delta v_0 \in \{\emptyset, -1, 0, 1\}$, hence resulting in the rule being writable as $(p \in S \wedge \delta v_0 = \text{opposite}) \implies \Delta x_0 \leq 3$. However, due to the driver's algorithm (see Table 2) and the value of the parameter d_ϵ (see Table 3), it is unlikely that rule 3 plays an actual role in determining drivers' behavior.

The analysis of the rules of Table 6 may suggest that some mechanism for detecting and cleaning ineffective rules may be beneficial in order to (i) increase the readability/understandability of the generated rules, and (ii) improve the evolutionary search. While we cannot make any meaningful prediction in this respect, we observe that, for the former goal, some automatic and domain-specific heuristic applied after the evolution may suffice—indeed a similar approach have been applied in [8] in the field of the automatic generation of rules for security policies.

We also analyzed our experimental results by looking at how individuals evolved across the 30 runs. Figure 5 summarizes the results of the evolutionary searches in terms of the fitness of the best individual in the population. In particular, Fig. 5a shows how the average (across all runs) best individual fitness varies during the evolution; Fig. 5b shows the histogram of the best individual fitness at the end of the evolution.

It can be seen from Fig. 5a that GE is in general able to decrease the fitness of individuals during the evolution: however, after approximately 20 generations, fitness decreases much more slowly. We speculate that some improvement to evolutionary search might be obtained by finely tuning the GE-related parameters, or maybe by using a different variant of GE (e.g., [7,9]). However, we also note that our scenario is characterized by a remarkably high stochasticity which could, at least, slow down the search of a good solution and, from a more practical point of view, makes experimentation and parameter tuning costly due to the long time needed to compute the fitness. In our case, running a single simulation took $\approx$ 10 s on commodity hardware and computing the fitness of a single individual (i.e., a set of rules) consisted in running 10 simulations, precisely to mitigate the impact of the high stochasticity in the simulations.

Figure 5b shows the histogram of the best individual fitness at the end of the evolution across the 30 runs. It can be seen that most of the runs resulted in fitness values close to 1, i.e., the distribution is skewed toward bad values. We analyzed the details of the runs and found that in some of those cases the search got stuck in a local minimum corresponding to a set of rules including one or more rules which, in practice, enforce drivers to stand still. Under those rules, no collision occurs (CpT = 0) and no one moves (ASR = 0), which is, clearly, one extreme of the trade-off between traffic efficiency and safety.

5 Concluding Remarks and Future Work

We proposed and assessed experimentally, by an extensive set of simulations, a method for synthesizing automatically a set of road traffic rules with the aim of maximizing such global indexes as road efficiency (high average speed) and safety (low number of collisions). We are motivated by a future scenario in which human and machine-based drivers will coexist on the roads, making current road regulation possibly unsuitable or inefficient. We are not aware of any similar proposal.

Our method is based on GE: individuals are sets of rules written according to a context-free grammar that we designed ad hoc to express quite expressive concepts such as, e.g., "stay on the rightmost free lane" or "slow down when approaching an intersection". The fitness of a candidate set of rules is given by a weighted sum of the traffic efficiency and safety resulting from the application of the rules set in a number of simulations, which makes this GE application highly stochastic.

Results of our experimental evaluation are promising, since generated rules result in simulated road traffic which is more efficient and safer than that regulated by hand-written rules or not regulated at all.

Our work may be extended in different ways, such as: (i) including a more fine-grained model (e.g., concerning intersections); (ii) considering a different way for expressing rules (e.g., with Linear Temporal Logic); (iii) better exploring GE parameters and/or variants. We plan to investigate some of these research lines in future works.

Acknowledgements. The authors are grateful to Lorenzo Castelli for his insightful comments.

References

1. Bartoli, A., De Lorenzo, A., Medvet, E., Tarlao, F.: Syntactical similarity learning by means of grammatical evolution. In: Handl, J., Hart, E., Lewis, P.R., López-Ibáñez, M., Ochoa, G., Paechter, B. (eds.) PPSN 2016. LNCS, vol. 9921, pp. 260–269. Springer, Cham (2016). doi:10.1007/978-3-319-45823-6_24

2. Brabazon, A., O'Neill, M.: Evolving technical trading rules for spot foreign-exchange markets using grammatical evolution. CMS **1**(3–4), 311–327 (2004)
3. Drake, J.H., Kililis, N., Özcan, E.: Generation of VNS components with grammatical evolution for vehicle routing. In: Krawiec, K., Moraglio, A., Hu, T., Etaner-Uyar, A.Ş., Hu, B. (eds.) EuroGP 2013. LNCS, vol. 7831, pp. 25–36. Springer, Heidelberg (2013). doi:10.1007/978-3-642-37207-0_3
4. Greene, J.D.: Our driverless dilemma. Science **352**(6293), 1514–1515 (2016)
5. Kirkpatrick, K.: The moral challenges of driverless cars. Commun. ACM **58**(8), 19–20 (2015). http://doi.acm.org/10.1145/2788477
6. Koza, J.R.: Genetic programming: on the programming of computers by means of natural selection, vol. 1. MIT press (1992)
7. Lourenço, N., Pereira, F.B., Costa, E.: SGE: a structured representation for grammatical evolution. In: Bonnevay, S., Legrand, P., Monmarché, N., Lutton, E., Schoenauer, M. (eds.) EA 2015. LNCS, vol. 9554, pp. 136–148. Springer, Cham (2016). doi:10.1007/978-3-319-31471-6_11
8. Medvet, E., Bartoli, A., Carminati, B., Ferrari, E.: Evolutionary inference of attribute-based access control policies. In: Gaspar-Cunha, A., Henggeler Antunes, C., Coello, C.C. (eds.) EMO 2015. LNCS, vol. 9018, pp. 351–365. Springer, Cham (2015). doi:10.1007/978-3-319-15934-8_24
9. O'Neill, M., Brabazon, A., Nicolau, M., Garraghy, S.M., Keenan, P.: πGrammatical evolution. In: Deb, K. (ed.) GECCO 2004. LNCS, vol. 3103, pp. 617–629. Springer, Heidelberg (2004). doi:10.1007/978-3-540-24855-2_70
10. Rizaldi, A., Althoff, M.: Formalising traffic rules for accountability of autonomous vehicles. In: 2015 IEEE 18th International Conference on Intelligent Transportation Systems, pp. 1658–1665. IEEE (2015)
11. Ryan, C., Collins, J.J., Neill, M.O.: Grammatical evolution: evolving programs for an arbitrary language. In: Banzhaf, W., Poli, R., Schoenauer, M., Fogarty, T.C. (eds.) EuroGP 1998. LNCS, vol. 1391, pp. 83–96. Springer, Heidelberg (1998). doi:10.1007/BFb0055930
12. Sanchez, J.J., Galan, M., Rubio, E.: Applying a traffic lights evolutionary optimization technique to a real case: "las ramblas" area in santa cruz de tenerife. IEEE Trans. Evol. Comput. **12**(1), 25–40 (2008)
13. Tachet, R., Santi, P., Sobolevsky, S., Reyes-Castro, L.I., Frazzoli, E., Helbing, D., Ratti, C.: Revisiting street intersections using slot-based systems. PLoS one **11**(3), e0149607 (2016)
14. Tumova, J., Hall, G.C., Karaman, S., Frazzoli, E., Rus, D.: Least-violating control strategy synthesis with safety rules. In: Proceedings of the 16th International Conference on Hybrid Systems: Computation and Control, HSCC 2013, pp. 1–10. ACM, New York (2013). http://doi.acm.org/10.1145/2461328.2461330
15. Vanholme, B., Gruyer, D., Lusetti, B., Glaser, S., Mammar, S.: Highly automated driving on highways based on legal safety. IEEE Trans. Intell. Transp. Syst. **14**(1), 333–347 (2013)
16. Wen, W.: A dynamic and automatic traffic light control expert system for solving the road congestion problem. Expert Syst. Appl. **34**(4), 2370–2381 (2008)

Solving Dynamic Graph Coloring Problem Using Dynamic Pool Based Evolutionary Algorithm

Gizem Sungu and Betul Boz[✉]

Computer Engineering Department, Marmara University, 34722 Istanbul, Turkey
gizem.sungu@marun.edu.tr, betul.demiroz@marmara.edu.tr

Abstract. Graph coloring problem is one of the main optimization problems from the literature. Many real world problems interacting with changing environments can be modeled with dynamic graphs. Genetic algorithms are a good choice to solve dynamic graph coloring problem because they can adopt to dynamic environments and are suitable for problems with NP-hard complexity. In this paper, we propose a dynamic pool based evolutionary algorithm (DPBEA) for solving the dynamic graph coloring problem, which contains a partition based representation to adopt to the dynamic changes of the graph and carry the valuable information obtained in history. The proposed algorithm uses a novel special purpose pool based crossover operator that targets to minimize the number of colors used in the solutions and a local search method that tries to increase the diversity of the solutions. We compared the performance of our algorithm with a well known heuristic for solving the graph coloring problem and a genetic algorithm with a dynamic population using a large number of dynamic graphs. The experimental evaluation indicates that our algorithm outperforms these algorithms with respect to number of colors used by the algorithms in most of the test cases provided.

Keywords: Graph coloring problem · Genetic algorithms · Dynamic graphs

1 Introduction

The graph coloring problem is one of the well-known optimization problems from the literature that tries to assign different colors to the vertices connected through an edge in a given graph. Its aim is to use minimum number of colors to color the vertices in the graph. This problem can be used to solve many practical and theoretical problems such as register allocation [1], frequency assignment [2] and scheduling applications [3]. The graph coloring problem is NP-Complete [4] and genetic algorithms are widely used to solve this problem [5,6].

In the static graph coloring problem, the input graph can be modeled with n number of vertices connected with edges having a probability of p and represented as $G(n, p)$ [7]. Genetic algorithms have been applied to solve static graph coloring problem [8,9].

© Springer International Publishing AG 2017
G. Squillero and K. Sim (Eds.): EvoApplications 2017, Part II, LNCS 10200, pp. 189–204, 2017.
DOI: 10.1007/978-3-319-55792-2_13

Most of the real-world optimization problems are changing over time [10] and can be modeled by using dynamic graphs [11]. The dynamic graph model used in this study adds the dimension of time to the graph $G(n, p, c_v)$ where c_v denotes *vertex change rate* as defined in [12]. In this work, vertex-dynamic graphs [11] that dynamically change in time by adding or removing vertices from the graph are used.

In this paper, we propose a solution to the dynamic graph coloring problem. Each individual in the population is represented with partitions [9] having non-conflicting nodes. When the graph changes, some of the nodes are added or removed from the graph. The individuals in the population can easily adopt to these changes by deleting the nodes from the partitions without changing the current non-conflicting groups, and adding new partitions for each newly added node. Our algorithm is able to keep the valuable information obtained in history and reshape this information with the current state of the graph. The number of partitions represent the number of colors used to color the graph, and the solution quality of each individual is different so the number of partitions in each representation is also dynamic. We propose a highly specialized and novel crossover operator that can easily deal with the dynamic representation of the individuals. It targets to maximize the number of non-conflicting nodes in the graph and place them to the same partition. The nodes having conflicts can not be directly placed in a partition so a pool is proposed to keep these nodes and place them to the most appropriate partition as soon as possible. As a result, the proposed pool based crossover operator can easily adopt to the dynamic changes of the graph. When we try to maximize the number of non-conflicting nodes in the partitions, we are also decreasing the search area, so to increase the diversity of the solutions in the population, we propose a local search method for checking the neighborhood solutions.

We conduct experiments with dynamic graphs to test the effectiveness of the proposed solution. The performance of our solution is compared with Degree of Saturation (DSATUR) [13] which is a well known and effcient greedy heuristic for solving the graph coloring problem and DGA [12] which is the first and recently published genetic algorithm that solves the dynamic graph coloring problem. DGA proposes a dynamic population that includes individuals with permutation based representation. It uses a standart crossover operator OX1 [14] and a mutation operator SWAP [15]. They mainly concentrate on the dynamics of the problem and dynamics of the algorithm and proposed populations suitable for dynamic graph coloring problem, so their genetic algorithm is pure and straightforward. Our experimental evaluation indicates that we have outperformed both of the algorithms from the literature.

The rest of this paper is structured as follows. The next section presents the details of the proposed solution. The experimental evaluation is given in Sect. 3. Finally, Sect. 4 summarizes our main conclusions.

2   Proposed Work

In the dynamic graph coloring problem, the dimension time is added to the graph so it changes over time. In our approach, only the current state of the graph is known and the solution from evolutionary algorithm is generated according to this state. The problem representation and operators of our algorithm are designed such that it can adopt to the dynamic changes of the graph.

The general procedure of our evolutionary algorithm is given in Fig. 1. The algorithm works on various number of dynamic graphs, and at time step $t = 1$ the first graph G_1 is created. The number of nodes in the initial graph will determine the number of color classes used by each individual in the initial population. According to the graph change step value, the current graph used by the algorithm will change and a new graph will be created. The algorithm gets the current state of the graph generated at time step t and continues for a predefined number of iterations working on the same graph. In each iteration, two individuals represented as *parent1* and *parent2* are randomly selected from the population and a new offspring is generated by applying the problem specific crossover operator from these individuals. The main objective of local search method is to add diversity to the newly generated solution by regrouping some of the randomly selected color classes, and it also tries to decrease the number

---

1. Generate an initial graph G_1.
2. **while** not predefined number of initial vertices created in G_1 **do**
3.   Create a vertex v.
4.   Assign a life time that is set randomly between t_{min} and t_{max} to v.
5.   Create edges between v and the vertices in G_1 with edge probability p.
6. **endwhile**
7. Generate an initial population S randomly according to G_1.
8. Evaluate S based on the given fitness function F.
9. **while** not predefined number of $GraphChangeStep(t)$ evaluated **do**
10.   **while** not predefined number of iterations evaluated **do**
11.   Select two parents from S randomly.
12.   Apply pool-based crossover to these parents to create an offspring.
13.   Mutate the offspring according to $MutationRate$.
14.   Evaluate the offspring based on F.
15.   Replace the offspring with the worst parent of S.
16.   **endwhile**
17.   Remove the vertices that have reached the end of their life times.
18.   Add new vertices to G_t according to $GraphChangeRate(c_v)$.
19.   Assign life times to the added vertices by using t_{min} and t_{max}.
20.   Create edges between the current and newly added vertices in G_t with p.
21. **endwhile**

Fig. 1. General algorithm of DPBEA

of color classes used in the offspring. Local search method may increase the number of colors used in the offspring generated after crossover, and in this case the offspring generated after crossover is used for replacement. Finally the fitness value of the offspring is calculated. The offspring is always replaced with the parent having the worst fitness value.

When the algorithm reaches the end of the iterations, it gives the best parent as the solution for the graph at time step t. The state of the graph is then changed to produce the graph at time step $t+1$ by removing nodes with its edges from the graph and adding newly generated nodes to the graph. Each node removed from the graph is also removed from all of the individuals, and a new color class is created for each newly generated node in all of the individuals in the population.

2.1   Graph Generation

Our input graph is modeled as $G(n,p)$ at time step $t = 1$ and is represented as G_1. When a vertex in the graph is created, a life time that is set randomly between two input parameters t_{min} and t_{max}, is assigned to the vertex. Throughout its lifetime, the vertex will exist on the graph. At each time step, the vertices in the graph are checked, and the ones that have reached the end of their life times are removed with their edges from the graph. While some vertices are removed from the graph, new vertices are added with graph change rate c_v. The number of vertices that can be added to the graph at time step t represented with G_t is determined randomly between 0 and $n \times c_v$. When a vertice is added to the graph, all of the vertices that are still alive are traversed and an edge is created between these two vertices with probability p.

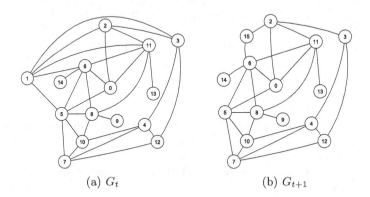

(a) G_t (b) G_{t+1}

Fig. 2. State of the dynamic graphs at graph change step t and $t+1$

Figure 2 shows the states of an input graph at time t as G_t and time $t+1$ as G_{t+1}. At time t, G_t has 15 vertices. At time t+1, $vertice_1$ has ended its lifetime and is removed from the graph with its edges $e_{1,2}$, $e_{1,3}$, $e_{1,5}$, $e_{1,6}$ and $e_{1,11}$. At the same time, $vertice_{15}$ is added with its edges $e_{15,2}$ and $e_{15,6}$ to the graph. Edges are only added or removed when the vertices are removed or added. The total number of nodes is the same for G_t and G_{t+1} but the total number of edges in the graph has decreased. These two graphs will be used in the following figures to describe our algorithm and to compare the performance of our algorithm with the algorithms from the literature.

2.2   Initial Population Generation

The initial population contains a predefined number of individuals and each individual is generated randomly. In our algorithm, each individual is represented with the partition method [9] as S_i where $S_i = \{R_0, R_1, ...R_{k-1}\}$ and k is the total number of colors used in the solution. Each color class R_i contains any number of conflict free nodes. In the dynamic graph coloring problem, the number of colors needed to color a given graph is not known a priori, and nodes can not be randomly assigned to color classes, because the classes should be conflict free. Due to these restrictions, each node is represented with a different color, and is assigned to a different color class R_i in the initial population. Thus k is equal to the total number of nodes only in the initial graph G_1. Once the grouping of the conflict free nodes starts, the number of colors used in the individuals will decrease and k will no longer be equal to n.

2.3   Crossover Operator

In this work, we propose a novel crossover operator *Dynamic Pool-Based Crossover* (DPBC) that increases the search space while generating each color class of the offspring. It also includes a pool which contains conflicting nodes that have not been assigned to any color class yet. DPBC is a variant of the *Pool-Based Crossover* (PBC) [16] operator that we have recently proposed. PBC operator is suitable for static and weighted graphs, whereas in this work the graphs are dynamically generated and the weights of the nodes are equal. The basic working principle of these operators is the same, but DPBC operator has major differences to adapt to the dynamics of the problem. Also in PBC operator, the number of colors to be used are fixed but in DPBC operator, the number of colors used by the algorithm changes as the solution evolves and gets better, or as the graph changes in time so is not fixed.

Our algorithm selects two parents with k partitions $S_1 = \{R_0^1, R_1^1, ...R_{k-1}^1\}$ and $S_2 = \{R_0^2, R_1^2, ...R_{k-1}^2\}$ randomly for the crossover operation. The proposed algorithm generates dynamic solutions and the number of color classes in S_1 and S_2 may not be equal but the total number of nodes in S_1 and S_2 are always equal. Initially the pool is emptied. In each step, DPBC operator selects one of the color classes from S_1 and S_2 randomly and combines the nodes in these color classes in R_i, which is the newly generated color class of the offspring. The nodes that are present in R_i are removed from the color classes of both of the parents S_1 and S_2. For each node in R_i, DPBC operator calculates the total number of conflicts and creates the maximum set of non-conflicting nodes by removing the nodes with the highest number of conflicts from R_i. If two nodes in R_i have the same number of conflicts, one of the nodes is selected randomly.

As soon as the conflicting nodes are removed from R_i and are placed in the pool, R_i becomes conflict free.

In the next step, the operator selects two random color classes that have not been selected from S_1 and S_2 again, combines the nodes in these classes with the nodes in the pool and places them to the next color class of the offspring. This process continues until all nodes in the parents are visited. If there are any nodes left in the pool, these nodes have not been assigned to a color class due to conflicts. Starting from the node with the highest number of conflicts in the original graph, a new color class is generated and the node is removed from the pool and added to this class. The remaining nodes in the pool are also checked and assigned to the new color class if they are not conflicting with the node/nodes currently assigned to the new color class. This process continues until all of the nodes left in the pool are assigned to a color class, and the pool becomes empty.

Figure 3 is an example of the crossover operator applied on two parents. In the first step of the algorithm, R_0^1 and R_2^2 are selected randomly and the nodes in these classes are combined in R_0. The selected nodes are removed from both of the parents S_1 and S_2. The conflicts between the nodes in R_0 are calculated by using the graph in Fig. 2(a) and $CF(m)$ denotes the total number of conflicts of each node m in the color class R_0. Node 5 has the maximum number of conflicts due to $e_{5,6}$ and $e_{5,10}$, so it is thrown to the pool. Once node 5 is removed from R_0, $CF(6)$ and $CF(10)$ are updated and are decreased by one. Each time a node is thrown to the pool, the total number of conflicts are recalculated. The nodes in R_0 are now conflict-free and are colored with $Color_0$.

In the next iteration, R_1^1 and R_0^2 are selected randomly and the nodes in these classes are combined with the nodes in the pool in R_1. This time node 5 and node 11 has the maximum number of conflicts, which is 4 and node 5 is randomly selected and is thrown to the pool. Node 5 is conflicting with node 0, node 1, node 7 and node 8, so the conflict numbers of these nodes are updated and CF_0, CF_1, CF_7 and CF_8 become 1, 2, 1 and 1 respectively. Node 11 still has 4 number of conflicts so it is also thrown to the pool. Node 11 has conflicts with node 0, node 1, node 8 and node 13, so CF_0, CF_1, CF_8 and CF_{13} become 0, 1, 0, 0 respectively. After the updates, there are still 4 conflicting nodes in R_1, which are node 1, node 3, node 4 and node 7. CF_3 and CF_4 are both 2, so node 4 is randomly selected and thrown to the pool and after the conflicts are updated node 1 is randomly selected and thrown to the pool.

In the third step, R_2^1 and R_3^2 are selected randomly, R_3^2 contains node 9 so it is combined with the nodes in the pool in R_2. In the previous iterations, all the nodes in the selected color classes are removed from both of the parents, and even if R_2^1 has never been selected before, it contains 0 nodes. Node 1 is conflicting with node 5 and node 11 and is thrown to the pool and the remaining nodes in R_2 are conflict free and colored with $Color_2$. Even though S_1 and S_2 has 4 color classes, all of the nodes in the graph are visited in three iterations and the parents become empty. Finally the algorithm checks the pool and creates new color classes for the nodes remaining in the pool. Node 1 is assigned to color class R_3 and colored with $Color_3$. Once the pool is emptied, the crossover operation is finished.

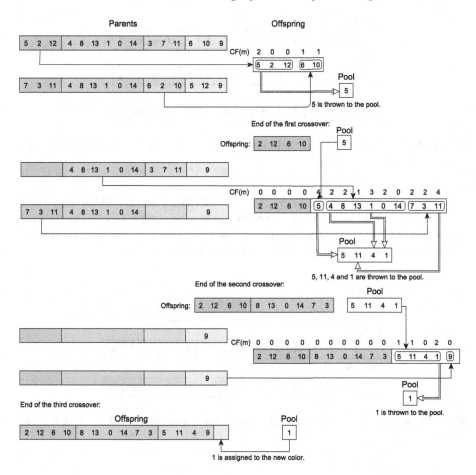

Fig. 3. Applying dynamic pool-based crossover on two parents using G_t. (Color figure online)

We have used the graphs in Fig. 2 to obtain the actual results of DPBEA, DGA and DSATUR algorithms which are given in Figs. 4 and 5 for the dynamic graphs G_t and G_{t+1} respectively. The results for DPBEA and DGA on the dynamic graphs are obtained after 2000 actual evolution steps. All three algorithms use 4 colors to color the graph in Fig. 2(a).

The aim of the DPBC operator is to group maximum number of nodes in the same color class and leave minimum number of nodes in the least used color classes. This property will bring the opportunity to decrease the number of colors used when the node/nodes that are present in the least used color are removed from the graph in the next graph change step. For example, node 1 is removed from G_{t+1} in Fig. 2(b) and the number of colors used in the offspring generated in Fig. 3 is reduced by one, even if node 15 is added to the graph. We would obtain the same performance if node 3 was removed instead of node 1,

DPBEA:

2	12	6	10	8	13	0	14	7	3	5	11	4	9	1

DGA:

11	1	4	12	9	13	10	7	0	5	2	8	14	6	3

DSATUR:

11	6	1	5	8	2	10	3	4	7	12	0	9	13	14

Fig. 4. Results obtained from actual runs of the algorithms on G_t (Color figure online)

and node 1 would be placed in R_1. In Fig. 5, DPBEA and DSATUR uses three color classes, whereas DGA uses 4 colors to color the graph G_{t+1}. The solution representation of the algorithms are not the same due to differences (partition-based vs. permutation-based) in individual representations.

DPBEA:

6	2	12	9	10	3	8	7	14	0	13	15	5	11	4

DGA:

0	6	15	11	14	12	13	9	2	5	3	8	4	7	10

DSATUR:

6	5	8	11	10	0	2	7	4	3	12	15	9	14	13

Fig. 5. Results obtained from actual runs of the algorithms on G_{t+1} (Color figure online)

The grouping of the nodes have these benefits, but the DPBC operator will group similar nodes in color classes after some number of evolution steps. For example, R_1^1 and R_1^2, R_2^1 and R_0^2 are two color classes that contain the same nodes in parents S_1 and S_2. To prevent producing offsprings with similar color classes and to increase diversity, local search is applied to the offspring with mutation probability.

2.4   Local Search Method

In local search phase, there is a mutation chance for every color class so each color class is visited to decide whether LS will be applied or not. A random number is generated for each color class of the offspring and local search is applied to the color classes depending on this number and the mutation probability. If mutation is applied to a color class, all the nodes in this class are thrown to the pool. The selected color classes become empty and are no longer used.

All of the remaining color classes that are not selected for mutation are visited. The aim is to increase the number of non-conflicting nodes in these color classes. Starting from the first color class, all of the nodes in the pool are added to the color class and combined with the nodes in this class. For each node, the number of conflicts are recalculated, and the nodes with highest number of conflicts are thrown to the pool as done in crossover operator. This process continues until all nodes in the pool are assigned to a color class.

If the number of colors used in the offspring increases after local search, the offspring created after crossover is replaced with the parent that has the worst fitness value, otherwise the offspring created after local search (even if it has worse fitness value than the offspring created after crossover) is selected for replacement to increase diversity.

2.5 Computation of Fitness Function

The number of colors used to color the dynamic graph in each graph change step is the basic criteria to compare the performance of the individuals. Two individuals may use the same number of colors, but one of them may have higher probability to generate a better offspring in the next graph change step, if the number of nodes is not evenly distributed between color classes. So our aim is to obtain individuals with fewest number of nodes in the three least used color classes. For each individual S_i, the fitness value F_i is calculated by Eq. 1 [12].

$$F_i = n^3 * c_i + n^2 * c_{i,1} + n * c_{i,2} + c_{i,3} \tag{1}$$

In this equation, n denotes the number of nodes currently available in the dynamic graph, c_i is the number of colors used, $c_{i,1}$, $c_{i,2}$ and $c_{i,3}$ are the number of nodes in the least, second least and the third least used color class. As we are trying to minimize the number of colors used, our algorithm tries to minimize the fitness function. The fitness values calculated for the solutions given in Fig. 4 are 13789, 14000, 13790 for DPBEA, DGA and DSATUR respectively. Even if all three algorithms use 4 colors, DPBEA and DSATUR have 1 node in the least used color class, so their fitness values are close to each other whereas DGA has 2 nodes in the least used color and has the worst fitness value.

3 Experimental Evaluation

In this section, the performance of our algorithm DPBEA is compared with DSATUR [13] and DGA [12] algorithms. We consider the number of colors used and the fitness values of the algorithms for comparison. The performance of the algorithms are evaluated using dynamic graphs. A graph generator running parallel with the algorithms creates the dynamic graphs. The graph generator takes six input parameters which are:

- *Graph Change Step:* Graph change step determines the number of dynamic graphs generated from the initial graph. The default value for graph change step is 50, but it can vary from 5 to 50 in the experiments.

– *Total Number of Nodes:* Total number of nodes in the graph is denoted by n. The default value for the number of nodes in the graph is 100. In the initial graph, there will be 0 to 5 nodes and according to graph change rate, minimum and maximum lifetime, the total number of nodes in each graph change step will change dynamically.
– *Edge Density:* Edge density is denoted by p. The default value of edge density is 0.75 but it can take values between 0.1 and 0.95.
– *Graph Change Rate:* Graph change rate denoted by c_v, is used to determine whether the dynamic change in the graph will be fast or slow. It affects the total number of nodes in the graph. If the graph change rate is low, the total number of nodes in the graph will change slowly. In Table 1, the relations between graph change rate and the number of nodes in the graph can easily be seen. The default value for graph change rate is 0.1, but in the experiments it can vary from 0.01 to 0.3.
– *Minimum Lifetime:* The minimum amount of iterations that a node is kept alive in the graph is the minimum lifetime of a node and is denoted by t_{min}.
– *Maximum Lifetime:* The maximum amount of iterations that a node is kept alive in the graph is the maximum lifetime of a node and is denoted by t_{max}.

The default values for the parameters of the evolutionary algorithm are mutation rate = 0.3, population size = 100 and generation size = 8000. In order to balance the number of nodes that are added and removed in each graph change step, the values for t_{min} and t_{max} are set to 3 and 13 respectively. These values are used in the experiments unless stated otherwise.

The initial graph has 0 nodes and in each graph change step, at most $n \times c_v$ number of nodes are added to the graph. When a node is created, a number between t_{min} and t_{max} is randomly generated to denote its lifetime, then all the nodes in the graph are traversed and an edge between these two nodes is created with probability p. In each graph change step, the graph is changed and is given as input to all three algorithms. In the first evolution step DSATUR algorithm produces its result, and in DGA and DPBEA the newly produced nodes are added to and the dead nodes are removed from the population. In DPBEA, the dead nodes are deleted from their color classes and for each newly produced node, a new color class is created and this node is the only node that is placed to this color class. Both DGA and DPBEA algorithms will evolve for 8000 evolution steps (denoted as e), where 8000 individuals are generated. The best individuals from DGA and DPBEA are recorded at the end of the graph change step. To compare the performance of the algorithms, this process continues for 50 graph change steps (from G_1 to G_{50}) working on one single dynamic graph and a total of 10 dynamic graphs are generated. The results are the mean of the number of colors and fitness values calculated by each algorithm for 500 different graph states.

In Figs. 6 and 7, the performance of three algorithms are evaluated and the results are given as percentage of the mean number of colors DSATUR algorithm used to see the relative performance of the algorithms clearly. The mean number

Table 1. Comparison of the algorithms by using dynamic graphs generated with different graph change rate values

c_v	# of nodes			# of colors used			Fitness values		
	Current	Added	Removed	DSATUR	DGA	DPBEA	DSATUR	DGA	DPBEA
0.1	5	8.2	0	2.4	2.4	2.4	106	106	106
	13.2	9.4	2.2	4.6	4.6	4.6	122×10^2	122×10^2	122×10^2
	20.4	10.2	3.2	5.6	5.4	5.4	584×10^2	553×10^2	553×10^2
	27.4	8.6	3.2	6.72	6.4	6.6	149×10^3	143×10^3	146×10^3
	32.8	10.2	3.6	7.6	7.08	6.96	280×10^3	263×10^3	260×10^3
	39.4	10.4	5.2	8.48	8.08	8	568×10^3	535×10^3	531×10^3
	44.6	9	8	9.8	8.92	8.64	991×10^3	892×10^3	859×10^3
	45.6	12.8	6.8	10	9.4	8.96	113×10^4	104×10^4	995×10^3
0.2	5	19.2	0	2	2	2	824	816	816
	24.2	19	4	6	6	6	114×10^3	109×10^3	109×10^3
	39.2	19.2	6	9	8.28	8	662×10^3	595×10^3	584×10^3
	52.4	21.4	7.8	10.6	9.92	9.6	164×10^4	153×10^4	149×10^4
	66	22.6	9	12.64	11.84	11.08	365×10^4	341×10^4	321×10^4
	79.6	21	10.6	15.04	14.36	13.56	837×10^4	798×10^4	759×10^4
	90	20	13	16.36	15.48	14.6	129×10^5	122×10^5	115×10^5
	97	19.4	12.8	17.04	16.6	15.56	160×10^5	156×10^5	146×10^5
0.3	5	29.6	0	2.6	2.6	2.6	247	246	246
	34.6	23.6	3.8	7.83	7.12	7	309×10^3	282×10^3	278×10^3
	54.4	27.8	5.8	10.92	10.52	9.92	175×10^4	168×10^4	159×10^4
	76.4	30.2	9	14.4	13.6	12.8	683×10^4	644×10^4	607×10^4
	97.6	31.4	14.4	17.48	16.72	16.08	179×10^5	170×10^5	164×10^5
	114.6	31	17.8	19.56	18.76	18.52	316×10^5	302×10^5	299×10^5
	127.8	32.4	21	21.28	20.84	20.2	488×10^5	477×10^5	462×10^5
	139.2	33.8	22.4	22.68	22.08	21.44	651×10^5	636×10^5	617×10^5

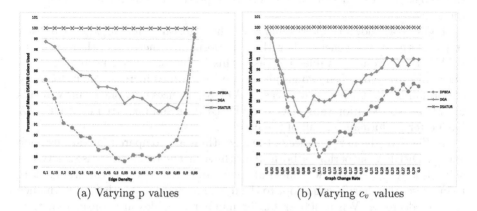

(a) Varying p values   (b) Varying c_v values

Fig. 6. Performance of DGA and DPBEA relative to DSATUR for variable edge probability and node probability values (Color figure online)

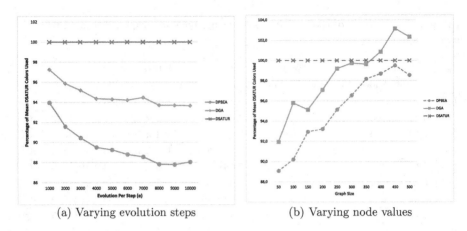

(a) Varying evolution steps   (b) Varying node values

Fig. 7. Performance of DGA and DPBEA relative to DSATUR for varying evolution steps and node values (Color figure online)

of colors used by DGA and DPBEA algorithms are scaled by the mean number of colors used by DSATUR algorithm.

In Fig. 6(a), the performance of the algorithms are compared for varying edge density values. As p values increase, the number of edges connecting the nodes in the graph are increased, so the number of colors used by the three algorithms also increase. The gap between DGA and DPBEA is variable and increased as p increases, but as p reaches 0.95, DGA and DPBEA nearly use the same number of colors.

In Fig. 6(b), the performance of the algorithms are compared for variable graph change rate values, that determine the probability of the number of nodes added to the graph at each graph change step. DPBEA outperforms DGA in nearly all of the cases (except 3 cases where they have equal performance), and this shows that our algorithm has better adaptation to the dynamic changes of the graph.

Figure 7(a) shows the performance of the algorithms for different evolution steps. Both of the genetic algorithms performance increase with respect to DSATUR as evolution values increase. This is due to generating higher number of offsprings between two graph change steps which increase the probability of obtaining a better result, whereas DSATUR produces only one result which is not related to evolution value. DGA and DPBEA have similar trend but DPBEA has better performance in all of the cases.

In Fig. 7(b) the performance of the algorithms are compared for various node values. DPBEA outperforms both algorithms in all of the test cases. DGA is suitable for graphs with few number of nodes, and as the nodes in the graphs start to increase, they hardly can adopt to the dynamic changes and their performance start to decrease. When 400 or higher number of nodes are considered, they show the worst performance. The results from the original paper of DGA show a similar trend. In the original paper, they use a smaller evolution size that is equal to 1000, and when 250 or higher number of nodes is considered, they have the worst performance.

Table 1 is used to show how the graph changes in 8 graph change steps (from G_1 to G_8). The values in this table are the mean values obtained from 15 different graphs having an edge probability 0.15, 0.3, 0.45, 0.6 and 0.75. For each edge probability value, 3 dynamic graphs are generated. This process continued for 3 different graph change rate values of 0.1, 0.2 and 0.3. So the total number of dynamic graphs used in this test is 45. t_{min} and t_{max} are set to 2 and 5 to see the affect of these parameters much more clearly. That is why in the first two graph change steps, the number of nodes removed from the graph is equal to 0. Starting from an initial graph with 5 nodes, the final graph contains 45.6 nodes, 97 nodes and 139.2 nodes for 0.1, 0.2 and 0.3 graph change rate values respectively. When we compare the algorithms, all three algorithms have the same performance in 5 test cases in the initial graphs. Once the graphs start to change dynamically, DPBEA outperforms DGA and DSATUR in 17 tests cases because it can adapt to these changes faster than DGA due to problem specific representation of the individuals and operators. In the remaining test cases, DGA outperforms DPBEA in 1 test case and DGA and DPBEA have equal performance outperforming DSATUR in 1 test case. When the fitness values are compared for the cases where all algorithms have the same performance, DGA and DPBEA find the same solution and in 2 test cases, their solutions are better than DSATUR.

In Tables 2 and 3 the performance of DPBEA algorithm that does not use local search (represented with DPBEA*) is also given to show the efficiency and cost of the operators used in DPBEA in much more detail. In both of the tests, initial graph contains 50 nodes and at each graph change step 50 nodes are added to the graph. None of the nodes are deleted from the graphs so t_{min} and t_{max} are not used in these tests. The results are the average values obtained from 5 different populations each running on 5 different graphs in Table 3.

Table 2 contains the number of colors used by DSATUR, DGA, DPBEA* and DPBEA algorithm for different evolution steps to show the affect of initial population, crossover and local search operators. In DPBEA each node is placed to one color class in the initial population and each individual in the population contains n number of color classes. In the first evolution step, DPBEA significantly outperforms DPBEA* because both crossover and local search is applied to the offspring generated in the first evolution. When the evolution is completed, the gap between the solutions obtained from DPBEA and DPBEA* decreases and DPBEA has better performance than DPBEA* in 2 cases, has equal performance in 2 cases and has worse performance in 1 case. This shows that our local search mechanism can be improved and the pool-based crossover mechanism is the main strength of our algorithm.

If we compare the initial solutions obtained by DGA and DPBEA, we see that there is a huge difference in the number of colors used. This is due to the differences in individual representation and the random node to color assignment DGA uses in initial population. Even if their initial population contains

Table 2. Comparison of the algorithms for varying node values and different evolution steps

Graph size	Evolution	# of colors used			
		DSATUR	DGA	DPBEA*	DPBEA
50	Before evolution	–	17.2	50.0	50.0
	1st evolution	17.4	17.1	35.0	26.4
	After evolution	17.4	16.0	15.0	15.0
100	Before evolution	–	30.4	65	65
	1st evolution	29.2	29.8	47	46.4
	After evolution	29.2	28.4	27	26.8
150	Before evolution	–	42.4	77	76.8
	1st evolution	41.2	41.8	59.2	52
	After evolution	41.2	40.2	38.6	38.6
200	Before evolution	–	54.4	88.6	88.6
	1st evolution	52.8	53.6	70.4	68.4
	After evolution	52.8	51.8	50	50.2
250	Before evolution	–	64.6	100.0	100.2
	1st evolution	62.8	63.7	81.2	80.6
	After evolution	62.8	61.4	60.2	60.0

better solutions, when the evolution is completed our algorithm outperforms DGA due to problem specific crossover operator. Both DGA and DPBEA can not outperform DSATUR when the results obtained after the first evolution is considered.

As the graph is dynamically changed, 50 nodes are added to the graph. DGA places these nodes randomly to its individuals, and the number of colors DGA uses is approximately increased by only 14, whereas DPBEA adds 50 new color classes, so the number of colors it uses is increased by 50 before the evolution of the new dynamic graph starts.

In Table 3 DPBEA outperforms DSATUR and DGA in all of the test cases provided. DGA shows the worst performance when 400 or greater number of nodes are considered, it can not easily adopt to the dynamic changes due to the structure of the problem representation and the operators it uses. DPBEA outperforms DPBEA* in 6 cases and they have equal performance in 1 case. Especially when the node number is equal to 300, local search significantly improves the quality of solution. When execution times are considered, DSATUR has very small amount of computational effort, and DPBEA shows the worst performance. If the execution times of DPBEA* and DPBEA are compared, we can see that local search method has a very high impact on the execution time.

Table 3. Detailed comparison of the algorithms for varying node values

n	# of colors used				Execution time			
	DSATUR	DGA	DPBEA*	DPBEA	DSATUR	DGA	DPBEA*	DPBEA
50	17.4	16.0	15.5	15.5	0.01	0.15	0.76	1.12
100	28.6	27.4	25.6	25.8	0.01	0.64	5.09	9.13
150	41.1	39.1	37.9	38.2	0.04	1.62	20.20	39.98
200	51.6	50.1	48.3	48.1	0.09	2.89	57.68	122.98
250	61.8	61.3	59.1	58.8	0.18	4.69	139.83	316.50
300	72.5	72.3	72.8	70.0	0.33	7.09	274.41	654.96
350	82.2	81.9	80.9	80.7	0.57	10.38	555.73	1276.75
400	91.6	92.4	90.3	90.4	0.87	14.20	1033.96	2369.62
450	100.6	102.7	100.3	100.1	1.28	18.22	1666.25	3866.60
500	110.6	113.2	109.2	109	1.94	24.80	2616.20	6207.40

4 Conclusions and Future Work

In this study, we propose a novel dynamic evolutionary algorithm for solving the dynamic graph coloring problem, that contains a novel crossover operator (DPBC) combined with a local search method that targets to increase the diversity of the solutions. We have used DSATUR, a well-known greedy algorithm for solving graph coloring problem, and DGA which is the first and to the best of our knowledge the only genetic algorithm targets to solve dynamic graph coloring problem, in the experimental study to evaluate the performance of our algorithm. Our algorithm outperforms DGA and DSATUR algorithms in most of the test cases with respect to total number of colors used when various graphs with different properties are considered.

Our algorithm has strengths and weaknesses. The most important strength is the efficient dynamic pool-based crossover operator it proposes, and the partition-based representation it uses. It is weak because it has the worst execution time. Nearly half of the computation time on DPBEA is spent on the local search mechanism that may not always yield to a better solution. As a future work, local search methods proposed in this study may be replaced with other efficient techniques to improve the quality of the solution. Also the performance of DPBEA can be investigated for edge-dynamic graphs, edge-vertex-dynamic graphs and dynamic graphs with different structures.

References

1. Briggs, P., Cooper, K., Torczon, L.: Improvements to graph coloring register allocation. Trans. Program. Lang. Syst. **16**(3), 428–455 (1994)
2. Aardal, K., van Hoesel, S.P.M., Koster, A.M.C.A., Mannino, C., Sassano, A.: Models and solution techniques for frequency assignment problems. Ann. Oper. Res. **153**(1), 79129 (2007)

3. Galinier, P., Hamiez, J.-P., Hao, J.-K., Porumbel, D.: Recent advances in graph vertex coloring. In: Zelinka, I., et al. (eds.) Handbook of Optimization. ISRL, vol. 38, pp. 505–528. Springer, Heidelberg (2013)
4. Garey, M.R., Johnson, D.S.: Computers and Intractability: A Guide to the Theory of NP-Completeness. W. H Freeman and Company, New York (1979)
5. Fleurent, C., Ferland, J.: Genetic and hybrid algorithms for graph coloring. Ann. Oper. Res. **63**, 437–461 (1996)
6. Dorne, R.Ë., Hao, J.-K.: A new genetic local search algorithm for graph coloring. In: Eiben, A.E., Bäck, T., Schoenauer, M., Schwefel, H.-P. (eds.) PPSN 1998. LNCS, vol. 1498, pp. 745–754. Springer, Heidelberg (1998). doi:10.1007/BFb0056916
7. Erdos, P., Renyi, A.: On the evolution of random graphs. Math. Inst. Hung. Acad. Sci. **5**, 17–61 (1960)
8. Fotakis, D.A., Likothanassis, S.D., Stefanakos, S.K.: An evolutionary annealing approach to graph coloring. In: Boers, E.J.W. (ed.) EvoWorkshops 2001. LNCS, vol. 2037, pp. 120–129. Springer, Heidelberg (2001). doi:10.1007/3-540-45365-2_13
9. Galinier, P., Hao, J.-K.: Hybrid evolutionary algorithms for graph coloring. J. Comb. Optim. **3**(4), 379–397 (1999)
10. Nguyen, T.T., Yang, S., Branke, J.: Evolutionary dynamic optimization: a survey of the state of the art. Swarm Evol. Comput. **6**, 1–24 (2012)
11. Harary, F., Gupta, G.: Dynamic graph models. Math. Comput. Model. **25**, 79–88 (1997)
12. Monical, C., Stonedahl, F.: Static vs. dynamic populations in genetic algorithms for coloring a dynamic graph. In: Proceedings of the 2014 Conference on Genetic and Evolutionary Computation, pp. 469–476. ACM, Vancouver (2014)
13. Brelaz, D.: New methods to color the vertices of a graph. Commun. ACM **22**(4), 251–256 (1979)
14. Starkweather, T., Mcdaniel, S., Whitley, D., Mathias, K., Whitley, D.: A comparison of genetic sequencing operators. In: Proceedings of the fourth International Conference on Genetic Algorithms, pp. 69–76. Morgan Kaufmann (1991)
15. Van Der Hauw, K.: Evaluating and Improving Steady State Evolutionary Algorithms on Constraint Satisfaction Problems. Master's thesis, Leiden University (1996)
16. Sungu, G., Boz, B.: An evolutionary algorithm for weighted graph coloring problem. In: Proceedings of the Companion Publication of the 2015 Annual Conference on Genetic and Evolutionary Computation, pp. 1233–1236. ACM, Madrid (2015)

General

Meta-heuristics for Improved RF Emitter Localization

Sondre A. Engebråten[1,2(✉)], Jonas Moen[1], and Kyrre Glette[1,2]

[1] Norwegian Defence Research Establishment,
P.O. Box 25, 2027 Kjeller, Norway
sondre.engebraten@ffi.no
[2] University of Oslo, P.O. Box 1080,
Blindern, 0316 Oslo, Norway

Abstract. Locating Radio Frequency (RF) emitters can be done with a number of methods, but cheap and widely available sensors make the Power Difference of Arrival (PDOA) technique a prominent choice. Predicting the location of an unknown RF emitter can be seen as a continuous optimization problem, minimizing the error w.r.t. the sensor measurements gathered. Most instances of this problem feature multimodality, making these challenging to solve. This paper presents an analysis of the performance of evolutionary computation and other meta-heuristic methods on this real-world problem. We applied the Nelder-Mead method, Genetic Algorithm, Covariance Matrix Adaptation Evolutionary Strategies, Particle Swarm Optimization and Differential Evolution. The use of meta-heuristics solved the minimization problem more efficiently and precisely, compared to brute force search, potentially allowing for a more widespread use of the PDOA method. To compare algorithms two different metrics were proposed: average distance miss and median distance miss, giving insight into the algorithms' performance. Finally, the use of an adaptive mutation step proved important.

Keywords: Search heuristics · Continuous optimization · Multilateration

1 Introduction

Radio Frequency (RF) emitters are becoming increasingly common in everyday use. Most people carry at least one RF emitter on them at any given time, for example a cellphone or smart watch. In the case of an emergency, the ability to locate people trapped in an avalanche or in distress, would greatly relieve the search effort and possibly save lives. Locating RF emitters can, for instance, be done using a number of inexpensive quadcopter sampling the RF signal at different points in space. Figure 1 shows 10 quadcopters sampling an RF signal at multiple points in space.

There are many different methods for locating or geolocating RF signals based on sampling of signal properties [1, 4, 10, 15, 17], including: Angle of arrival,

© Springer International Publishing AG 2017
G. Squillero and K. Sim (Eds.): EvoApplications 2017, Part II, LNCS 10200, pp. 207–223, 2017.
DOI: 10.1007/978-3-319-55792-2_14

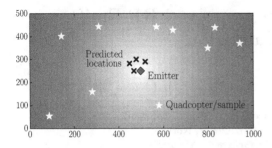

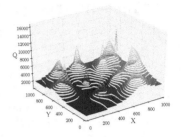

Fig. 1. Illustration of predicting the location (crosses) of an RF emitter (diamond) using 10 quadcopters/sampling locations (stars). Lighter areas have stronger signal.

Fig. 2. An example search landscape; lower Q values are better. The example shown is for 10 spatially different measurements with noise.

Time difference of arrival, Power difference of arrival, and Frequency Difference of arrival. Most methods for geolocation require the RF signal to be sampled at multiple distinct locations in order to achieve a prediction of the emitter location. The different methods all have their strengths and weaknesses, in practical applications it is likely that multiple methods or a combination of methods will be applied [17]. Regardless of the method applied, it is important for an implementation to be as efficient as possible.

One method of locating an RF emitter is based on Received Signal Strength (RSS), or Power Difference of Arrival (PDOA) [4, 10]. This method can be implemented using cheap and readily available sensors, based on simple power measurements. An issue with this method is the high amount of computation required in order to make a prediction of the emitter location. The computational requirements includes the brute force minimization of a function over a discrete grid. This minimization can be implemented on a hardware accelerated system [4]. For many applications, where locating RF emitter would be useful, the use of hardware acceleration may be impossible due to energy constraints or inability to carry a specialized computing unit for this purpose.

The goal of this work is to reduce the computational requirements of PDOA geolocation in order to facilitate implementation, on simple and energy restricted platforms. By reducing the required computational resources it would be possible to implement this using minimal hardware, for instance on a small board computer. Evolutionary computation methods or numerical methods may assist in solving the minimization problem faster and more efficiently. The use of evolutionary computation methods would also allow for potentially infinite resolution, compared to a brute force solver.

In this work, a few of the most common heuristics for continuous optimization are compared for performance on this RF emitter localization problem. These were chosen for being common and frequently used algorithms in the literature, and were used without significant modification or customization. The algorithms chosen are examples of hill-climber methods, population based methods and higher-order search algorithms. The tested heuristics are: Random sampler, Nelder-Mead (NM) [12], Preselect NM, Genetic Algorithm (GA) [3,6], Covariance Matrix Adaptation Evolutionary Strategies (CMA-ES) [7,8], Particle Swarm Optimization (PSO) [2], and Differential Evolution (DE) [16].

This is the first paper to our knowledge describing the application of search heuristics in an effort to make the minimization of the error function more effective. Several papers exists on the topic of locating RF emitters [1,10,15,17]. Contrary to previous work, we apply evolutionary computation methods, instead of a brute force optimization, in order to increase the speed and precision of the emitter location predictions. A GA have previously been applied to optimize the location of the sampling points, both for the static and dynamic cases [4]. Using RSS to locate RF emitters have also been attempted in the context of a swarm system [13]. However, in this paper the focus is shifted from optimizing the behavior and positioning of the sample locations, to increasing the efficiency of the location prediction algorithm itself using meta-heuristics instead of a brute force optimization.

Section 2 describes the problem of locating RF emitters and defines a benchmark. Section 3 defines the heuristics used for this optimization problem. Section 4 describes the test cases used and the extensive parameter variation required for optimal algorithm performance. Sections 5 and 6 features results, with multiple metrics for comparison, and discussion. Finally, Sect. 7 concludes the paper.

2   RF Emitter Localization

In locating objects in space, there are three common exploitable methods: triangulation, trilateration and multilateration [1,15]. Triangulation estimates the location of an unknown object by measuring the angle towards the object from multiple directions. This gives an intersection where the object is estimated to be located. Trilateration uses the distance from at least three points to find an intersection between circles (in 2D) to locate an object. Multilateration combines measurements of the differences in distances, at multiple known points, in order to estimate the location of the object. These fundamental geolocation methods makes up the basis of the search for an RF emitter. There are multiple ways of locating an RF emitter [1,4,10,15], including:

1. Angle of arrival (triangulation)
2. RSS (trilateration)/PDOA (multilateration)
3. Frequency difference of arrival (triangulation)
4. Time of arrival (trilateration)/Time difference of arrival (multilateration)

Using a simple RSS method is problematic as it is fairly common that the power of the emitter is not known. Many transceivers (radio transmitters and receivers) today implement power saving schemes, where they vary emitted power. By varying the emitted signal strength, using only RSS for geolocation (with trilateration) becomes impossible. However by combining multiple RSS measurements and using PDOA it is possible to remove the unknown emitted effect at the cost of additional complexity.

2.1 Power Difference of Arrival

PDOA compares the RSS at multiple distinct locations in order to get an estimate for the emitter location. This is based on an estimation of the loss in signal strength at a given distance. A common model for propagation loss of an RF signal is the path loss model [10,11,14]. This model gives the RSS L at a distance r and can be expressed as follows:

$$L(r) = L_f(r_0) - 10\alpha \log_{10} \frac{r}{r_0} \tag{1}$$

$$P(r) = L(r) + \mathcal{N}(0, \sigma) \tag{2}$$

$L_f(r_0)$ is signal strength "a short distance" from the emitter; this is typically determined experimentally and is a fixed value. For these experiments the distance r_0 was set to 1. $P(r)$ is a sample, with added noise, a distance r from the emitter. By attaining a number of samples $P(r)$ of the RSS at multiple different points in space it is possible to estimate the location of an RF emitter. The exact constant value of $L_f(r_0)$ is irrelevant, as it is canceled out when calculating the difference between pairs of samples.

Simulated samples are generated by adding white noise to the estimated signal strength $L(r)$, where σ is the standard deviation of the white noise. α is the path loss factor, depending on the environment this constant may vary from 2 to 6. Free space/line-of-sight gives an α of 2.0.

There are several methods of using the attained power measurement to obtain a prediction of the emitter location [10]. Some examples are: Non-Linear Least Squares (NLLS), maximum likelihood, and discrete probability density. All of these methods are fairly computationally expensive, in the order of $O(I \cdot J \cdot M^2)$. $I \cdot J$ is given by the grid resolution and M is the number of measurements. The physical sensors used for PDOA are capable of gathering several hundred samples per second. Using all the information available will result in a large M, making the optimization slow.

NLLS can be expressed as an optimization to minimize the error, given a set of measurements. By comparing the measured difference in RSS to the expected signal strength, an expression for the error can be formulated [10] as:

$$P_{kl} = P_k - P_l \tag{3}$$

$$Q(x, y) = \sum_{k < l} [P_{kl} - 5\alpha \log \left(\frac{(x - x_l)^2 + (y - y_l)^2}{(x - x_k)^2 + (y - y_k)^2} \right)]^2 \tag{4}$$

The proposed location of the emitter is (x, y). k and l denotes indexes into the list of samples. Predicting, or finding, the most likely emitter location can be done by minimizing the function $Q(x, y)$ over the desired area. Analytic methods are problematic for this expression due to the non-linearity found in the expression. Figure 2 is an example of the search landscape as defined by $Q(x, y)$. The search landscape is smooth and can be highly multi-modal.

The conventional way of solving this problem would be to use regular grid, over which the function is evaluated and the smallest value located. Using a grid suffers from a number of undesirable features; such as finite resolution and high computational cost. Practical implementations may even have problems defining the grid boundaries, over which to minimize the function, as this makes an assumption about the emitter location before any predictions have been made. It is also impossible to predict a location outside of the grid.

2.2 Error Metric

In order to evaluate the performance of each algorithm, a suitable benchmark metric has to be defined. All of the search and optimization algorithms will return a single best solution found through the search, the position in which $Q(x, y)$ takes on the least value seen. This solution is used to calculate an error measurement (e_{avg}), given as follows:

$$d_i = ||S_i - S_{ref}|| \tag{5}$$

$$e_i = \begin{cases} d_i, & \text{if } Q_i > Q_{ref} \\ 0, & \text{otherwise} \end{cases} \tag{6}$$

S_i is the best found solution (by the search algorithm) and S_{ref} the solution calculated by brute force using 40.000 evaluations (a fine grid of 200 by 200 cells). Both of these are two-dimensional coordinates. The Euclidean distance between the two solutions is d_i, for a single run of the optimization algorithm. An error e_i is calculated, only penalizing those solutions that have worse fitness value Q_i compare to the reference Q_{ref}. All of the errors are aggregated and an average is calculated, indicating the performance of the given algorithm on the given case. For the same set of values e_i, median and standard deviation is also calculated.

It is important to note that the true emitter location, where the emitter was placed during simulation, may not be the location of the global optimum. Due to the noise added to the samples (Eq. 2), the global optimum may shift away from the true emitter location. For this reason, the global optimum has to be located using a brute force search.

2.3 Error Bound for Brute Force Search

Brute force divides the grid into a number of cells, this limits the maximal error e_i by the size of the grid cell. Similarly, it is possible to estimate the expected error assuming a uniform distribution of global optima. Two independent uniform distributions X and Y give the x and y coordinates, respectively. The exhaustive grid search (brute force) will divide the area of interest into bins of equal dimensions. Since all the bins are equal, we only need to consider the case of a single bin to find the expected miss distance. A 2D-grid of size (G_x, G_y) is divided equally into bins of size (B_x, B_y). We can then define the uniform distributions of X and Y as follows:

$$X = \text{Uniform}(-\frac{1}{2}B_x, \frac{1}{2}B_x) \tag{7}$$

$$Y = \text{Uniform}(-\frac{1}{2}B_y, \frac{1}{2}B_y) \tag{8}$$

$$D = \sqrt{X^2 + Y^2} \tag{9}$$

Monte-Carlo simulations were used to determine the expected average miss distance $E(D)$.

Table 1. Metrics ($B_x = B_y = 100$)

Miss dist.	Estimated	Expr.
Avg.	38.3	$0.383B_x$
Median	39.9	$0.399B_x$

$$N_{\text{eval}} = \frac{G_x^2}{B_x^2} = \frac{0.15G_x^2}{D_{\text{avg}}^2} \tag{10}$$

The expression, in Table 1, for average expected miss distance was determined numerically, using regression on a number of different values for B_x and B_y. Using this expression it is possible to devise the resolution required (using a discrete grid optimization) to achieve any desired maximal error.

In Eq. 10, N_{eval} is the number of evaluations required to achieve an average prediction error of D_{avg}. For example, if the desired average miss should be less than 20 m, at least 375 evaluations would be required. The area of interest (G_x, G_y) was set to $(1000, 1000)$, as used for the test cases.

This is a tight and optimistic bound for the average error. Most algorithms will not be able to attain this bound. Experiments found that even with a reasonably fine grid, the global optimum would not be sampled close enough. This resulted in choosing a local optimum instead, with a better fitness value. Missing the global optimum, and instead choosing a local optimum, gives a severe penalty to the average distance miss. The local optima are often located far away from the global optimum (See Fig. 2).

3   Optimization Heuristics

Seven different common optimization heuristics were implemented in this paper: Random sampling, NM, Preselect NM, GA, CMA-ES, PSO and DE. For all of the heuristics tested, the solutions are encoded as a 2D real-valued vector. Some of these algorithms had standard implementations found in the DEAP framework [5]. The full source code can be found here[1].

For comparison, a basic random sampler was implemented. This uses a uniform distribution in x and y dimensions to generate a random sampling of solutions within the area of interest. The best solution, of the random selection, is returned by this method. This is similar to the brute force method, but does not restrict the solutions to a regular grid.

The NM algorithm [12] is a continuous numerical optimization algorithm, that does not require gradient information in the fitness space. The initial step of the NM algorithm requires a simplex to be defined. A simplex is a set of three points, for a two dimensional search landscape. Further iterations will manipulate the simplex through reflection, expansion and contraction, eventually converging to a small area of the search landscape. NM has four parameters governing the rate of contraction and simplex permutation; Alpha, Gamma, Sigma, and Phi. In the case of multiple minima, NM can get stuck or fail to converge to a single solution. For the problem as described, the fitness landscape may have more than one minimum. This makes the NM algorithm a poor choice by itself, but is included for comparison.

NM will typically struggle on non-smooth landscapes, or in cases where there are multiple optima. If the NM algorithm could be initialized in a way as to exclude these two problems, this algorithm could be a prime contender due to very fast convergence to a single solution. Choosing the simplex carefully it may be possible to reduce or even eliminate the adverse properties of the NM method alone. The Preselect NM method samples a (large) number of points in the search space before applying the NM method. These points are used to select the initial simplex for the NM algorithm. From the points sampled, the three best solutions (according to $Q(x, y)$ values) are chosen and given to the NM method. This allows the algorithm to start closer to the global optimum and may assist in reducing the chance of getting stuck in local optima.

In this paper, the GA [3,6] is applied as a search heuristic in the two-dimensional optimization problem defined in the previous sections. A direct real encoding is used, and the fitness function is $Q(x, y)$ as defined in the problem description. Furthermore, to apply a GA to this problem a suitable mutation, crossover and selection operator has to be chosen. Tournament selection is used as a selection operator. The mutation operator is implemented as a simple Gaussian additive mutation, which requires a sigma to be specified. The crossover operator takes two parent solutions and creates two children by selecting two new random solutions on the line segment joining the two parent solutions. In total,

---

[1]   https://github.com/ForsvaretsForskningsinstitutt/Paper-NLLS-speedup.

the GA requires five parameters to be specified: Mutation probability, Mutation sigma, Crossover probability, number of elites, and finally, a population size.

CMA-ES [7,8] is described as a second degree method building on Evolutionary Strategies [9]. As opposed to the GA, this method does not use a crossover operator, only a mutation operator and selection. The CMA-ES algorithm will attempt to adapt the mutation step size dynamically (from an initial guess), maximizing the likelihood that favorable solutions are generated by the mutations. This is an important feature, as it allows for rapid convergence once an area of solutions with good fitness has been found. The main drawback of this method is the use of a population size of 1 (in the standard implementation). Having only a single individual makes the algorithm prone to getting stuck in local optima, converging prematurely. The same properties that make the algorithm exceptional at quickly converging and find a good solution are a disadvantage in respect to robustness when faced with multi-modal fitness landscapes. CMA-ES requires two parameters: a population size and an initial permutation standard deviation.

The concept of the PSO [2] is to have a number of particles moving in the N-dimensional space and being attracted to the various optima that both the particle itself finds, and the global optimum as found by all the particles. This algorithm required minimal modification to suit the described problem, but has a number of parameters that will significantly impact the performance of the algorithm. The parameters are: population size (number of particles), attraction weight toward local best (ϕ_1), attraction weight toward global best (ϕ_2) and a maximum particle speed.

DE [16] is a variation of an evolutionary optimization method. The main difference is the use of a differential operator as a mutation operator. In short, the mutation step used by DE is defined by the difference between two solution vectors. This allows the mutation step size to adapt and converge as the solutions in the population converge to a single optimum. DE uses three parameters: F a scaling factor for the mutation size, CR for controlling the chance of a mutation, and the population size.

4   Testing Methodology

50 cases were randomly generated, in order to make sure that algorithms excelling at a single problem instance were not preferred. Each case consists of 10 distinct randomly located simulated PDOA samples with randomly generated noise (Eq. 2). In this work free space/line-of-sight was assumed, α of 2 and σ of 3.0. The optimization area (G_x, G_y) is $(1000, 1000)$. For all of the test cases the true emitter location is in the middle of the search area, but the location of the global optimum will vary depending on the noise added. In a real-world implementation of PDOA, averaging may be used to reduce the percieved standard deviation of the noise (σ). Varying the position of samples and measured RSS will drastically alter the fitness landscape. All the algorithms are benchmarked on the exact same cases. Due to the non-determinism found in several of the

heuristics, each algorithm was tested 50 times on each case, using a new random seed for each trial. For all experiments algorithms were given a limited number of function evaluations, effectively limiting the number of iterations. The number of test cases and samples per case was limited by the computational resources available.

4.1   Heuristics Parameters

Most of the analyzed algorithms require one or more parameters to be defined. Common for all the population based methods is a population size, which inevitably affects the number of iterations, as each algorithm is limited in the number of function evaluations. Deciding the best set of parameters for each algorithm is non-trivial and may require expert knowledge about both the fitness landscape and the properties of the search algorithm. In this paper, a fairly extensive set of parameter combinations were tested for each algorithm. The best set of parameters, for any given algorithm, depends heavily on the metric used for comparison. The optimal set of parameters may also vary depending on the limit on function evaluations.

Table 2. Parameters for all experiments and algorithms

Algorithm	Parameters
NM	Alpha 1.0, Gamma 2.0, Sigma 0.5, Phi -0.5
Preselect NM	NM evals. 10%, Alpha 1.0, Gamma 2.0, Sigma 0.5, Phi -0.5
GA	Pop. size [200 160 100 80 50 40 20 10], Mut. sigma [25.0 50.0], Mut. prob. [0.1 0.2], Crossover prob. [0.4 0.6], Elites max(2, 5%), Tournament N=2
CMA-ES	Pop. size [200 160 100 80 50 40 20 10], Sigma [100.0 125.0 150.0 200.0]
PSO	Pop. size [200 160 100 80 50 40 20 10], ϕ_1 [1.0 2.0], ϕ_2 [1.0 2.0], Speed max [20.0 50.0]
DE	Pop. size [200 160 100 80 50 40 20 10], Crs [0.25 0.50], Fr [0.5 1.0]

Based around recommended settings, the parameters seen in Table 2 were used for the different algorithms. Experiments were conducted for all the possible combinations of parameter settings. This resulted in each algorithm having around 32 different sets of parameters to test. The exception to this was the NM algorithm, which was only run with the single parameter set recommended for the algorithm. The default parameters were found to work well for this problem.

All algorithms were compared on the 50 test cases. As a baseline; a brute force optimizer, i.e. grid search, was also implemented. The brute force optimizer used an additional 450 randomly generated test instances (in addition to the 50 used for the other algorithms). Without the additional cases, brute force would

216   S.A. Engebråten et al.

only have 50 sample points (compared to 2500 for each of the other algorithms), as it is a fully deterministic algorithm.

In addition, the effect of the function evaluation limit was tested. Tests were run for 100, 200, 400, 800, and 1600 evaluations per optimization run. The performance of each algorithm will vary depending on the number of evaluations allowed to solve the problem. In total approx. 500.000 optimization runs were conducted, evaluating 300 million solutions in the search space.

5   Results

One of the main challenges for this problem, is to determine the optimal parameters for each algorithm. These parameters may change depending on evaluation budget size. In order to address this problem, extensive parameter variation tests was conducted based on values given in Table 2. Initially, the case of a fixed evaluation budget of 400 evaluations will be examined, before extending the same methods and analysis to a set of different and variable evaluation budgets.

5.1   Fixed Evaluation Budget Size

A histogram over error values (e_i) can be made for each algorithm and parameter set tested using a fixed evaluation budget size. An example of this can be seen in Fig. 3 for the random sampler using 400 evaluations. For most trials, a simple random sampling will succeed in finding a good solution to the problem instance.

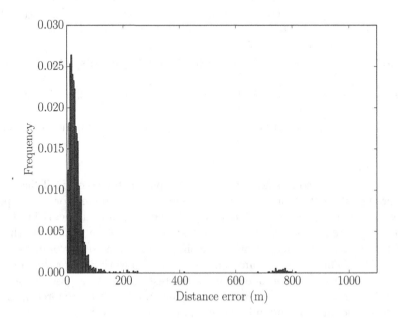

Fig. 3. Random sampling - Error distribution for 2500 tests using 400 evaluations

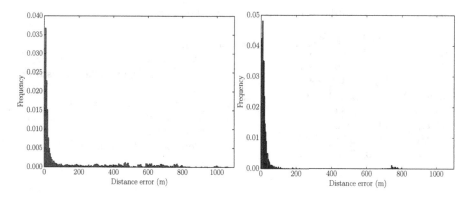

Fig. 4. Example of error distribution for 2500 tests using 400 evaluations and a single set of parameters - GA (left) and DE (right)

Most of the weight of the distribution is found at less than 100 m away from the reference solution S_{ref}. In some cases, a random sampling will miss the global optimum and instead choose a local optimum. This can be seen at a distance 750 m in Fig. 3.

Left part of Fig. 4 shows an example of the error distribution for the GA for a single set of parameters. The GA has a similar distribution as the random sampling, but is more likely to get stuck and converge prematurely in the given example. This can be seen by the long and heavy tail of the distribution.

DE outperforms both a random sampling and the GA and has more consistent performance. Right part of Fig. 4 shows an example where the DE often is able to converge to the global optimum as defined by S_{ref}. This distribution does not have the same tail as the random sampling and the GA, indicating that it is less likely to get stuck in local optima.

However, none of the histogram plots are symmetric distributions. This leads to problems when attempting to rank the methods and generate useful statistics. In particular, the average miss of each algorithm will be significantly skewed by the outliers, favoring reliable algorithms. By using the median as a measure for comparison, this is mitigated, but it also hides some of the issues when using search heuristics on the problem. For some applications, the loss of reliability may be acceptable, but not in others. Table 3 shows performance on the metrics median, average and standard deviation for selected parameter combinations. The parameters associated can be found in Table 3. This is based on Euclidean distance, as defined in Eq. 6. The selected subset of combinations was chosen based on its performance on the median metric. Normally, the average metric would give a better indication of performance, but in this case, the average metric is insufficient.

The search landscape is smooth (an example can be seen in Fig. 2), but still poses a challenge for search algorithms. Multi-modality makes these problem instances hard, and often makes the search heuristic converge prematurely, or

Table 3. Results overview - 400 evaluations

	Med	Avg	Stddev
Brute force	19.7	25.9	53.9
Random	26.1	43.9	100.8
NM	0.0	164.7	290.4
Preselect NM	0.0	17.1	103.6
GA	16.8	148.0	240.9
CMA-ES	0.0	84.0	222.7
PSO	15.7	67.8	173.5
DE	0.0	35.8	140.6

Algorithm	Params
GA	Population 10, Elites 2, Mut. prob. 0.2, Mut. Sigma 50.0, Crossover prob. 0.6
CMA-ES	Population 20, Sigma 200.0
PSO	Population 10, Phi1 1.0 , Phi2 1.0, Smax 20.0
DE	Population 10, Cr 0.5, F 0.5

get stuck in local optima. For this problem, the average metric is indicative of the likelihood for getting stuck. A single miss (on the global optimum) gives a severe penalty to the average. If the average was used to select the best parameter for each algorithm, a single generation/iteration with the maximum possible number of evaluations would be preferred for many algorithms. With such parameter settings, any heuristic becomes a random search.

An alternative to focusing on a single metric, such as median or average, could be to use a combination of metrics, as commonly done in multi-objective optimization. The metrics are defined as follows:

1. Probability of getting stuck in a local minimum
2. Average Euclidean distance error, given that the global minimum was found

The first of these two metrics acts a filter, effectively removing the outliers seen in the histogram plots. In order to quantify the chance of getting stuck, a solution has to be classified as either a part of a local optimum or the global optimum. While classifying the solutions like this is non-trivial, a simple approach would be to define some radius around the global minimum, and use this as a selection threshold. Based on the clustering of solutions seen in the experiments (Figs. 3 and 4), a radius of 100 m was selected. This is a relaxed limit and includes most, if not all, solutions that were in the basin of attraction of the global optimum.

Figure 5 shows the different algorithms-parameter combinations and how they perform on the two objectives. Preselect NM is able to approach the origin, i.e. reference solution. CMA-ES shows excellent ability to find equal or better solutions as the reference solution, but lacks in reliability; as seen by a fairly high chance of missing the global optimum completely. DE is the opposite of CMA-ES and is very reliable, but lacks somewhat in its ability to converge to solutions equal or better than the reference.

5.2   Variable Evaluation Budget Size

Another interesting view of this problem would be to examine the performance of each algorithm across evaluation budget sizes. All the algorithms were tested

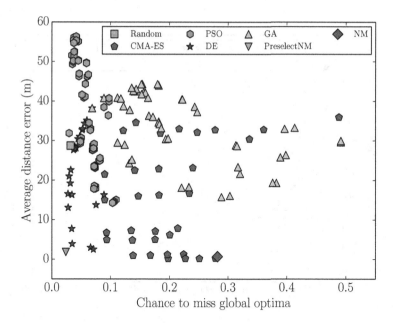

Fig. 5. Algorithm comparison using two alternative metrics. Each dot represent a parameter configuration. Clustered dots from the same algorithm typically share parameters significantly affecting performance.

with 100, 200, 400, 800 and 1600 evaluations, and the number of evaluations are likely to affect the performance of the algorithm. Figure 6 shows a comparison across evaluations using the average metric. In this figure, the parameters for each algorithm were selected based on average metric.

Only DE and Preselect NM manage to compete with brute force search on the average metric. The rest of the heuristics were found *on* or *above* the line for random sampler and are excluded from the plot for readability. Preselect NM performs well across all numbers of evaluations; particularly in the area of 200 to 800 evaluations, where it is comparable to using twice as many evaluations on a brute force search. In other words, applying the Preselect NM algorithm resulted in a speed-up of at least 2x on this real-world problem.

In Fig. 6 a plus (+) signs indicate the positive result of a Wilcoxon Rank and Sum test, testing the Brute force algorithm against Preselect NM using comparable number of evaluations. This test was applied for each number of evaluations as indicated in the figure. The distribution of errors, between Preselect NM and the Brute force algorithm, was found to be significantly different at the level of 0.01 for all tests applied. The results are the same for the median plot because the underlying dataset is the same.

The challenge of this real-world problem is not to find a good solution, but to find the best solution. For several of the heuristics this is problematic, as they readily will converge to local optima. Yet, the problem may greatly benefit

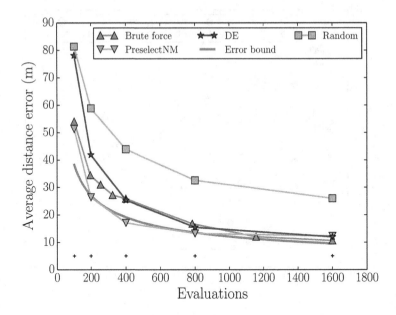

Fig. 6. Comparison of algorithms across number of evaluations using average metric. Plus signs indicate statistical significant difference between Preselect NM and Brute force algorithms for the given number of evaluations.

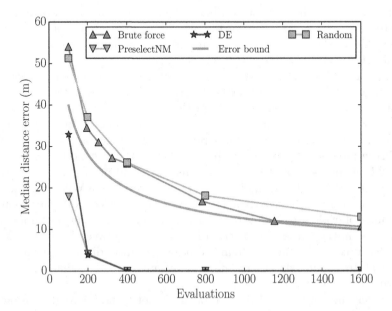

Fig. 7. Comparison of algorithms across number of evaluations using median metric.

from a heuristic in converging to the global optimum from nearby areas in the solution space.

Using a median metric shows another view of the algorithms performance (Fig. 7). This plot highlights the benefit of using a search heuristics in providing solutions that often are better than the reference solution found by a brute force optimization using 40.000 evaluations. Parameters were here chosen based on median. DE and Preselect NM are repeatedly able to find solutions that outperform a brute force optimization with an equal number of evaluations.

Finally, considering the effect of increasing the number of evaluations for Fig. 5 is a gradual tendency for all points in the plot to converge on the origin. As more evaluations are allowed, most algorithms and parameter combinations perform better (i.e. provide better solutions). Decreasing the limit has the opposite effect.

6 Discussion

For this particular real-world problem, finding a suitable metric for comparing algorithms and parameter combinations proved challenging. With the average miss as the metric, many of the search heuristics had problems caused by their unreliability to find the global optimum. Using the median metric instead allows for a partial solution to this problem, but will camouflage how unreliable each algorithm is to a certain degree.

Many of the heuristics are able to often find solutions that outperform those found by a brute force search using several orders of magnitude more resources. In particular, DE, Preselect NM and CMA-ES proved to excel at this. What differentiates these algorithms from the remaining (PSO and GA) is the use of adaptive step lengths when converging on an optimum. In order to maximize the solution performance, this proved an important trait. It becomes clear that there is a trade-off between the reliability of an algorithm and the ability to narrow in on an optimum. With a limited evaluation budget a heuristics cannot do both, and depending on parameters, may focus on one or the other.

One of the main premises for using search heuristics is that there is no guarantee that the optimal solution will be found. For some problems this may be acceptable, and not for others. In this case, it depends on the application scenario of the method. In presenting a prediction of the location of an RF emitter to a user, there is an expectation of reliability and predictability. Automated systems may to a greater degree be able to accept the chance that, in certain cases, a prediction might miss, as long as the miss is not too great or too frequent. In future work it would be interesting to investigate the use of a search heuristic, as described in this paper, in a context of swarm system. Commonly, swarm systems rely on simple and cheap units with limited capabilities. In such a context, the acceptance of suboptimal performance (a chance to miss) may be unavoidable and must be dealt with on a higher algorithmic level.

In the case of a miss being unacceptable and absolute reliability required, significant performance increase is still possible using a search heuristic. As shown for Preselect NM, a no-cost speed-up can be achieved, effectively giving double the performance on limited resources. As described previously, the issue of a suitable metric camouflages some of the characteristics of the search heuristic. For this particular case, the use of a hill-climber allows a system implementing this to be at least as reliable as a system using twice the amount of resources on a brute force search. In addition, the system gains an infinite resolution. What previously was limited to the resolution of the brute force grid is only limited by the resolution of the number representation, and how quickly the hill-climber can converge. This is an important result of this work.

7   Conclusions

This paper shows the viability of using search heuristics on the problem of geolocating RF emitters. By using a search heuristic, multiple favorable attributes can be achieved, such as: infinite resolution, reduced and flexible computational cost, and greater robustness against deceptive objective functions when restricted in computational resources. Comparing a number of common search algorithms, such as GA, PSO and CMA-ES, it is clear that these strategies may not always be the best option given a limited computational budget. The challenge for these algorithms is to converge quickly enough while at the same time avoiding local optima. If the search space is reasonably small, applying the NM algorithm with a preselect may be an option resulting in high performance even with little resources.

One of the biggest issues in this particular problem was the multi-modality of the fitness landscape. Multiple local optima made this a deceptive problem and required algorithms that were robust and had an exploratory behavior.

This work may not only allow for a practical real-world implementation of a system locating RF emitters, but also a wider range of concepts to be explored. The ability to locate an RF emitter can also be used as part of a higher level simulation, investigating into the behaviors or how multiple agents should interact. One intriguing idea is a swarm of flying platforms able to autonomously locate RF emitters. This is a topic for future research.

Acknowledgments. We would like to thank Ingebjørg Kåsen and Eilif Solberg for their assistance with the statistical issues in this paper and Jørgen Nordmoen for enlightening discussions and excellent feedback.

References

1. Berle, F.: Mixed triangulation/trilateration technique for emitter location. IEE Proc. F Commun. Radar Signal Process **133**(7), 638–641 (1986)
2. Eberhart, R., Kennedy, J.: A new optimizer using particle swarm theory. In: Proceedings of the Sixth International Symposium on Micro Machine and Human Science, MHS 1995, pp. 39–43. IEEE (1995)
3. Eiben, A.E., Smith, J.E.: Introduction to Evolutionary Computing. Springer Science & Business Media, Heidelberg (2003)

4. Engebråten, S.A.: RF Emitter geolocation using PDOA algorithms and UAVs. Master's thesis, Norwegian University of Science and Technology (2015)
5. Fortin, F.-A., De Rainville, F.-M., Gardner, M.-A., Parizeau, M., Gagné, C.: DEAP: evolutionary algorithms made easy. J. Mach. Learn. Res. **13**, 2171–2175 (2012)
6. Goldberg, D.E., Holland, J.H.: Genetic algorithms and machine learning. Mach. Learn. **3**(2), 95–99 (1988)
7. Hansen, N., Müller, S.D., Koumoutsakos, P.: Reducing the time complexity of the derandomized evolution strategy with covariance matrix adaptation (CMA-ES). Evol. Comput. **11**(1), 1–18 (2003)
8. Hansen, N., Ostermeier, A.: Adapting arbitrary normal mutation distributions in evolution strategies: the covariance matrix adaptation. In: Proceedings of IEEE International Conference on Evolutionary Computation, pp. 312–317. IEEE (1996)
9. Huning, A., Rechenberg, I., Eigen, M.: Evolutionsstrategie. optimierung technischer systeme nach prinzipien der biologischen evolution (1976)
10. Jackson, B., Wang, S., Inkol, R.: Emitter geolocation estimation using power difference of arrival. Defence R&D Canada Technical report DRDC Ottawa TR, 40 (2011)
11. Levanon, N.: Radar Principles, 320 p. Wiley-Interscience, New York (1988)
12. Nelder, J.A., Mead, R.: A simplex method for function minimization. Comput. J. **7**(4), 308–313 (1965)
13. Nordmoen, J.: Detecting a hidden radio frequency transmitter in noise based on amplitude using swarm intelligence. Master's thesis, Norwegian University of Science and Technology, 6 (2014)
14. Saunders, S., Aragón-Zavala, A.: Antennas and Propagation for Wireless Communication Systems. John Wiley & Sons, Chichester (2007)
15. Staras, H., Honickman, S.N.: The accuracy of vehicle location by trilateration in a dense urban environment. IEEE Trans. Veh. Technol. **21**(1), 38–43 (1972)
16. Storn, R., Price, K.: Differential evolution-a simple and efficient heuristic for global optimization over continuous spaces. J. Global Optim. **11**(4), 341–359 (1997)
17. Wang, Z., Blasch, E., Chen, G., Shen, D., Lin, X., Pham, K.: A low-cost, near-real-time two-UAS-based UWB emitter monitoring system. IEEE Aerosp. Electron. Syst. Mag. **30**(11), 4–11 (2015)

Automated Design of Genetic Programming Classification Algorithms Using a Genetic Algorithm

Thambo Nyathi[✉] and Nelishia Pillay[✉]

School of Mathematics, Statistics and Computer Science,
University of KwaZulu-Natal, Pietermaritzburg, South Africa
vuselani@gmail.com, pillayn32@ukzn.ac.za

Abstract. There is a large scale initiative by the machine learning community to automate the design of machine learning techniques to remove reliance on the human expert, providing out of the box software that can be used by novices. In this study the automated design of genetic programming classification algorithms is proposed. A number of design decisions have to be considered by algorithm designers during the design process and this is usually a time consuming task. Our automated design approach uses a genetic algorithm to automatically configure a genetic programming classification algorithm. The genetic algorithm determines parameter values and sets the flow control for the classification algorithm. The proposed system is tested on real world problems and the results indicate that induced classifiers perform better than manually designed classifiers.

Keywords: Data classification · Automated machine learning · Genetic programming · Genetic algorithms

1 Introduction

A significant amount of research has been carried out in the domain of data classification resulting in the development of numerous classification algorithms. The application of heuristic based methods such as Evolutionary Algorithms (EAs) [1] to data classification problems has gained traction. EAs are population based algorithms that emulate the Darwian principles of natural evolution to solve problems. Genetic programming(GP) [2] an EA has proved to be very effective at inducing classifiers particularly for binary data classification problems [3]. GP requires a number of parameters to be defined to have a functional system. A combination of GP parameters that results in a functional system define a configuration. Setting the configuration of GP as a classification algorithm entails searching for parameter values and component combinations that will lead to the algorithm evolving optimal classifiers. It is widely accepted that the effectiveness of an EA to solve a problem at hand depends on the design decisions taken to configure the EA [4]. Finding the best configuration is a manual

© Springer International Publishing AG 2017
G. Squillero and K. Sim (Eds.): EvoApplications 2017, Part II, LNCS 10200, pp. 224–239, 2017.
DOI: 10.1007/978-3-319-55792-2_15

search process that is usually carried out empirically using trial runs on subset instances of a problem. This manual process is considered to be a non trivial menial task that consumes a lot of man-hours [1]. Sabar et al. [5] argue that effective manual design requires detailed knowledge of both algorithm design and the problem domain, which is not always possible. During manual design not all possible design decisions are considered but the few that are, are selected based on the experience and intuition of the algorithm designer. The effect of this is a search in a limited search space which may not be effective as other unexplored areas may contain parameters likely to lead to optimal classifiers. The design of GP classification algorithms that yield optimal classifiers remains a challenge.

In this research we propose the automation of the design process through the use of an EA namely a Genetic Algorithm (GA) to evolve classification algorithms. We use a GA to search for a GP configuration that will lead to GP inducing good classifiers. The search is conducted in a search space of GP configuration parameters including GP classification algorithm design components. The purpose of this work is to automate the design of GP classification algorithms. We hypothesise that automatically designed GP classification algorithms are competitive when compared to human designed algorithms. Our contribution is an automated approach to designing GP classification algorithms. The automated design approach will reduce the man-hours spent on the design process which involves parameter tuning, through trial and error. This will free the designer to attend to other tasks as the design process will be automated. The user of this system does not require expert knowledge of genetic programming but they need knowledge of the classification problem they need solved. Therefore the system can be used by novice users. It is important to point out that the objective of our approach is not to reduce the time of the design process. The system creates a GP algorithm and tunes the parameters therefore long run-times are anticipated. The aim is to automate the process of designing the genetic programming approach, while producing classifiers that perform at least as good as that generated by the manually designed genetic programming approach.

The rest of this paper is structured as follows. Section 2 provides a brief overview of GP, and classification. Section 3 provides an overview of related work and in Sect. 4 we present the proposed system. In Sect. 5 the experimental setup is presented. Section 6 describes and analyses the results, and Sect. 7 draws conclusions and presents future work.

2   Background

2.1   Classification

A classifier is a predictive model extracted when a classification algorithm analyses a collection of labeled attributes (training set). In [6] a classification algorithm is described as a computational procedure that receives a set of attributes and attempts to discover a predictive relationship between them. The effectiveness of a classifier is tested on unseen instances of data (test data set) that is similar to the training set. Among a number of methods proposed for inducing classifiers, genetic programming has also proved to be popular [3].

2.2 Genetic Programming and Classification

As a classification algorithm GP searches for the best classifier in a population of randomly initialized classifiers, these are evolved until a stopping criterion is met. The problem being solved influences the tree representation used in the algorithm and this also influences the contents of the function and terminal sets. When configured to model decision trees the GP algorithm function set consists of nominal variables from the data set and the terminal set contains the classes and classification evaluation is a top down process. Arithmetic tree GP classification algorithms output a numerical value, hence a preset threshold is used to separate the classes based on the output [2]. The function set contains functions that are used to manipulate numeric data and the terminal set has variables that index attributes of the classification problem. The function set for logical tree representation normally contains logical operators while the terminal set will have variables indexing the data set. One of the advantages of using GP as a classification algorithm is that it can represent a number of classification models such as classification rules, decision trees, discriminant function and other classifier models. This benefit arises from the flexibility provided by a tree representation. In [7] Koza demonstrated how GP can model decision trees. Bojarczuk et al. [8] used logical trees to evolve rules to classify medical data while in [9] arithmetic tree representation was used in credit scoring. Another advantage of GP is that it is able to perform feature selection during the evolution process. Since a classifier is evolved from the data instances it is not possible to use the same classification algorithm configuration across different problem domains or problem instances. To evolve good classifiers the configuration of classification algorithms is a data specific process and therefore we cannot use the same configuration across different data instances and expect optimal results. A comprehensive review of the application GP in the area of classification is provided in [3]. In the next section we review related work.

3   Related Work

A significant amount of similar research has been carried out in the broader area of evolutionary algorithms. Research can be found under parameter tuning, parameter control and hyper-heuristics. In this section we review only approaches in the literature that are closely related to our proposed approach. Genetic algorithms have been used to tune other metaheuristics. In [10] a genetic algorithm is used to evolve parameter settings for an Ant Colony Optimization (ACO) metaheuristic to solve the orienteering problem, a form of the traveling salesman problem. Real numbers are used to encode the chromosome. Each gene of the chromosome represents a specific parameter of the ACO metaheuristic. Stochastic universal selection is the preferred selection method while uniform crossover (90%), random bit mutation (0.1%) and elitism (2%) are used as the genetic operators. The GA is used to search for parameter values that yield the best ACO solution to solve the problem at hand. The effectiveness of each ACO is measured using a measure referred to as solution quality (SQ). The SQ metric is also used as the fitness function of the associated GA individual that evolved the configuration. The best GA trained ACO settings are compared to manually tuned parameters by applying them to unseen instances of the orienteering problem. Results show that the GA evolved ACO algorithms perform better than those manually tuned.

In [11] a decision tree is decomposed into its basic components and an evolutionary algorithm is used to recombine the components. Accuracy and the f-measure [6] are used as the fitness functions. Twenty data sets are used to compare the performance of the automatically designed classifiers to those evolved using C4.5 and CART. The automatically evolved classifiers perform better than the CART and C4.5 classifiers. Oltean et al. [12] present a GA to evolve an evolutionary algorithm. Each gene of the chromosome is structured to contain a pair of elements. The first element defines how the genetic operators are applied to generate an offspring. The second element defines the strategy employed for inserting the generated offspring into the new population. The GA chromosome is a sequence of 8 genes, each gene indexes a complete EA. The fitness of the best evolved EA is used as the fitness of the evolving GA. The evolved EAs are tested on function optimization problems and the results indicate that the evolved EAs produced competitive results when compared to standard function optimization schemes. Our proposed work differs from the presented work in that we create new GP algorithms and parameter tune them for classification problems. In the next section we present the proposed system.

4   Automated Design of GP Classification Algorithm Using GA

This work proposes the use of a GA to evolve GP classification algorithms. To the best of our knowledge there is no work in literature which follows this proposed approach to automate the design of GP classification algorithms.

4.1   Genetic Algorithms

Genetic algorithms (GA), are also classified under EAs [13]. They are widely used to solve optimization and search problems. Algorithm 1 is a high level overview of a generational GA algorithm. A detailed presentation of genetic algorithms is provided in [13].

4.2   GP Design Components and GA for Automated Design

In this section we provide a brief review of the design decisions considered during the configuration of a GP classification algorithm. We also provide a description

---

Algorithm 1. Genetic Algorithm

1: Create initial population
2: Calculate fitness of all individuals
3:     **while termination condition not met do**
4:         Select fitter individuals for reproduction
5:         Recombine between individuals
6:         Mutate individuals
7:         Evaluate fitness of all individuals
8:         Generate a new population
9:     **end while**
10: **return** best individual

---

of how the components are encoded in our GA chromosome. The GP classification algorithm is decomposed into a pool of low-level configuration design components. A component may be a numerical parameter (e.g. population size) or categorical (e.g. selection type). We predefined the range of possible values for each component based on typical values found in literature.

4.3   GA Chromosome Representation

For this study we considered 14 GP design components. Therefore our GA individual is encoded as a 14 gene fixed length chromosome as illustrated in Fig. 1. The 14 chromosome genes are labeled from g_0 to g_{13}. A gene represents a parameter (design component) of a classification algorithm. Gene values are encoded as integer values. As stated parameters can be numerical or categorical and the value of each gene can index a specific categorical component or be the value for that parameter. The 14 design components are presented as follows:

Representation in [14] the importance of representation is emphasized and the authors assert that representation acts as a link between the conceptual algorithm and real-world problem. The commonly used representations when evolving classifiers using GP are arithmetic trees, logical trees and decision trees. This component is represented by g_0 in the chromosome for GP representation and can be one of three integer values, 0 for arithmetic trees, 1 for logical trees or 2 for decision trees.

Population size represents the search space, a small population size means a small search space and the algorithm might converge prematurely while too large a population size may lead to slow or no convergence. Research has been carried out on classification problems using population sizes as low as 50 to as high as 5000 [15]. The value of g_1 is the population size in our encoding scheme. For our study population size can either be 100, 200 or 300.

Fig. 1. GA chromosome representation

Tree generation method is encoded by g_2. The three common methods found in literature for tree generation are, the full method which constructs balanced trees with branches of equal size, the grow method which constructs irregular trees and the ramped half-and-half which constructs half of the trees using the full method and the other half using the grow method at each level of tree depth. Values of g_2 can be 0 - full, 1- grow and 2 - ramped half and half.

Maximum initial tree depth an initial maximum depth limit has to be defined for tree growth for the initial population. This value can be as small as 2 as used in [15] to evolve decision trees, or as high as 17 as used in [16] for text classification. The value of g_3 defines the maximum tree depth at initialization and possible values can be set within the range [2–15], except if the specified tree type is 2 (decision trees) then the range is set to [2–8]. This restricts the size of our decision trees.

Offspring tree depth is defined by g_4 and the range of values are defined as [2–15]and [2–8] for decision trees.

Selection method gene 5 denoted by g_5 can be 0 or 1 representing selection methods, fitness proportionate and tournament selection respectively.

Tournament size is defined by g_6 and can have a value in the range [0–100] which determines the size of the tournament. If the selection method determined by g_5 is not tournament selection then g_6 is ignored.

Reproduction rates are defined by g_7 which sets the crossover rate. This by default also sets the mutation rate and is given by the evaluation of (100 - crossover). Crossover rates as high as 90% have been used and mutation as low as 1%. In our system these are randomly generated within the range [0–100].

Mutation type. The eighth gene, g_8 specifies the mutation type and can be 0 indicating grow mutation or 1 for shrink mutation. Grow mutation in which a randomly selected subtree is replaced by a randomly created one and shrink subtree mutation which replaces a subtree with a random terminal.

Mutation depth is relevant if the selected mutation type is grow mutation and is represented by g_9 and can be assigned a value in the range [2–6].

Pool of operators this design component is defined by g_{11} and indexes a pool of predefined genetic operators listed in Table 1 and explained as follows; if the value of this gene is 0 the application rates of genetic operators rates are set as defined by g_7, if the value is 1 the whole generation is evolved by crossover only, if the value is 2 then mutation only is applied to evolve the complete generation. If the value is 3 a random pair of rates is selected from (crossover, mutation) [{ *10,90; 20,80; 30,70; 40,60; 50,50; 60,40; 70,30; 80,20; 90,10*}]. If the gene is set to 4 then a new population is evolved by first mutating all the members of the previous population and then applying crossover at a randomly determined rate. Operator 5's functionality is similar to that of operator 4 albeit starting with crossover and operator 6 randomly creates a new population.

Operator sequence this design component defined by g_{10} is responsible for determining how an operator is used to evolve a generation. If this component's value is set to 0 all the generations of a run are evolved using the genetic operator specified in g_{11}. However if the value is 1 a random operator is selected to evolve each generation from the pool of operators in Table 1.

Table 1. GP pool of operators

Index	Operator
0	Crossover $= g_7$
1	Crossover $= 100\%$
2	Mutation $= 100\%$
3	Random selection preset rates*
4	100% mut then (rand)% of crossover
5	100% cross then (rand)% of mutation
6	Create new population

Fitness functions predictive accuracy is the most common choice of fitness function used in classification. The authors in [17] argue that predictive accuracy is overused as a fitness function. In some domains (medical/financial) reducing misclassification can be more desirable than improving accuracy. Other metrics from the confusion matrix [6] such as *sensitivity, specificity*, have been used as fitness functions [8]. Research in which different combinations of these measures has been presented, for example Barros et al. [11] use the *f-measure* given by

$$f = 2 * \left(\frac{sensitivity * specificity}{sensitivity + specificity} \right) \tag{1}$$

as a fitness function for classification of unbalanced data sets. In this study 5 fitness functions were defined and are indexed as outlined in Table 2. Index 0 defines accuracy and index 1 defines the f-measure. In [18] a weighted fitness function is proposed using 50% of the true positive and 50% of the true negative rates, we adapt the same principle however we weight accuracy and f- measure using the same 50% and that fitness function is fitness function 2. Three is a similar principle however the weighting rates are set randomly, and finally 4 is the true positive rate. The fitness function design component is specified by g_{12}

Number of generations defined by g_{13} which can lie in the range of [50–200] sets the actual value of the number of generations.

The GP design components considered in this study and the range of possible values are summarized in Table 3

Table 2. Fitness functions

Index	Method
0	Accuracy
1	f-measure%
2	$weighted = 0.5 * accuracy + 0.5 * fmeasure$
3	$weighted_{rand} = rand * accuracy + rand * fmeasure$
4	True positive rate

Table 3. Design components

Gene #	Param. Description	Range of possible values
0	Representation	0 - arithmetic, 1 - logical, 2 - decision
1	Population size	100, 200, 300
2	Tree generation	0- full, 1- grow, 2- ramped half and half
3	Initial tree depth	2–15 (decision tree 2 -8)
4	Max offspring depth	2–15
5	Selection method	0 - fitness proportionate, 1 - tournament selection
6	Selection size	2–10
7	Reproduction rates	0 - 100 crossover (mutation = 100-crossover)
8	Mutation type	0 - grow mutation, 1 - shrink mutation,
9	Max mutation depth	2–6
10	Reproduction sequence	0 - fixed 1 - random
11	Operator pool	0–6
12	Fitness type	0–4
13	Number of generations	50, 100, 200

4.4 Initial Population Generation

An initial population of chromosomes (individuals) is randomly generated. The value of each gene of the chromosome is randomly set from the range of possible values defined in Sect. 4.3. Each individual is a configuration of a GP algorithm for evolving classifiers. The effectiveness of each individual is evaluated by the GP algorithm inducing classifiers using the configuration defined by the individual and the best testing classification value (accuracy) from the classifiers is assigned as a fitness of that individual.

4.5 Selection

Fitness proportionate is used to select parents that will take part in the reproduction of offspring for the next generation. This selection of parents is based on the fitness of each individual in the population.

4.6 Genetic Operators

The population of the next generation of configurations is determined by reproduction operators. For this system uniform crossover where random genes can be copied from either of the selected parents is used as the crossover operator. While the mutation method used is bit mutation where each bit has a random chance of being altered and assigned a value within the domain of defined ranges in Sect. 4.3. Application rates of both crossover and mutation have to be set. Elitism is also applied where a stipulated percentage of the population is allowed to progress to the next generation.

5 Experiment Setup

In this section we describe the experimental setup used to evaluate the effectiveness of automatically designed classification algorithms when compared to those manually designed. We selected eleven data sets with real-world data and binary class attributes from the UCI machine learning repository [19]. We chose data sets from different domains and with diverse characteristics such as both balanced and unbalanced class distributions. This enables us to asses the suitability of automated designed classifiers to adapt to different data characteristics. Each dataset was randomly split into 70% for training and 30% for testing. Table 4 outlines the selected data sets and their attributes.

Table 4. Summary of selected data sets

Dataset	# attributes	# numeric	#nominal	# instances
Australian credit data	14	8	6	690
Appendicitis	7	7	0	106
Breast cancer (Ljubljana)	9	0	9	277
Cylinder band	19	19	0	365
Diabetes (pima)	8	8	0	768
German credit data	20	7	13	1000
Heart disease	13	13	0	270
Hepatitis	19	19	0	80
Liver disease (Bupa)	7	7	0	345
Mushroom	22	0	22	5644
Tictactoe	9	0	9	958

For each training data set 30 runs of the GA were performed. The GA was configured with a population size of 20, we used fitness proportionate as the selection method. Uniform crossover at 80% and bit mutation 10% were the genetic operators. We used 10% elitism to preserve good configurations. The population control model used was generational. These values were obtained empirically through performing test runs. A population size higher than 20 did not improve the search whilst a significantly lower population size yielded poorer results. Beyond generation 50 in most cases the algorithm was found to have converged. We termed the automatically designed classifiers autoDesign. The same GA settings were used for all the training data sets.

We compared the performance of the best autoDesign configured algorithm to three human designed baseline GP classification algorithms. The three GP classification algorithms were distinct in the representation used in each namely arithmetic tree, logical tree and decision tree representations.

The baseline algorithms were designed based on the generational GP algorithm presented in Algorithm 2. Tournament selection was used as the selection

Algorithm 2. Generational Genetic Programming Algorithm

1: Create initial population
2:    **while termination condition not met do**
3:        Calculate fitness of all individuals
4:        Select fitter individuals for reproduction
5:        Apply genetic operators to selected individuals
6:        Replace the current population with the offspring
7:        **end while**
8:    **return** best individual

Table 5. Manual algorithm parameter values

Dataset	Tree type	Parameter values	Dataset	Tree type	Parameter values
Aus credit data	Arithmetic	8, 10, 4, 60, 40, 5	Appendicitis	Arithmetic	8, 10, 12, 90, 10, 6
	Logical	8, 10, 8, 80, 20, 5		Logical	8, 10, 8, 85, 15, 4
	Decision	2, 5, 8, 80, 20, 3		Decision	2, 4, 8, 70, 30, 3
Breast cancer	Arithmetic	3, 10, 4, 80, 20, 6	Cylinder band	Arithmetic	3, 15, 4, 60, 40, 6
	Logical	4, 12, 8, 60, 40, 5		Logical	2, 10, 4, 60, 40, 6
	Decision	2, 5, 4, 70, 20, 3		Decision	3, 5, 4, 80, 20, 3
Diabetes	Arithmetic	8, 10, 4, 60, 40, 6	German credit data	Arithmetic	6, 10, 4, 70, 30, 6
	Logical	4, 10, 4, 70, 30, 6		Logical	3, 10, 4, 80, 20, 4
	Decision	3, 5, 4, 70, 30, 3		Decision	2, 4, 4, 80, 20, 3
Heart disease	Arithmetic	8, 10, 8, 70, 30, 4	Hepatitis	Arithmetic	4, 12, 4, 65, 35, 8
	Logical	6, 10, 4, 80, 20, 4		Logical	3, 10, 8, 80, 20, 6
	Decision	2, 5, 4, 70, 30, 4		Decision	2, 5, 4, 70, 30, 3
Liver disease	Arithmetic	7, 15, 8, 85, 15, 4	Mushroom	Arithmetic	8, 10, 12, 60, 40, 4
	Logical	8, 10, 8, 70, 30, 5		Logical	6, 12, 8, 80, 20, 6
	Decision	4, 5, 4, 70, 30, 4		Decision	3, 5, 4, 70, 30, 4
Tictactoe	Arithmetic	5, 10, 4, 90, 10, 6			
	Logical	4, 12, 4, 60, 40, 6			
	Decision	2, 5, 8, 80, 20, 3			

method and crossover and mutation were the genetic operators. For each of the human designed algorithms, parameters were determined empirically using trial runs for each dataset. The following settings were used for all manual configurations; Population size = 300; Tree generation = ramped half-and-half; Selection method = tournament; Mutation type = grow; Maximum generation = 200; Fitness function = accuracy. The numerical values used for *initial tree depth, maximum tree depth, selection size, crossover rate, mutation rate and mutation depth* are listed respectively for each algorithm per dataset in Table 5.

Arithmetic tree algorithm function set =$\{ +, -, *, /(\text{protected})\}$, terminal set = one variable for each attribute in the dataset. Logical tree algorithm function set = $\{\text{AND,OR,EQUAL,DIFFERENT,NOT}\}$, terminal set = one variable for each attribute in the dataset. Decision tree algorithm function set = one variable for each attribute in the dataset, terminal set = class 0 and class 1.

The specification of the computer used to develop the software is as follows: Intel(R) Core(TM) i5-3337U CPU @ 2.7 GHz with 4GB RAM running 64bit Linux Ubuntu. The simulations were performed using the CHPC (Centre for High Performance Computing) Lengau cluster. Java 1.8 was used as the software development platform on the Netbeans 8.1 Integrated Development Environment. In the next section we present the results.

6   Results and Discussion

Table 6 shows the training results obtained from applying the four algorithms to the data sets. Each row refers to a dataset while a column is the applied algorithm. The best training accuracy $\pm$ standard deviation over 30 runs is presented for each algorithm. The number of generations each algorithm takes to reach convergence is shown in brackets. From the results the autoDesign algorithms trained better on 3 data sets and tied on 2 while the logical tree algorithms were also better on 3 data sets and tied on 2. The arithmetic tree representation algorithms performed well on 1 dataset and tied on 4. On average across all data sets the decision tree algorithms converged quicker followed by the autoDesign algorithms and then arithmetic tree algorithms which were marginally better than logical tree algorithms

The best evolved classifiers were tested by applying them to unseen instances in the test data sets. Table 7 shows the classification accuracy of the arithmetic tree, logical tree, decision tree and autoDesign algorithms. It outlines the accuracy $\pm$ standard deviation of the best classifiers over 30 runs. From the results the

Table 6. Training results

Dataset	Arithmetic	Logical	Decision	autoDesign
Aus credit	$0.89 \pm 0.01(151)$	$\mathbf{0.91 \pm 0.01}(183)$	$0.86 \pm 0.01(94)$	$0.89 \pm 0.01(48)$
Appendicitis	$\mathbf{0.97 \pm 0.02}(117)$	$0.89 \pm 0.02(96)$	$0.89 \pm 0.02(138)$	$0.95 \pm 0.02(148)$
Breast cancer	$\mathbf{0.98 \pm 0.01}(103)$	$0.97 \pm 0.01(178)$	$0.94 \pm 0.02(86)$	$\mathbf{0.98 \pm 0.01}(121)$
Cylinder band	$0.74 \pm 0.01(97)$	$\mathbf{0.77 \pm 0.01}(116)$	$0.64 \pm 0.01\ (58)$	$0.75 \pm 0.01(101)$
Diabetes (pima)	$\mathbf{0.78 \pm 0.07}(171)$	$\mathbf{0.78 \pm 0.07}(191)$	$0.69 \pm 0.07(110)$	$0.75 \pm 0.01(104)$
German credit	$0.76 \pm 0.06(187)$	$0.76 \pm 0.06(163)$	$0.73 \pm 0.06(91)$	$\mathbf{0.85 \pm 0.07}(94)$
Heart disease	$0.92 \pm 0.01(103)$	$\mathbf{0.94 \pm 0.01}(131)$	$0.79 \pm 0.01(56)$	$0.87 \pm 0.01(72)$
Hepatitis	$\mathbf{0.98 \pm 0.03}\ (171)$	$\mathbf{0.98 \pm 0.03}(167)$	$0.88 \pm 0.02(111)$	$0.93 \pm 0.02(182)$
Liver disease	$\mathbf{0.80 \pm 0.01}(169)$	$0.73 \pm 0.01(193)$	$0.62 \pm 0.01(186)$	$\mathbf{0.80 \pm 0.01}(161)$
Mushroom	$0.86 \pm 0.00(192)$	$0.86 \pm 0.00(102)$	$0.60 \pm 0.00(99)$	$\mathbf{0.88 \pm 0.00}(108)$
Tictactoe	$0.87 \pm 0.07\ (157)$	$0.84 \pm 0.07(169)$	$0.72 \pm 0.07\ (152)$	$\mathbf{0.94 \pm 0.07}(138)$

Table 7. Testing results

Dataset	Arithmetic	Logical	Decision	autoDesign
Aus credit	0.83 ± 0.01	0.84 ± 0.01	0.85 ± 0.01	$\mathbf{0.88 \pm 0.01}$
Appendicitis	0.84 ± 0.03	0.78 ± 0.03	0.85 ± 0.03	$\mathbf{0.91 \pm 0.03}$
Breast cancer	$\mathbf{0.97 \pm 0.02}$	0.93 ± 0.03	0.90 ± 0.04	$\mathbf{0.97 \pm 0.02}$
Cylinder band	0.66 ± 0.01	0.68 ± 0.01	0.69 ± 0.01	$\mathbf{0.75 \pm 0.01}$
Diabetes (pima)	0.64 ± 0.01	$\mathbf{0.75 \pm 0.01}$	0.69 ± 0.01	0.70 ± 0.07
German credit	0.65 ± 0.01	0.65 ± 0.01	0.65 ± 0.01	$\mathbf{0.68 \pm 0.01}$
Heart disease	$\mathbf{0.77 \pm 0.02}$	0.64 ± 0.02	0.44 ± 0.01	0.72 ± 0.02
Hepatitis	0.67 ± 0.03	$\mathbf{0.75 \pm 0.03}$	$\mathbf{0.75 \pm 0.03}$	$\mathbf{0.75 \pm 0.03}$
Liver disease	0.64 ± 0.01	0.64 ± 0.01	0.44 ± 0.01	$\mathbf{0.71 \pm 0.01}$
Mushroom	0.78 ± 0.00	0.75 ± 0.00	0.66 ± 0.00	$\mathbf{0.81 \pm 0.00}$
Tictactoe	0.73 ± 0.01	0.76 ± 0.01	0.65 ± 0.01	$\mathbf{0.86 \pm 0.01}$

autoDesign evolved classifiers generalised better on 7 of the 11 data sets. While arithmetic trees and logical trees induced classifiers were better on 1 data set each. On the remaining data sets no algorithm induced classifiers outperformed the others.

To evaluate the statistical significance of the testing results we use the non-parametric Friedman test as recommended by Demšar [20] for evaluating multiple algorithms on multiple data sets. We ranked each algorithm based on performance and calculated the average rank for each algorithm the best performing algorithm is ranked 1st and the worst 4th. If there were any ties the ranking was averaged between the equal algorithms. Table 8 shows the evaluated ranks.

Table 8. Average ranks for testing accuracy

	Arithmetic	Logical	Decision tree	autoDesign
Average ranks	2.90	2.68	3.09	1.32

The critical value F(3,30) degrees of freedom at $\alpha = 0.05$ (5%) is 2.92. Using the average rankings in Table 8 we evaluate our F_f to 6.04. This leads to the rejection of our null hypothesis which states that autoDesign algorithms perform the same as human designed algorithms since our calculated value is greater than the critical value of 2.92. We then carry out a pairwise comparison of the autoDesign algorithm to the baseline algorithms using the Nemenyi post-hoc test. The critical difference at $\alpha = 0.05$ for the Nemenyi test for 4 classification algorithms is evaluated to be 0.447. The differences in average ranks of the autoDesign and arithmetic tree algorithm is 1.58, autoDesign and logical tree algorithm is 1.36 and autoDesign and decision tree algorithm is 1.77. All the average differences

Table 9. autoDesign configurations

Dataset	Configuration
Aus credit data	0, 200, 2, 8, 10, 0, 6, 21, 1, 5, 0, 3, 0, 55
Appendicitis	0, 200, 2, 3, 10, 0, 8, 57, 1, 4, 0, 0, 0, 153
Cylinder band	2, 300, 2, 3, 5, 0, 5, 31, 1, 3, 1, 2, 0, 161
German credit data	1, 200, 0, 6, 5, 0, 5, 33, 1, 5, 0, 2, 0, 109
Liver disease	0, 200, 0, 3, 9, 0, 6, 77, 1, 3, 0, 5, 3, 170
Mushroom	0, 200, 2, 8, 11, 0, 9, 60, 0, 4, 1, 5, 3, 138
Tictactoe	1, 100, 0, 3, 9, 0, 4, 55, 0, 5, 0, 0, 2, 156

are greater than the critical difference which means autoDesign performs better than the human designed algorithms for accuracy.

Table 9 presents the 7 configurations evolved by autoDesign that outperformed the baseline algorithms. Out of the 7 configurations 5 used arithmetic tree representation, 1 decision tree and 1 logical tree. Five configurations set a population size of 200, 1 with 300 and 1 with 100. Ramped half-and-half was used as the initial population generation method on 4 of the 7 and grow method on the other 3 data sets. The values for initial tree depth were well spread from 3 to 8. A value of size 3 was used 4 times and 8 twice and 6 once. Maximum offspring depth value of 5 was used twice, 9 twice, 10 twice and 11 once. Surprisingly all 7 configurations used fitness proportionate as the selection method, this is in contrast to the intuitive norm that tournament selection is better. On 5 of the 7 configurations g_{10} was set to 0 which means the same randomly selected operator was used to complete a run for GP. Crossover was applied using higher rates than mutation on 3 of 5 configurations. Shrink mutation was used for 5 of the 7 data sets. The 2 configurations that used grow mutation used a mutation depth of 4 and 5 respectively. Operators from the pool were only effective on 2 data sets and the selected operators were mutation and 100% crossover and random mutation. Four of the 7 configurations used accuracy as the fitness functions while the weighted random fitness function was used twice and the 50% weighted function used once. Only 1 configuration had a low maximum generation value which was set as 55 the other configurations had values higher than 100 although none had the maximum value possible which was 200. As anticipated with the proposed approach high run-times were experienced during the automated design process. The lowest runtime experienced for a single data set was 16 h and the highest 36 h. Compared to a manual approach this period of time was considered to be acceptable. The automation is also able to configure algorithms in an unbiased manner as shown in the results where crossover is applied at 57%, a rate a human designer is unlikely to configure. Table 10 presents a comparison of the autoDesign algorithms accuracy to other methods found in literature. The following section draws the conclusion and proposes future work.

Table 10. Comparison of autoDesign accuracy to other methods

Dataset	GP approaches	Other state-of-the-art	autoDesign
Aus credit data	89.00 [9]	90.50(ANN) [21]	88.00
Appendicitis	86.01 [22]	90.60(GA) [23]	91.00
Breast cancer	71.80 [24]	99.51(SVM) [25]	97.00
Cylinder band	78.69 [22]	88.30(OOB) [26]	75.00
Diabetes (pima)	67.96 [27]	84.20(FNN) [28]	70.00
German credit data	85.80 [29]	87.57(ANN) [30]	68.00
Heart disease	72.20 [31]	90.00(ANN) [28]	72.00
Hepatitis	81.00 [11]	79.40(GA) [32]	75.00
Liver disease	68.00 [31]	72.78(SVM) [33]	71.00
Mushroom	94.00 [27]	88.40(SVM) [33]	81.00
Tictactoe	74.21 [27]	95.00(SVM) [33]	86.00

7 Conclusion and Future Work

This paper proposed an automated approach to designing GP classification algorithms. The developed automated approach was compared to three human designed classification algorithms. The comparison was carried out on 11 data sets selected from the UCI data repository. The results suggest that automated design is able to evolve classification algorithms that perform better than human designed algorithms. The main benefit of automated design is that it enables a user who lacks knowledge of genetic programming to produce genetic programming classifiers. The runtimes for the autoDesign algorithm on the considered data sets ranged from 16 h to 36 h. This may seem high but it allows the human designer to attend to other tasks and therefore reduces man-hours on the design process. In the future we plan to parallelize the algorithm in order to reduce the runtime. The promising results also open up the possibility of increasing the number of design decisions as well as applying automated design to multi-classification problems. The results presented in the paper suggest that automating the design of GP classification algorithms is feasible.

References

1. Back, T.: Evolutionary Algorithms in Theory and Practice: Evolution Strategies, Evolutionary Programming, Genetic Algorithms. Oxford University Press, Oxford (1996)
2. Banzhaf, W., Nordin, P., Keller, R.E., Francone, F.D.: Genetic Programming: An Introduction, vol. 1. Morgan Kaufmann, San Francisco (1998)
3. Espejo, P.G., Ventura, S., Herrera, F.: A survey on the application of genetic programming to classification. IEEE Trans. Syst. Man Cybern. Part C Appl. Rev. **40**(2), 121–144 (2010)

4. Eiben, Á.E., Hinterding, R., Michalewicz, Z.: Parameter control in evolutionary algorithms. IEEE Trans. Evol. Comput. **3**(2), 124–141 (1999)
5. Sabar, N.R., Ayob, M., Kendall, G., Qu, R.: Automatic design of a hyper-heuristic framework with gene expression programming for combinatorial optimization problems. IEEE Trans. Evol. Comput. **19**(3), 309–325 (2015)
6. Han, J., Pei, J., Kamber, M.: Data Mining: Concepts and Techniques. Elsevier, USA (2011)
7. Koza, J.R.: Concept formation and decision tree induction using the genetic programming paradigm. In: Schwefel, H.-P., Männer, R. (eds.) PPSN 1990. LNCS, vol. 496, pp. 124–128. Springer, Heidelberg (1991). doi:10.1007/BFb0029742
8. Bojarczuk, C.C., Lopes, H.S., Freitas, A.A.: Discovering comprehensible classification rules using genetic programming: a case study in a medical domain. In: Proceedings of the 1st Annual Conference on Genetic and Evolutionary Computation, vol. 2, pp. 953–958. Morgan Kaufmann Publishers Inc. (1999)
9. Ong, C.S., Huang, J.J., Tzeng, G.H.: Building credit scoring models using genetic programming. Expert Syst. Appl. **29**(1), 41–47 (2005)
10. Souffriau, W., Vansteenwegen, P., Berghe, G.V., Van Oudheusden, D.: Automated parameterisation of a metaheuristic for the orienteering problem. In: Cotta, C., Sevaux, M., Sörensen, K. (eds.) Adaptive and Multilevel Metaheuristics. SCI, vol. 136, pp. 255–269. Springer, Heidelberg (2008)
11. Barros, R.C., Basgalupp, M.P., de Carvalho, A.C., Freitas, A.A.: Automatic design of decision-tree algorithms with evolutionary algorithms. Evol. Comput. **21**(4), 659–684 (2013)
12. Diosan, L.S., Oltean, M.: Evolving evolutionary algorithms using evolutionary algorithms. In: Proceedings of the 9th Annual Conference Companion on Genetic and Evolutionary Computation, pp. 2442–2449. ACM (2007)
13. Goldberg, D.E.: Genetic Algorithms. Pearson Education India, New Delhi (2006)
14. Eiben, A.E., Smith, J.E., et al.: Introduction to Evolutionary Computing, vol. 53. Springer, Heidelberg (2003)
15. Aitkenhead, M.: A co-evolving decision tree classification method. Expert Syst. Appl. **34**(1), 18–25 (2008)
16. Agnelli, D., Bollini, A., Lombardi, L.: Image classification: an evolutionary approach. Pattern Recogn. Lett. **23**(1), 303–309 (2002)
17. Cios, K.J., Swiniarski, R.W., Pedrycz, W., Kurgan, L.A.: The knowledge discovery process. In: Data Mining, pp. 9–24. Springer, New York (2007)
18. Bhowan, U., Zhang, M., Johnston, M.: Genetic programming for classification with unbalanced data. In: Esparcia-Alcázar, A.I., Ekárt, A., Silva, S., Dignum, S., Uyar, A.Ş. (eds.) EuroGP 2010. LNCS, vol. 6021, pp. 1–13. Springer, Heidelberg (2010). doi:10.1007/978-3-642-12148-7_1
19. Frank, A., Asuncion, A., et al.: Uci machine learning repository (2010)
20. Demšar, J.: Statistical comparisons of classifiers over multiple data sets. J. Mach. Learn. Res. **7**, 1–30 (2006)
21. Yao, X., Liu, Y.: Ensemble structure of evolutionary artificial neural networks. In: Proceedings of IEEE International Conference on Evolutionary Computation, pp. 659–664. IEEE (1996)
22. Cano, A., Ventura, S., Cios, K.J.: Multi-objective genetic programming for feature extraction and data visualization. Soft Comput., 1–21 (2015)
23. Raymer, M.L., Punch, W.F., Goodman, E.D., Kuhn, L.A., Jain, A.K.: Dimensionality reduction using genetic algorithms. IEEE Trans. Evol. Comput. **4**(2), 164–171 (2000)

24. Bojarczuk, C.C., Lopes, H.S., Freitas, A.A., Michalkiewicz, E.L.: A constrained-syntax genetic programming system for discovering classification rules: application to medical data sets. Artif. Intell. Med. **30**(1), 27–48 (2004)
25. Akay, M.F.: Support vector machines combined with feature selection for breast cancer diagnosis. Expert Syst. Appl. **36**(2), 3240–3247 (2009)
26. Bylander, T.: Estimating generalization error on two-class datasets using out-of-bag estimates. Mach. Learn. **48**(1–3), 287–297 (2002)
27. Espejo, P.G., Romero, C., Ventura, S., Hervás, C.: Induction of classification rules with grammar-based genetic programming. In: Conference on Machine Intelligence, pp. 596–601 (2005)
28. Kahramanli, H., Allahverdi, N.: Design of a hybrid system for the diabetes and heart diseases. Expert Syst. Appl. **35**(1), 82–89 (2008)
29. Cao, V.L., Le-Khac, N.-A., O'Neill, M., Nicolau, M., McDermott, J.: Improving fitness functions in genetic programming for classification on unbalanced credit card data. In: Squillero, G., Burelli, P. (eds.) EvoApplications 2016. LNCS, vol. 9597, pp. 35–45. Springer, Cham (2016). doi:10.1007/978-3-319-31204-0_3
30. West, D.: Neural network credit scoring models. Comput. Oper. Res. **27**(11), 1131–1152 (2000)
31. Jabeen, H., Baig, A.R.: Depthlimited crossover in GP for classifier evolution. Comput. Hum. Behav. **27**(5), 1475–1481 (2011)
32. Raymer, M.L., Doom, T.E., Kuhn, L.A., Punch, W.F.: Knowledge discovery in medical and biological datasets using a hybrid bayes classifier/evolutionary algorithm. IEEE Trans. Syst. Man Cybern. Part B (Cybern.) **33**(5), 802–813 (2003)
33. Mangasarian, O.L., Musicant, D.R.: Lagrangian support vector machines. J. Mach. Learn. Res. **1**, 161–177 (2001)

Author Index

Printed in the United States
By Bookmasters